BIG BUT
CHRISTIANS

Overcoming Our Excuses

D1607952

DR. T. S. WISE

Big But Christians: Overcoming Our Excuses

Scripture quotations taken from the New American Standard Bible®,
Copyright © 1960, 1962, 1963, 1968, 1971, 1972, 1973,
1975, 1977, 1995 by The Lockman Foundation
Used by permission." (www.Lockman.org)

First Edition
ISBN: 978-0-9860613-1-8

Published by
Servant Communications, Inc.
Kirksville, MO 63501

Cover picture © Ariwasabi | Dreamstime.com - Man Showing Sign Surprised.
Used with permission.

Cover picture © Mack2happy | Dreamstime.com - Golden Antique Background.
Used with permission.

Cover & Interior Design: Lissa Auciello-Brogan

Printed in the United States of America.
14 13 12 11 10 / 10 9 8 7 6 5 4 3 2 1

DEDICATION

*Dedicated to those whose sole desire in life is to pursue
God with all their heart, soul, mind, and strength, and who
are willing to examine their own life in that pursuit.*

May your courage be blessed by our Lord.

*Dedicated to those whose hearts seek cleansing from the plethora
of flimsy conditions, justifications, excuses, and behaviors
that cause so much havoc along the spiritual journey.*

*May you experience freedom and joy to serve
God faithfully and effectively.*

*Dedicated to those who relentlessly pursue the elimination
of Big But vocabulary, thinking, and behavior.*

May you hear the clarion voice of God and obey His call upon your life.

*Dedicated to those who yearn for authenticity and
purity in their relationship with the living God.*

May you experience the abundant life in Christ.

CONTENTS

PREFACE

The notion of Big But Christians is an entertaining idea. Friends and colleagues laughed at the catchy phrase and wondered what in the world I was talking about. After explaining the concepts behind the play on words, I was encouraged to write a book about it. So I did.

While the catchy play on words helps to get my point across, the thrust of this book is significant. How do we make sense of all that we see and experience in the Christian life? When we compare *what is* with *what ought* to be, we realize there is a disappointing gap between the two. We readily see this chasm in the life of others, and if we are honest with ourselves, we acknowledge the discrepancies in our own life as well. How do we rid ourselves of the many conditions, justifications, excuses, and behaviors that hinder us from following and experiencing God?

One of the ways I cope with these discrepancies and flimsy excuses is through laughter. Humor helps me manage what is evident to all of us. After all, we don't live in a utopian society. Writing *Big But Christians* is my way of trying to make sense of the incongruity between what we are and what we ought to be in a way that enhances our pursuit of God.

Most Christians I have met earnestly desire to live a life pleasing to our Lord. While the desire is present, their Big But seems to get in the way all too often and their spiritual journey takes the form of one step forward and two steps backwards. This book is intended to help you on your spiritual journey. Rather than sugarcoat serious issues, I expose them for what they are and provide a pathway for wholeness. My high hope is that your desire to please God would intensify and your life would be lived in alignment with the Creator.

The tone of this book is simple, friendly, and relaxed, as though I am sitting in your living room conversing over a hot beverage. In Chapter 1, I define "Big But Christians" and share true stories that help illustrate the point. Big But examples from both the Old and New Testament are examined in Chapter 2. In Chapter 3, I take those biblical examples and develop a Big But Cluster List that helps us understand and identify problematic areas in our lives. In Chapter 4, I explore shining examples of Tiny But behavior in both the Old and New Testament. Finally, in Chapter 5, I present the Big But Cleansing Cycle, a powerful cleansing process for removing harmful contaminants from our thoughts and behaviors.

TSW
Kirksville, MO 2015

THE BIG BUT PROBLEM

Introducing Big Buts

You have to be either blind or deaf to escape the "Big Buts" some Christians walk around with these days. "How rude," you say with a puzzled look upon your face, "How dare he say such a thing?" In all honesty, I am trying to be nice. Now I might as well do away with all pretense and just say it like it is: many Christians have humungous Buts; not just Big Buts, but gargantuan Buts that interfere with how they walk, how they function, how they influence others, and how others view them (or, more precisely, can't help but view them).

Big But Christians are like floating icebergs in the North Atlantic Ocean. Though beautiful from a distance, it is the enormous portion beneath the water-line that is so dangerous. Stay your distance and navigate around them, or a collision could land you on the ocean floor.

Let's be honest; when Mr. Big But Christian talks to you about following Jesus, do you really listen? Are you paying attention? Do you give credence to his words? Of course not! His Big But is in the way. You aren't tuned in to what Mr. Big But Christian is saying. Instead, what captures your attention is the grotesque image of his Big But. Though you try to get that picture out of your mind, you just can't. Like the branding of a Texas steer, his Big But is seared into your memory.

Everything Mr. Big But Christian says and does is offset by the inescapable memory of his colossal But. As he drags Mt. Everest behind him wherever he goes, his ability to effectively minister to others is endlessly hindered. Like the emperor who wore no clothes, everyone except Mr. Big But Christian seems to notice.

After just a few introductory paragraphs, you are either 1) angry at my political incorrectness and ready to initiate a class action lawsuit on behalf of overweight Christians throughout the world, 2) laughing hysterically at my insensitivity and audacity to write such things, or 3) amused, but also confused, wondering where I am going with such But-speak.

A Big But What?

Before we go farther, let me explain what I mean by "Big But Christians." Hoping to capture your attention, I use a play on words to help you remember the main thrust of this book. During law school, I utilized numerous memory devices to retain important points of law. For instance, "ABC FITT" helped me remember the list of intentional torts:

- Assault
- Battery
- Conversion
- False imprisonment
- Intentional infliction of emotional distress
- Trespass to land
- Trespass to chattel

Similarly, I use "Big But Christians" as a humorous memory jogger to help you recall the point of this book. First, let's explore what I mean by the word "But."

I Said But, Not Butt!

Notice that I did not say "Big *Butt* Christians," but rather "Big *But* Christians," hence, the play on words. Had I been referring to the size of a person's derrière, offense may have been taken. The actual size of a person's buttocks is absolutely, totally irrelevant. Some folks have large bottoms, some small bottoms, some flat bottoms, and some buy implants and become surgical bottoms. Whatever kind of bottom you possess, celebrate it and live with it. It's you, so move on and recognize how insignificant the size of your backside happens to be.

I still chuckle remembering the day not long ago when I was being fitted for a new suit. There seemed to be enough room for a small refrigerator in the backside of my baggy trousers. Something needed to be done. Finally, as though she were making the greatest of discoveries, the frustrated clerk looked up, and with a pin stuck between her teeth, exclaimed, "Sir, you have no butt!"

In all my years I have never heard a store clerk, or anyone else for that matter, say something like that to me. She was merely verbalizing what I already knew. It is a Wise trait. My dad had no butt, his dad had no butt, and like all Wises before me, I inherited a flat bottom like all the others. From generation to generation this trait was passed down. I want to design a pair of jeans for people like me. I will call them "flat-bottom" jeans with a concave backside! With all joking aside, do you know what having a flat bottom actually means? Absolutely nothing! I have a flat bottom, you have a round one, another has a big one, and others have a small one. Who cares? I certainly don't! Of all the things in life worthy of conversation, the actual size of one's backside isn't even on my list.

I Forgive You . . . BUT

When I say "Big But Christians," I am not referring to the size of that thing we sit on. I am referring to something far more menacing and debilitating to our spiritual health. The Big But Christians I have in mind are those who put a "but" in the middle of their sentences. I love you, *BUT. . .*, I forgive you, *BUT. . .*, I will follow God, *BUT. . .*, I will obey, *BUT. . . .* Like clockwork, they always condition their obedience, their commitment, their love, their forgiveness, etc., on a gigantic "but" in the middle of their sentences. I refer to this problem as the Big But problem, the Big But Syndrome, Big But-ology, Big But-itis, But-speak, But tsunami, But-ness and other But-worthy words and phrases.

> Big But-itis . . . a perspective or behavior that conditions, justifies, or excuses our conduct and thinking, or reveals discontentment with God.

Big But-itis is revealed in many ways, not only by saying the word "but" in a sentence. Words are merely symptoms of a much deeper issue. Any time we do something, say something, or believe something that acts as a condition, justification, and excuse, or reveals discontentment with God, it becomes an inflammation of But-ness. In this book, I define "Big But-itis" as *a perspective or behavior that conditions, justifies, or excuses our conduct and thinking, or reveals discontentment with God.*

This Big But Syndrome is spiritually devastating and prevents us from experiencing God with the fullness He desires. In reality, But-ness is nothing more than a lame excuse masquerading in religious attire. When the word "but" is connected to a spiritual phrase like "I forgive you," it seems, at first, to lend credence to what is being said. Upon closer examination, however, we realize it is merely a false support structure—a facade masking the true intent of the speaker. Holding God hostage to seeing and doing things their way, Big But Christians extensively utilize "but" as a means of conditioning obedience to the Lord's directives or to excuse sinful behavior. They desire the *appearance* of being spiritual without *actually* being spiritual, an attitude that is Pharisaical at best and demonic at worst.

Big But Beginnings

Our Lord encountered the Big But Syndrome. With a smirk on his face, the devil announces to Jesus, "Why of course you are the Son of God, *but* prove it by jumping off this Temple." The unbelieving Jews proudly assert, "We will attest to your authority, *but* give us a sign so we can believe." The religious elite feign half-hearted interest with, "We will follow you, *but* first answer this question, should we pay taxes to Caesar?" The staunch protectors of crusty rules and regulations, cob-webbed for decades, declare, "We know that You speak the truth, *but* why do You break all of our traditions?"

The Big But Syndrome has been around since the beginning of time. It even influences Adam and Eve. With God's searchlight upon his soul, Adam responds with, "Oh yes God, I ate the apple, *but* Eve made me do it." Eve's response is no better, "I ate the apple, *but* the devil made me do it." We notice Big But-itis in Cain as he justifies killing Abel, "Yes, I killed Abel, *but* my offering should have been accepted too." Scripture is replete with examples of But-ness.

What if the tables were turned? In other words, what if God played the Big But game with us? "Oh, I forgive your sins all right, *but* there are a few of them that need additional work on your part in order to completely wipe the slate clean. Of course heaven is absolutely reserved for you, *but* if you falter in any way, I will cancel your reservation in a heartbeat. Sure, I will be with you in the hard times, *but* if I feel that you contributed to your own downfall in any way, I will allow you to suffer alone."

If God engaged in But-speak with us, our hope would crumble and complete devastation would overcome us. We would be nothing more than a tiny rowboat floating in a Big But sea without an anchor to God's comforting promises or a lifeline to His sure Word.

Big But Stories

Big But stories abound everywhere despite culture, continent, color, or denomination. We have all been squashed by the Big But of professing Christians and have personally experienced But-ness to some degree in our own lives. Truth be told, not only have we experienced the negative effects of Big But-ology, we have also squashed others with our own Big Buts. Let me share a few Big But stories that come from the real world of my own life.

Big But Bob's Trousers

Florida is the land of shorts and flip-flops. Soaking up every ray of sunshine I could during my ministry days in the sunshine state, I loved the casual dress, warm days, Gulf breezes, walks on the beach, beautiful sunsets, and all that Florida had to offer.

Along with its wonderful climate and fun-filled activities, the state largely consists of transplants from other states. This transitory element means that Florida churches are a hodgepodge of individuals from all over the country and from various denominational backgrounds. Florida is also a home to cowboys—a remnant, I suppose, from its early days as a land to be tamed. People love their horses, acreages, and big trucks.

My church was no different than most—dwindling in the summer as winter snowbirds flew north to cooler weather and swelling in the winter as they moved south to escape the frigid air. The church coffers were depleted as attendance waned during the hot summer but mushroomed during winter months when attendance peaked. Florida winters meant more people, more opinions, and more of just about everything, both good and bad.

Big But Bob traveled down from Ohio every year, a practice he maintained for a long time. He was now reaping the retirement benefits of a fruitful career and accumulated wealth. Bob was used to getting his way. In fact, he built his fortune by being in control and directing his own affairs. He was smart and outgoing, but he had little patience with things for which he disagreed. He sat in the same church pew every Sunday wearing an impeccable suit and an off-color toupee. He drove a fancy new car every year. He was old school.

When others didn't show their respect for God the way he did, it bothered him immensely. Sunday was "dress up for God" day, and that meant wearing a suit and tie. As a leader in the church, he expected others to wear a suit and tie as well. Anything less was considered unacceptable and disrespectful.

It was bound to happen, and I was waiting to see how long it would take before the new deacon who helped out with communion and offering would be criticized. After all, there he was, standing in front of the entire congregation wearing Durango boots, denim jeans, cowboy shirt with bolo tie, and a big smile on his face. His blonde, flowing hair was noticeably far too close to his shoulders for people like Big But Bob. The new deacon thought he was wearing his cowboy best to church, but Bob considered it a total disgrace and lack of respect for the Lord.

Big But Bob's face reflected his inner tension and for some reason reminded me of the worried parent of an elementary school basketball player. It wasn't the father's place to coach the team, choose the starting lineup, or make derisive comments about his daughter's lack of playing time, but you could see it on his face—yearning to give the coach a verbal beating, but somehow holding back.

One sunny Sunday morning, Big But Bob blew a gasket. Like Yellowstone's Old Faithful, he finally exploded, blurting his feelings about leaders in the church. Maybe his influence would carry the day. Maybe his pocketbook would sway others; after all, people knew he was a generous giver. Maybe he could convince others by his longevity in the church. Maybe he could command them like he ordered his own business affairs. If that didn't work, maybe he could phrase his words in such a manner as to gently shame others into acquiescence.

As though he was holding court in the church foyer, breathing heavy with excitement and ready to pronounce his final decree on the matter, Big But Bob pontificated, "I know that God looks at the inside of a man's heart and we are not to judge a person by the clothes they wear, *but* it is disrespectful and wrong for a leader in this church to wear jeans on Sunday morning."

What? Really? Were my ears deceiving me? He acknowledged God's view on things, and even stated it in his own terms, "God looks at the inside of a man's heart." Then came the Big But eruption, "*but* it is disrespectful and wrong for a leader in this church to wear jeans on Sunday morning." I was disheartened. Here was a statesman in his sunset years, a long-time Christian who contributed to the church in many ways, making such an infantile statement. Did he not grasp the gravity of his words? His personal choice of Sunday morning trousers was undermining the clear teaching of Scripture, and he really didn't seem to care.

Imagine an 80-year-old gentleman standing in the middle of the foyer sporting a clean, fresh diaper, wearing a lopsided and off-color toupee, acknowledging the teaching of Scripture on a particular subject, articulating that teaching with clarity, and then raising his plastic rattle in one hand and baby bottle in the other, declaring at the top of his lungs that Scripture is to be set aside for his personal Sunday morning trouser preference!

Fortunately, in this situation, church leaders stood firm, unwilling to make a mountain out of a molehill. Think about how often this happens in the church, how often well-meaning Christians show off their Big Buts. Unfortunately, when local churches succumb to Big But-ology, the end result is a weakening of Scripture and the growing of bigger Buts. The church becomes nothing more than a dusty, meaningless Bible on the one hand and a large and lengthy But-list on the other hand. All too often, the But-list is used to interpret the Bible, not the other way around.

But-ness demands that even Scripture become subservient to its coercion. Quite often, Big But Christians accept the holy writings as authoritative, and believe they should be obeyed—that is, until that obedience runs smack into a Big But wall. When biblical teaching collides with Big But-itis, the Bible most often gets plowed under; not because it is inherently weak or faulty, but because Big But Christians are unwilling to place themselves under the authority of Scripture. But-ness sets forth ultimatums and insists upon the acquiescence of others. Our personal preferences *should* bow to the truth of Scripture, yet the Big But Syndrome requires that all else yield to its demands. This nullifies the writings, or at least selects which portions to believe and obey.

Like Big But Bob, we often know quite clearly what Scripture teaches and can even articulate it with great skill. Yet, when that teaching is at odds with our personal preferences, we toss in the "but" word, intending to hold God hostage to our personal likes and dislikes while forcing others to succumb to our way of thinking. Somehow we feel this mitigates our refusal to obey.

Big But Bubba's Apology

Far from Florida is the state of Minnesota, the land of ten thousand lakes. Alligators give way to loons, while shorts and flip-flops succumb to down-filled winter coats declaring war on arctic cold fronts. It is a beautiful state.

Just one glance at this Iron Range town revealed its outdated 1950s persona, frozen in time since the decline of the mining industry. The sniff test of acceptance from town folks took a long time for new people. When my secretary moved to the community many years ago, her new neighbor asked how the unpacking was coming along, to which my secretary responded, "Very slowly. I am procrastinating." The neighbor had never before heard the word "procrastinating." What was this big, fancy, high-faluting vocabulary being used by the arrogant newcomer? My secretary failed the sniff test, and the neighbor never spoke to her again. I was warned, as the new pastor in town, "You will never be accepted in this community until you bury a loved one here."

The beauty of Northern Minnesota is juxtaposed against ruggedness, not only in the landscape, but also among its people. Rugged Bubba was an inspector for the county. Set in his beliefs and understanding of life, no one, not even God, was going to tell him any differently. Bubba and his family sat in the same pew every Sunday morning. We are all creatures of habit with preferred Sunday morning seating choices, but in this case, I knew Big But Bubba didn't come to hear from God; he came to protect the congregation from people like me who might challenge their thinking and beliefs. His role, as he saw it, was to evaluate, judge, and pronounce a verdict on the worthiness of every sermon I preached. Each Sunday, he mentally scoured his doctrinal and behavioral checklist to determine if my words aligned with his perfect understanding of Scripture and life.

While preaching one Sunday from a passage in Ephesians, I could tell from Bubba's body language that my message didn't pass muster. His head shook in disappointment throughout the entire sermon, as though he were watching a Wimbledon tennis match. And I heard about it afterwards!

Big But Bubba saw himself as a leader, a standard-bearer for how Christians should believe and act. He was a domineering, overbearing father and husband. His wife barely spoke for fear of chastisement. He commanded his children to rise at five in the morning for family devotions, and compelled his wife and daughter to bake bread for the day. While the children didn't say much growing up (how could they?), the ramifications of Big But Bubba's approach to family life would come back to bite him in future years. I suppose the term "Christian dictator" might be a more appropriate term for Rugged Bubba.

Unfortunately, his dictatorial demeanor wasn't limited to the church or to his family; it affected the community as well. As a consistent attender of city council meetings aired on local television, Dictator Bubba's reputation preceded him and his presence made life miserable for all who attended. I was embarrassed—embarrassed for our church, for our community, for Bubba, for the council members, and for God Himself. Who acts like this? Where is the love and grace of God demonstrated in his life? Why is he so angry? What happened in his life that makes him this way? Doesn't he understand how detrimental his behavior is to the cause of Christ in the community?

> Big But-ology allows us to feign spirituality without ever having to deal with the demanding truths of reality.

Big But Bubba made life miserable for me as a pastor, and on one particular Sunday he exploded. His hot-blooded words ran me over like a semi-tractor trailer. He then backed the rig up and ran me over again and again ensuring my emotional demise. He was nasty, his words always stinging, his judgments fundamentally twisted, and it hurt, both me and my family. Instead of backing down, I called him on his behavior. I doubt anyone ever stood up to Dictator Bubba, let alone a pastor.

The following week I traveled to Denver for a large denominational gathering and was quite surprised when a thick envelope was delivered to my hotel room. It was from Bubba. Oh no, what was this? Was I being tracked down like America's most wanted only to receive his malicious blows courtesy of the United States Postal Service?

It was an eight-page handwritten letter. Maybe God's Spirit miraculously penetrated Bubba's petrified shell and touched his heart. After reading the first paragraph, I was encouraged. Bubba actually apologized for his behavior. Praise God! Was this some sort of turnaround many had hoped for? My elation was short-lived as I read paragraph two, then three, and then the rest of the letter. I couldn't believe what I was reading: one paragraph of apology and over seven pages of Big But justification.

The letter was nothing more than a litany of reasons why *I caused* his behavior. In essence, Big But Bubba said, "Sure my behavior wasn't the best, *but* if you were a better pastor . . . , *but* if you saw things my way . . . , *but* if you preached the truth . . . , *but* if you left the church . . . , I wouldn't have acted this way." I was absolutely floored—stunned beyond belief. In his mind, I was the one responsible for *his* behavior. I *caused* him to react in an ungodly manner. How is it that a grown man, who views himself as a spiritual giant, can be so deceived? It was the worst Big But letter I have ever received.

You see, Big But-ology allows us to feign spirituality without ever having to deal with the demanding truths of reality. Big But Bubba became a rubberized man. Truth bounced off of him. The work of God's Spirit bounced off of him. Not even the love and concern of others could penetrate Big But Bubba's protective insulation. The Big But suit did not protect anything worthwhile; in fact, it was a deceptive hindrance that locked Bubba into a constant state of But-ness. Damaging and damning at the same time, Big But-itis prevented him from identifying and following the Spirit's leading, being used by God to bless and minister to others, and becoming a positive and fruitful influence in the community. After all, who wants to be like Bubba? If Bubba represents the inviting change Christ can make in a person's life, I would rather become an atheist.

Big But-ology warps the way we perceive ourselves, God, and others. As our Buts become enlarged, we step into the realm of "specology," where we focus on the tiny speck in another's eye. God, however, calls us to be "logologists," examining the log in our own eye that prevents us from seeing things accurately. Yet, we insist on being the "specologist" so aptly described in Matthew 7:1–5:

> Do not judge so that you will not be judged. For in the way you judge, you will be judged; and by your standard of measure, it will be measured to you. Why do you look at the speck that is in your brother's eye, but do not notice the log that is in your own eye? Or how can you say to your brother, "Let me take the speck out of your eye," and behold, the log is in your own eye? You hypocrite, first take the log out of your own eye, and then you will see clearly to take the speck out of your brother's eye.

Dictator Bubba went through life with a very Big But. He wouldn't change, never saw the need for it, and instead, insisted that everyone else change. In the end, his Big But got the best of him and over time you know what happened . . . it all came back to bite him in the butt!

Big But Boss' Dollar Eyes

I have worked for several bosses throughout my career. Many of their behaviors and decisions were brilliant, some mediocre, and others just plain ridiculous. One thing is for certain: I gained a boatload of knowledge just by watching them operate. What an education!

In any leadership position, constant tension exists between political pressure and walking with integrity. I once was asked to turn around an unprofitable, stagnate organization into a thriving, productive, revenue-generating entity. With the Lord's help and that of many others, this was accomplished in a relatively short period of time. In the division I directed, more profit was produced in one year for the organization than in all the previous years combined. At the end of every fiscal year, senior executives battled over excess year-end money which had always been miniscule and inconsequential. Imagine two grown men arguing over a penny they find in the parking lot. Amidst this culture of scarcity, financial success was attained with great jubilation.

Early on, I realized there was little accountability for spending and no financial model from which to operate, so I quickly developed both of these. Upon my arrival, a budget proposal containing large increases to my operating budget awaited my approval. But how could I approve a budget increase when expenses exceeded income? This may be how the federal government operates, but it isn't my philosophy or practice. I didn't have to be an accountant to realize the numbers didn't add up, so I asked to examine this nonsensical approach and generate my own recommendations.

After some contemplation, I designed a plan for obtaining all the personnel needed to move the division forward while still remaining under the previous year's budget. This allowed me to make necessary adjustments for growth while saving the corporation large budget increases. While explaining this to my boss, I pointed out that a vital part-time position remained unfilled. I outlined the various strategic options for him. To go left meant one thing, and to go right meant another. Neither path pleased him. The last option available was for me to fill the role on a temporary basis until the right individual could be hired.

Already sustaining long hours and a hectic schedule, I agreed to accept the increased responsibilities, workload, and time commitment with a corresponding increase in remuneration for the additional expectations. My boss beamed with excitement and responded, "If you can rearrange your personnel, come under last year's budget, and save the organization this kind of money, I will agree to increase your pay for taking on the additional responsibilities." We agreed on an amount, and the deal was sealed. I saved the organization significant dollars and strategically rearranged personnel while adding additional responsibilities to an already full plate.

Would my boss actually honor his word and pay the promised amount, or would his memory conveniently fail? Unfortunately, his Big But got in the way, and he later declared, "I would pay someone else to do the job, *but* since you are already on salary, I can't pay any more than I am already paying you." *What about our agreement? What about honoring your word to me? I honored my word and did what I told you I would do, why won't you do the same?* As Christians, honoring our word to one another is what we are supposed to do, isn't it? His Big But cost me thousands of dollars. Was I to take him to court or file a grievance with the organization? He lied to me, and it meant financial loss. Even though I was wronged, I let it go and moved on. Life isn't always fair; how we react to Big Buts is a test of our own character.

My Big But Boss would face another convenient memory failure. When the organization was deteriorating and barely able to stand, he boldly promised to split with my division any positive margin I could generate. This addressed the cash flow urgency while allowing me to reinvest in progressive initiatives for growth. But when record-breaking revenue was produced, his pupils turned to dollar signs, the agreement was altered, and his memory conveniently failed him once again. I did not receive all of the reinvestment dollars promised.

> In its bare essence, a Big But is nothing more than situational ethics wrapped in a cloak of self-righteousness.

The situation reminds me of my uncle, a born salesman. He sold western clothing and cowboy boots for a living. In an attempt to steal him away from his current job, an alluring company promised hearty commissions and a large territory. He accepted their offer. In fact, he was wildly successful and made more money than the executives thought he should, so they cut his territory down. They used glittery financial incentives to attract him, never really believing he would be so effective. By cutting the size of his territory, they lost both him and the revenue he generated. Sheer lunacy!

You see, the Big But Syndrome has a lot to do with integrity of one's character. In its bare essence, a Big But is nothing more than situational ethics wrapped in a cloak of self-righteousness. When it is convenient to have a memory failure, we can escape the honoring of our word and still justify and rationalize our actions as God-honoring. How naive do we think God is? Do we really believe He doesn't notice such shenanigans?

I once worked for a Christian boss who had both a great sense of ministry and tremendous business savvy. When he moved in a direction that made sense from a business standpoint but wasn't biblical or ethical, he rationalized, "It has to be done because it makes good business sense." Yet, when he sought to embark on a course that didn't make good business sense, he remarked, "It has to be done because it is a spiritual decision." He knew how to play his cards, didn't he? How can you lose when you hold all the aces? In any given situation, he is able to do as he desires by utilizing a Big But called "business sense" or "spiritual right," whichever one best fits his purpose at the time.

The Pharisees in Jesus' day utilize Big But-ology in the same way. They are unwilling to accept the teaching of Jesus and are reluctant to follow God with their whole heart. They don't care about others or about helping them commune with the living God. They care mostly for themselves. When you don't really care about God or others, they merely become tools for what you really do care about.

The Pharisees *do* care about the applause of men. They *do* care about their reputation and status in the eyes of others. They *do* earnestly desire to be seen as teachers of the law while perceiving themselves to be above the law. They *do* long to be regarded as spiritual giants, without actually being spiritual.

In reality, they wouldn't recognize God's voice if He spoke to them face-to-face. In fact, that is exactly what happened. The Father sent Jesus to physically walk among them. According to traditional Christianity, God actually put on human skin to show them what He is like and how they should live, yet they stubbornly refuse to acknowledge Jesus. Instead, they incite crowds against Him, attempt to trick Him, and combine their efforts to discredit Him. Jesus is attracting larger crowds and they will have none of it. With one final crescendo, they speak in one accord, "Crucify Him!"

When our life contains Big Bad Buts, our integrity is undermined and our perspective becomes warped to the point where we no longer recognize God's voice. As a result of seeing things incorrectly, we behave badly; our behavior is always tied to our thinking.

Big But Becky The Secretary

God has always blessed me with competent administrative assistants for which I have been extremely grateful. To this point in my career, each has been an ISFJ on the Myers Briggs Type Indicator, a personality type instrument I use often. ISFJ's are often detailed individuals with caring hearts. They enjoy structure, organization, and are wired to serve. Because they are introverted, standing around the water fountain spending precious hours yacking away in fruitless conversation isn't a worry. Becky was no different, except she had a Big But about her that was difficult to ignore.

Early on in my tenure with the organization, Becky was all smiles with little reason to show off that Big But of hers. In due time, however, her Big But would become prominent enough to be considered a noticeable and permanent fixture of her demeanor. It's hard to conceal a Big But!

One particular transaction sums up her Big But perspective. A fellow employee became extremely agitated with her immediate supervisor and exploded verbally and behaviorally. The scene was ugly and left a bad taste in everyone's mouth. I was minutes away from the office when I received the news. Upon my arrival, the visibly upset employee was on her way out of the building with boxes of personal effects in her arms. The situation had been boiling for some time, and today was the day everything fell apart.

Words can uplift and heal or destroy and crush one's spirit. The words spewing from her lips that day cut like a razor. In a calm and inquiring voice I asked what was happening, providing her ample opportunity to vent. Maybe I could bring sanity and tranquility to the situation. I had worked hard to develop trust and favor with her. On one occasion, upon entering her office, the guest chair was stacked with papers, books, and files, so I sat on the floor. Before you know it, she was sitting there with me. Here we were, two professionals sitting on her office floor having a cogent and friendly conversation.

Her understanding and commitment to Christ was extremely fragile. Her personal life had taken some sharp turns and, shaken to the core, she was trying to wrap her arms around these experiences and come out safely on the other side. She respected me and felt comfortable talking with me. I had high hopes that our Christian work environment would minister to her soul and provide a loving and kind atmosphere. Given time, I was optimistic that her understanding, appreciation, and commitment to Christ would deepen. However, the explosion occurred, and all was in jeopardy.

To make matters worse, she was overseeing several important assignments that, had she left immediately, could have cost the organization thousands of dollars. Was there a way for me to redeem the situation, reduce the organization's financial risk, and bolster the employee's commitment to Christ? With emotions running so high, it was a tall order.

"I can't take it anymore," her voice crackled, "I will not be talked to like that and treated that way." The more we talked, the more I realized the inevitability of parting ways was fast approaching. After helping her cool down, I asked if she was willing to report directly to me and complete her projects before leaving the organization. Fortunately she agreed, and disaster was averted. I treated her with respect and continued being the feet and hands of Jesus to her troubled heart. The projects were completed with no financial loss to the organization.

While my intervention seemed to produce positive results for both the employee and the organization, it was not to the liking of Big But Becky, and she let me know it. It was too much for her to absorb and accept. Things didn't go her way. When she could no longer contain her displeasure, she stomped into my office, noisily pulled up a chair, sighed numerous times in disgust, and proceeded to tell me how I mishandled the situation. How could I keep the employee around after behavior like that? What was wrong with me? I was setting a bad example. This was a Christian organization, and negative behavior should be punished. What in the world was I thinking? I should have immediately dismissed her with firmness and resolve. Becky's Big But was revealed in this statement: "I know you are the Vice President and can do what you want, *but* you made a bad decision. How could you do this?" Yada . . . yada . . . yada, on and on she went.

The funny thing about Big But Christians is that while they want control of the world around them, they have no inclination to control themselves.

Did she recognize her own inappropriate behavior? Should I have treated her insolence with the same firmness she wanted me to treat other inappropriate behavior? Was she willing to extend the same grace to others that I extended to her? One dishonored Christ with her scorching words and explosive behavior, and the other dishonored Christ with her insolence and veiled desire for control. She was unyielding, and even after I provided a rationale for my decision, she continued with her cross-examination. She left my office in a huff because she was unable to control a situation handled in a manner that was displeasing to her. As she left the room, I couldn't help but notice her Big But.

That's the thing about Big But Christians—they crave control. Everything and everyone must align with their thinking, their understanding, and their conclusions about people, places, events, and circumstances. Big But-itis is nothing more than a "my way or the highway" mentality. The funny thing about Big But Christians is that while they want control of the world around them, they have no inclination to control themselves. In fact, it doesn't even occur to them. Why would they need to control themselves? After all, in their mind, they always see things correctly. They are all for God moving in mighty ways, *but* He first better get their permission to do so.

The desire to take control away from God is a hideous sin—so ugly that to look upon it in its raw form is too much to bear. Big Buts, however, know how to dress it up, apply perfume and makeup, outfit it with a pinstriped skirt, and spin it so its repugnancy is concealed. You can take a coffin, paint it with your favorite colors, line it with silk, and attach gold plated hardware, but inside is still a dead body.

When my tenure came to a close and the Lord called me to a different ministry, Big But Becky was unable to say goodbye in an appropriate manner. She was in charge of all goodbyes and if you were valued by her, attended her church, liked by her, gossiped with her, and didn't interfere with her Big But, you received a party with lots of gifts, cake, and hoopla.

Learning of my upcoming departure gave her hope that she could push my replacement around with her Big But. My goodbye party was merely another opportunity for Big But Becky to reveal her displeasure with me. My last day consisted of a large event welcoming newcomers to the organization. I introduced the staff, uplifting each member in the presence of the group, building up their loyalty to the organization and their commitment to serve the newcomers.

My kind parting words must have hit a nerve with Becky. The guilt of her actions, or lack of them, began to take root. She treated me with disrespect and acted inappropriately, allowing her Big But to get the best of her—and she knew it. Later that evening, I received an email containing these Big But words: "I wanted to get you a card and a meaningful gift before you left, *but* I failed to do that in time. I hope you know I still care."

Over the years, I have discovered two important things about people: First, people do what they want to. We always seem to find the time, money, and energy to do what is important to us, and what is important to us is seen in our actions, not in our words. Secondly, people always seem to follow the path of least resistance, unless they are led by the Spirit of God.

Big But Becky had a final opportunity to do the right thing, but she couldn't bring herself to do it. My upcoming departure was known for some time, during which she wrestled internally with an inflammation of Big But-itis. Would she do the right thing or justify her Big But behavior? In the end, she did what she wanted to do and took the path of least resistance. This is the way it always goes if one is not led by the Spirit of God. While she justified it in her mind, her behavior betrayed her.

The Big But Syndrome seeks entry into every situation no matter how small the opening, unless a life controlled by the Spirit of God keeps it out. Till the very end, Big But Becky yearned for control. She sent an intentionally hurtful message that screamed, "I am not going to give you a decent sendoff because all you did was stifle my Big But!" It's true; I didn't allow her Big But to reign, and she massaged her guilt by sending a Big But note at the last possible moment to cover her tracks.

My Own Big But

The Big But scenarios I have shared are typical, everyday Big But stories. They are neither sensational in nature, nor obscure in their occurrence. They are illustrative of how Big But perspectives enter everyday life and hinder our relationship with God and others.

It wouldn't be right for me to point out everyone else's Big But and neglect my own. Nobody likes the gym rat showing off his six-pack stomach and large pectoral muscles while everyone else is sweating profusely on the treadmill and gasping for air. To be honest, I don't have large pectoral muscles, and rather than the coveted six-pack, washboard look, my stomach is a one-pack. Hey, why carry around six packs when you can carry around one?

As much as I hate to admit it, I too have a Big But. I am on the treadmill right next to you trying to work on my own protruding But. While I struggle to keep it in check, it pops out at the most inopportune times. It is challenging to control

But size, and about the time I think my But is getting thinner and smaller, BANG—it bursts right out again!

I find myself looking in the mirror quite often these days. The reflection allows me to check my But size on a regular basis. I give the precious Holy Spirit permission to search me, examine me, move me, convict me, and change me. It is never easy to see one's reflection in a mirror and observe all the flaws staring back. Yet, smoothing rough edges and reducing But size is good work that moves us closer to Christ. Though it is painful, it is productive and necessary.

The time when I think my But was biggest and most dangerous to my spiritual health came after nearly ten years of full-time pastoral ministry. I was worn out. Had I been a shoe, I would have been a sole-less one. The sides were there, my toes were covered, and shoe strings were present, but my shoes had no bottom. I was walking around on bare feet covered with shoestrings and loose leather flapping in the wind, all the while believing I was wearing shoes. When you walk around like that for a long time, your feet become sore, cut, bruised, and bloody. You notice every uneven piece of concrete, and each rock you step on produces pain. When you finally reach soft grasses with the hope of finding relief, you discover burs, bugs, and barbs. The promise of comfort and normalcy quickly fades away.

Granted, I was a rookie minister, unrefined in my thinking and ministerial skills, but I was gifted from the Lord and willing to charge hell with a water pistol and a bucket of water. I wanted to serve with all my heart, preach the Scriptures, and be an instrument of God for touching hurting lives. God commandeered that desire of mine and asked me to shepherd two of the most difficult churches in the district. He certainly has a sense of humor, doesn't He?

The first assignment was a "key city project" church. In those days, cities were selected across the United States for establishing denominational church plants. A building and parsonage were purchased, and the newly formed congregation struggled to survive under the huge load placed upon its shoulders. With nearly all income utilized for debt reduction, outreach efforts were limited and collective energies focused upon survival. This is not a smart church planting strategy. Yet, in a state where more people were leaving than coming, this small "key city project" church doubled in size, cut the cords of district subsidy, and financially stood on its own feet. Yet, it was not without cost.

In every church, there seems to be at least one antagonist whose goal in life is to torment the minister. I wonder if these folks go to bed at night dreaming up ways to hurt and maim God's shepherds. Antagonists see themselves as protectors of the church—gatekeepers of God's little local body. Yet, it never dawns on them that instead of protectors, they are destroyers—not gatekeepers, but gate-closers who shut seekers out of the kingdom.

Here I was, ready to charge the hill, conquer the enemy, and advance the kingdom, arm-in-arm with fellow believers. I knew the enemy was at the top of the hill, but I never expected to be shot at by those at the bottom of the hill or those charging the hill with me. How do you survive *that*? When bullets are flying from the enemy in front, you can duck, hide behind a tree, or crouch near the ground. However, when knives are thrust in your torso by those at your side and shots ring out from among your own ranks, all aimed at you, it becomes apparent that you are no leader; you are a target with a big red bull's-eye on your chest. Serving in this local church was about target practice, not advancing the kingdom in any significant way.

The church paid me very little. I saved a few dollars for taxes and schooling and wound up living on nothing but love and hope with two children in diapers. Those were the days when I prayed someone might ask us to their home for dinner or take us out after church so we could enjoy a decent meal.

As I moved on to a larger church, complete with a Christian school, new education wing and gymnasium, I thought to myself, "Surely, things will be better here." During my interview, I asked the governing board how they encouraged their pastor. After looking at each other with wide eyes, stunned glances, and complete astonishment, one elder piped up, "Well, we make sure to tell him what he is doing wrong." Wow! If this was their encouragement, what was I in for? It didn't take long before I found out.

Why would you accept such a church, you ask? At that time I did what most pastors do—jumped from the frying pan into the fire. The heat from the frying pan drains you, and antagonists are difficult to deal with on a daily basis. In the end, it is easier to jump from a difficult situation to a more hopeful one. Moving on becomes the path of least resistance, the path with the least pain. When you're wounded on the battlefield you want to go home and tend to your wounds.

Sure, the new church meant higher pay, a larger congregation, and closer proximity to family, but in reality, I wanted to escape the heat. Being stuck on a hill and shot at from all sides made little sense to me. I wanted to work with others in advancing the kingdom, not become a moving target on the firing range. I was eager to move on to those who desired ministry rather than rebellion. So when I heard the words, "Well, we make sure to tell him what he is doing wrong," I suppressed them, made excuses for the board, and chalked it up to not knowing how to respond. I jumped from a hot frying pan directly into the fire, a situation far worse than the first.

The difficulties of my new church were intense. I was a little wiser to them now that this was my second full-time ministry position, but they were no less painful. If the former church produced antagonists of the average kind, this church produced antagonists on steroids. Yet, despite the adversities, I sensed a calling to both churches. Each experienced substantial ministry, and each experienced significant battles from within. For many, I was a godsend, and to others, I was a devil. Which one was it?

My mind struggled to understand the nasty folks in the church. Were they even Christians at all, or were they just badly behaved ones? After serving this congregation for nearly five years, I was asked to leave, not for theological or moral grounds, but for ugly, insignificant minutia amounting to excuses, not reasons. In justifying their behavior, church leaders pointed to Paul and Barnabas each going their own way (Acts 15:36–41). They reasoned that if Paul and Barnabas could part ways, they also had the biblical green light to ask for my departure. Church growth produces change, change produces threat, threat produces conflict, and it is easier to ask one person to leave than to actually deal with Big But issues in a biblical manner. In one phone call, I lost my church, my income, my home, and my community. I nearly lost my dignity after being forced to move in with my generous in-laws.

The district superintendent, a man with considerable years of ministry under his belt, and who would later become a college and denominational president, said to me, "I have never met anyone in ministry who has gone through as much as you have." He paused, looked me straight in the eye and continued, "But you have handled it well." He understood the arduous landscape I was traversing and affirmed that my responses to such rough terrain were God-honoring.

> Lying on the battlefield all bloodied and bowed, you begin to ask "why" questions—disturbing questions about the very existence and nature of God.

I began to weep, because his opinion mattered. I respected him, and that kind of remark made the next leg of my journey a bit easier. There were plenty of times when I could have laid in to people, opened them up and exposed them, and improperly used spiritual authority to undermine, manipulate, and frustrate their evil purposes. Had I been in charge of sending people to heaven during those difficult days, many of them would have been on the very first bus!

But I didn't. I couldn't. To do so would have lowered me to their level, and I purposed deep in my heart that no matter how difficult my circumstances, they would not undermine my commitment to Christ. I had handled it well. God was proud of me. Though it nearly broke me, I did the right thing, at the right time, and in the right way.

Now comes the Big But part. If you have been wounded in battle, suffered great loss, or experienced severe pain, you know exactly what I am referring to. Wounded people begin to question the battle, the war, their role in it, and whether the fight is worth the effort. Lying on the battlefield all bloodied and bowed, you begin to ask "why" questions—disturbing questions about the very existence and nature of God.

Is there really a God? Why does He allow evil to exist? Is He in some way culpable for all the pain in this world, including my own? Why did God allow me to go through this? What did I ever do to deserve such pain when all I wanted in life was to serve Him with my whole heart? Is God really a good God? Where is His power to help me?

It would be five years before I could celebrate communion again, and still more years before my heart could sing. The scars stand as a constant reminder of a painful past, and although faded, the memories remain. What *has* changed is my perspective: how I view the scars, pain, trials, and their meaning and significance in my life. I am convinced that God uses greatly those who have been wounded deeply. Mine were scars of faithfulness and commitment to my Lord, no matter who inflicted them.

In his quest to draw us away from our Creator, Satan uses difficult circumstances against us. He entices us to question God's nature and purposes in our life. He tried this on Job, and he hit me with it as well, but I was not as successful as Job.

My personality pursues understanding. It's my nature. It's how I am wired. I love learning, perceiving, interpreting, growing, and comprehending. While I want to wrap my arms around all there is, draw it close to me, and seek to understand, I have come to the conclusion that I *don't* know everything. I *won't* understand everything, even though I *want* to, and that's just the way it is in this world. Why God allowed me to experience such deep pain in ministry, I doubt I will fully understand in this life.

What I do know is this: because of my experiences I am more patient, caring, forgiving and less judgmental toward others. I have sifted through the fluff of Christianity and hold loosely to matters of personal preference, minutia, and doctrinal issues where well-meaning Christians can differ. My commitment to God is no longer a mile wide and an inch deep. Rather than a thin layer of superficiality, my faith is deeper and more focused than ever. I know what I am willing to die for and what I am not. I realize God is God, and I am not.

Sounds pretty simple, doesn't it? A fellow goes through a difficult time, learns some life lessons, and moves on. While true, it oversimplifies things and diminishes the painful journey. It misses the "But trimming" and minimizes the time, energy, and emotions involved. In my life, the rough edges were being smoothed down in the Lord's workshop, and one couldn't possibly ignore the thunderous buzzing sound.

During the five years it took for me to feel comfortable celebrating the Lord's Supper again, I wrestled with the Big But Syndrome. Getting rid of a Big But is no easy task. It is challenging, like pulling a dandelion up from the ground. You have to go down deep and pull it out by the root, or it quickly grows back again. In a spiritual way, getting rid of a Big But is really pulling up roots.

> I thought He was doing a pretty poor job of being God and if I were His boss, I would fire Him for incompetence.

My ministry didn't go as I had planned, and when pain ran me over like a freight train, I whipped out my Big But: "God, I trust You, *but* this doesn't seem like a good path to travel. I am committed to You, *but* this is ridiculous. I know You are a loving God, *but* You sure have an odd way of showing it. I am willing to follow You, *but* there has to be an easier way. God, what is wrong with You, *but* hey, just saying. At least one of us is being faithful, *but* I could be wrong." My But-list got larger and louder.

I was questioning the goodness of God, the power of God, the sovereignty of God, the nature of God, the love of God, and nearly everything about God. I thought He was doing a pretty poor job of being God and if I were His boss, I would fire Him for incompetence. I was hurt and didn't understand the larger picture, so I blamed Him. I didn't want anything to do with the church, and yes, I would still follow Him, but I would hang my head, kick my heels, and pout like a spoiled adolescent so He knew how upset I was. Yes, I had a Big But, and I used another Big But to justify my Big But. In essence, I had a double Big But. My heart was turning to stone, and I needed God to be patient with me while His love melted the concrete barrier surrounding my heart.

God was patient with me back then, and He is still patient with me today. There are times when I climb into the Father's lap, beating my fists upon His breast while claiming right to my Big But. As He wraps His loving arms around me, my strength gives way, my anger turns to tears, and soon my fists stop flailing as He draws me close, once again embarrassed of my Big But. Will I ever learn? I hope so, but until I do, I am sure glad God is more patient with me than I am with Him.

BIBLE BIG BUTS

2

We know two things for certain: 1) that other Christians have Big Buts, and 2) so do we. What I observe so readily in others is also apparent in my own life. Think about it: from *our* perspective, everyone else is in the "other Christians" category, and we immediately identify their obnoxious Big But behaviors. Yet, from *their* perspective, we are included in the "other Christians" category. Simply put, no one is immune; we all have issues with the Big But Syndrome.

Big But-itis is not some quirky cultural phenomenon or a new twenty-first century spiritual predicament. Quite the opposite is true. But-ness has been around for quite a long time. Don't believe me? Even a modest survey of the Bible will prove me right. Both Old and New Testaments contain abundant examples of Big But-itis. A sampling of key Bible Big Buts should easily convince us that the problem is far greater than we might have initially imagined.

New Testament Big Buts
Big But Satan: *Pride*
Matthew 4:1–11

> Then Jesus was led up by the Spirit into the wilderness to be tempted by the devil. And after He had fasted forty days and forty nights, He then became hungry. And the tempter came and said to Him, "If You are the Son of God, command that these stones become bread." But He answered and said, "It is written, 'Man shall not live on bread alone, but on every word that proceeds out of the mouth of God.'" Then the devil took Him into the holy city and had Him stand on the pinnacle of the temple, and said to Him, "If You are the Son of God, throw Yourself down; for it is written, 'He will command His angels concerning You'; and 'On their hands they will bear You up, so that You will not strike Your foot against a stone.'" Jesus said to him, "On the other hand, it is written, 'You shall not put the Lord your God to the test.'" Again, the devil took Him to a very high mountain and showed Him all the kingdoms of the world and their glory; and he said to Him, "All these things I will give You, if

You fall down and worship me." Then Jesus said to him, "Go, Satan! For it is written, 'You shall worship the Lord your God, and serve Him only.'" Then the devil left Him; and behold, angels came and began to minister to Him.

Satan, or Lucifer as he is called in the Old Testament, possesses such a corpulent But that it eventually causes his downfall. He lost a significant role in heaven, is booted from the presence of God, and now spends his time growling at the children of God.

Satan's initial Big But is triggered by pride and feeling discontent with his appointed position. Instead of serving the Creator, he drools and craves a more lofty position; he aspires to be God. He thinks more highly of himself than he ought, and playing second fiddle is unacceptable in his eyes. He sees a throne and wants to sit upon it.

As the perfect, holy, and infinite Creator and Sustainer of life, God is worthy of receiving praise and adoration from His creation. Satan's role in the heavenly realms, many Bible teachers believe, was to protect the glory of God as a Seraphim angel. But Satan can never be as high, lofty, important, and glorious as the Creator, for he is merely a created being. Like a lump of clay on the potter's wheel, Satan is shaped by the craftsman's skilled hands to be a jug. Unfortunately, the jug doesn't want to be a jug; it wants to be the potter himself. Instead of being filled with the contents of its purpose, the jug is filled with pride and dissatisfaction.

Not much is known about Satan's heavenly role prior to his downfall, but many Bible teachers believe Isaiah 14:12–14 indicates the reason for such calamity:

How you have fallen from heaven, O star of the morning, son of the dawn! You have been cut down to the earth, you who have weakened the nations! But you said in your heart, "I will ascend to heaven; I will raise my throne above the stars of God, and I will sit on the mount of assembly in the recesses of the north. I will ascend above the heights of the clouds; I will make myself like the Most High."

The five "I wills" rising from Satan's heart reveal a jug brimming with pride and dissatisfaction at his created status.

1. *I will ascend to heaven.*

2. *I will raise my throne above the stars of God.*

3. *I will sit on the mount of the assembly.*

4. *I will ascend above the heights of the clouds.*

5. *I will make myself like the Most High.*

Keep in mind that Big But-itis is revealed in many ways, not just by saying the word "but." The deadly disease is exposed when we use "but" in sentences designed to condition, justify, excuse, or reveal discontentment. Yet, *Big But-itis is much more than the use or non-use of the "but" word; it is a perspective or behavior that conditions, justifies, or excuses our conduct and thinking, or reveals discontentment with God.*

Satan didn't use "but" in his statements, yet we easily read between the lines an underlying Big But attitude. Whether "but" is utilized or not, just beneath the surface we find a common denominator—the deteriorating posture of one's heart. Rephrasing Satan's "I wills" with the "but" word helps us see the underlying attitude at hand.

1. *God, You are in heaven now, but that is where I want to be.*

2. *God, Your throne is in heaven above the stars, but that is where I want to be.*

3. *God, You sit on the mount of assembly, but I want to sit there.*

4. *God, You are above the heights of the clouds, but that is where I want to be.*

5. *God, You are the Most High, but that is what I want to be.*

Jesus taught that words not only flow *from* the heart, they also reveal what is *in* the heart (Mt. 15:18–20). Satan's words reveal an ugly and evil Big But perspective.

According to Revelation 12:9, Satan is cast out of heaven: "And the great dragon was thrown down, the serpent of old who is called the devil and Satan, who deceives the whole world; he was thrown down to the earth, and his angels were thrown down with him." His Big But attitude eventually seals his doom in Revelation 20:10: "And the devil who deceived them was thrown into the lake of fire and brimstone, where the beast and the false prophet are also; and they will be tormented day and night forever and ever."

Big But perspectives have consequences—perhaps not as severe as Satan's final doom, but consequences nonetheless. When discontentment fills the heart, our relationship with the Father is hampered, spiritual growth is impeded, and our view of God is obstructed. We reap the consequences of sowing such attitudes and deeds, and they are never positive.

Satan's heavenly fall did little to change his outlook as noted in I Peter 5:8: "Be of sober spirit, be on the alert. Your adversary, the devil, prowls around like a roaring lion, seeking someone to devour." Satan doesn't learn his lesson even after being expelled from heaven. Instead, his But grows to portly proportions, and his entire mission in life is that of prowling and pouncing on God's people. Like our adversary, when we continue down the wrong path refusing to learn important lessons, our Buts become more expansive and problematic.

The devil even tries his hand with Jesus. It is yet another opportunity to demonstrate his prowling and pouncing prowess, this time with the Son of God. He will fail once again, but his devouring desire is revealed in his Big But.

Soon after being baptized by John the Baptist, Jesus "was led up by the Spirit into the wilderness to be tempted by the devil" (Mt. 4:1). He remains in the wilderness forty days and nights facing and conquering all that Satan hurls at Him. This is an important season in His life—a time of testing and calling forth obedience. It is Satan's opportunity to inflict damage and embarrassment upon the One he despises. Will Jesus make a mistake? Will He fail? Will He sin? Will Satan mock and embarrass the Creator? Will the flow of God's sovereignty be disrupted? Will Satan's Big But instigate a coup d'état? Will the enemy force a realignment of God's purposes? Well, of course not, but Big Buts always have to give it a try, despite the odds. That's the deceptive power of the Big But Syndrome; like a riptide forcefully pulling us out to sea, we often rebel against God's will thinking the odds are forever in our favor. They never are.

Jesus can easily accomplish all that Satan proposes. Without effort, our Lord can turn stones into bread or jump from the Temple pinnacle without injury. But that isn't the real issue, is it? Jesus will go on to raise dead men to life, turn water into wine, feed five thousand people with five loaves of bread and two fish, heal multiple diseases, and be resurrected from the dead. Turning stones into bread is no big feat for Him. The issues go much deeper than stones and bread. The devil's But-speak can be seen in his "if" challenges to Jesus.

1. *If You are the Son of God, command that these stones become bread.*

2. *If You are the Son of God, throw Yourself down, for God will take care of You.*

3. *If You are the Son of God, bow down and worship me, and I will give You all kingdoms.*

Jesus recognizes But-speak when He hears it, and He sees through the repulsive attitude underlying these "if" phrases. They are nothing more than veiled Big But words—a jug dissatisfied with its purpose and overflowing with pride and dissatisfaction. Rephrasing Satan's temptations with "but" words help us discern the underlying Big But attitude.

1. Of course You are the Son of God, aren't You? You shouldn't question your Sonship even though God led You into a dessert without food, *but* just to make sure, You could turn these stones into bread to prove who You are.

2. Why, of course You are the Son of God. You shouldn't question God's leading, Your abilities, Your mission, or why You are without food in a desert, *but* You could jump off the Temple pinnacle to see if He will really protect You, just to be sure of God's calling.

3. See all the kingdoms I oversee and all the power I possess? I will give them all to You, *but* first, You must bow down and worship me.

Realizing his plan is once again failing, Satan's last temptation exposes his true intent: seeking to be worshipped. The insolent jug wants to be the potter rather than the clay. And once again, he fails; a second-time loser. As an example to the rest of us, Jesus sees through it, exposes it, and endures it to the glory of the Father.

Satan tops the list of Bible Big Buts. His Big But perspective leads to an unsuccessful rebellion and ejection from the heavens. Once fallen, he attacks the Son of God and continues prowling and pouncing on believers today. Big Buts, a problem then, and a problem now.

Big But Disciples: *Unbelief*
Matthew 15:32–38

And Jesus called His disciples to Him, and said, "I feel compassion for the people, because they have remained with Me now three days and have nothing to eat; and I do not want to send them away hungry, for they might faint on the way." The disciples said to Him, "Where would we get so many loaves in this desolate place to satisfy such a large crowd?" And Jesus said to them, "How many loaves do you have?" And they said, "Seven, and a few small fish." And He directed the people to sit down on the ground; and He took the seven loaves and the fish; and giving thanks, He broke them and started giving them to the disciples, and the disciples gave them to the people. And they all ate and were satisfied, and they picked up what was left over of the broken pieces, seven large baskets full. And those who ate were four thousand men, besides women and children.

Jesus' public ministry attracts booming crowds, and according to Matthew 7:28–29, "the crowds were amazed at His teaching; for He was teaching them as one having authority, and not as their scribes." Folks recognize a difference in Jesus—a difference that renders Him attractive and winsome. But amazement at His teaching isn't the only reason so many come out to see Him.

People sense that Jesus actually cares for them—that He is a compassionate and knowledgeable individual. Rather than abuse, use, and manipulate others for His own personal gain, He initiates a healing ministry as one way to demonstrate His benevolence toward them. News of His ministry spreads like wildfire.

In this particular passage, Jesus hikes up a mountain to garner some time for Himself. Instead of solitude, a great multitude arrives with their sick, lame, blind, dumb, and crippled. Moved with compassion, Jesus heals them. Quite a crowd must have gathered, for He was ministering to them for three consecutive days. Realizing the group has been without food all this time, Jesus is again moved with compassion, not to heal them, but to feed them. Not wishing to send seekers away hungry, He turns to His disciples for a solution to the food shortage.

> Focusing on our circumstances instead of God's ability creates fertile breeding grounds for Big But-itis.

For the disciples, this is a moment of testing, a moment to call forth faith. Yet, after witnessing the miraculous healing power of Jesus to cure the sick, restore sight to the blind, cause the dumb to speak, and make the lame whole again, they don't have enough foresight and faith to believe He can feed four thousand people. Somehow, the disciples don't connect His power with their need. It would have been exciting had they exclaimed, "Lord, You have the power to feed all these people with only seven loaves of bread and a few fish. That's all we have, but we believe in You. We have watched You perform miracle after miracle these last three days. With faith, let's feed this crowd and continue ministering to them."

Our Lord is sounding the depth of their faith, and instead of a glorious moment of spiritual success, it is simply another Big But failure. For three days Jesus is healing everyone who comes to Him and displays of miraculous power occur right under their noses. Now it is their moment to shine, to show forth what they have learned and observed. Sadly, their Big But gets the best of them as they reply, "Where would we get so many loaves in this desolate place to satisfy such a large crowd?" (Mt. 15:33).

This is But-speak. In essence, they are saying, "Lord, why are You looking to us for an answer to the food problem? We understand there is a great need with so many people, but after all, we are in a desolate place and the options are limited. We don't see an answer. I guess we should dismiss them and let them go home hungry." Do you recognize their Big But perspective?

The disciples display the Big But of unbelief. Though they are in the center of a flurry of miraculous activity, they never see how that power applies to their need. They miss what God is doing, how He is moving in their own lives, and how He can use this situation to demonstrate His power. Their focus is on the desolate location and its lack of resources rather than on the power of God to meet their present need. Focusing on our circumstances instead of God's ability creates fertile breeding grounds for Big But-itis. Even the disciples, those closest to Jesus, faced the Big But Syndrome. No one is immune.

Big But Rich Man: *Materialism*
Matthew 19:16–22

> And someone came to Him and said, "Teacher, what good thing shall I do that I may obtain eternal life?" And He said to him, "Why are you asking Me about what is good? There is only One who is good; but if you wish to enter into life, keep the commandments." Then he said to Him, "Which ones?" And Jesus said, "You shall not commit murder; you shall not commit adultery; you shall not steal; you shall not bear false witness; honor your father and mother; and you shall love your neighbor as yourself." The young man said to Him, "All these things I have kept; what am I still lacking?" Jesus said to him, "If you wish to be complete, go and sell your possessions and give to the poor, and you will have treasure in heaven; and come, follow Me." But when the young man heard this statement, he went away grieving; for he was one who owned much property.

Jesus always has a way of getting to the heart of the matter. Instead of dancing around issues, engaging in political spin, or appeasing crowds with what tickles their fancy, Jesus penetrates deeper, pinpoints issues, and leaves listeners with choices to be made.

He does this very thing during His famous Sermon on the Mount (Mt. 5–7). While everyone believes the sheer outward physical act of adultery is sinful, Jesus pinpoints the matter as an issue of the heart: "But I say to you that everyone who looks at a woman with lust for her has already committed adultery with her in his heart" (Mt. 5:28). When others feel it is the mere outward act of killing another that is iniquitous, Jesus pinpoints the matter as an issue of the heart: "But I say to you that everyone who is angry with his brother shall be guilty before the court" (Mt. 5:22).

In Luke 18:9–17, Jesus shares a tale about a slithering, self-righteous Pharisee and a self-condemning, penitent tax collector. It is quintessential teaching between that which is external and seen by others and that which is internal and valued by God.

Two different individuals go to the Temple to pray. One is dripping with religious pride; the other is dripping with humility. One thinks highly of himself; the other feels unworthy. One engages in all the right outward religious acts, such as praying and giving, while the other struggles to do any of it. One looks down upon other people; the other looks down upon himself. One feels superior by comparing himself to other folks, while the other senses a great chasm between what he is and what God wants him to be. One exalts himself; the other lowers himself. With pride billowing in his heart, one declares, "God, I thank You that I am not like other people: swindlers, unjust, adulterers, or even like this tax collector. I fast twice a week; I pay tithes of all that I get" (Lk. 18:11–12). The other, feeling insignificant and unable to even lift his eyes toward heaven, stands at a distance, beats his breasts in shame, and desperately cries out, "God, be merciful to me, the sinner!" (Lk. 18:13).

The contrast between these two men couldn't be more distinct. Speaking of the lowly and despised tax collector, Jesus summarizes the account: "I tell you, this man went to his house justified rather than the other; for everyone who exalts himself will be humbled, but he who humbles himself will be exalted" (Lk. 18:14). Once again, Jesus pinpoints the real issue as one of the heart.

There is no religious sect called "Pharisees" in our modern age, yet we understand the parable and identify with the message Jesus is conveying. While we lack Pharisees and a Jewish Temple, we are not without an overabundance of pride. Severe privation of humility permeates our world, and in that regard, our age is not much different than the days of Jesus.

We find individuals today who are all too eager to whip out their scroll of biblical rules, mandates, and legislation. For them, following Jesus is a matter of strictly adhering to a set of rules and mandates. The Bible is nothing more than a legislative book—a collection of codified laws to obey. In their view, we become godly Christians by knowing all the rules, obeying all the rules, and helping others obey all the rules. The more rules we know and obey, the better Christians we become. Rules are easy to quantify. As we keep track of our rule-keeping prowess, we can compare our "obedience quotient" to that of others who may not be as good at memorizing and obeying the biblical manual of legislative mandates. If we obey 295 rules and our neighbor only obeys twenty-nine, we consider ourselves spiritually superior and feel pretty good about our level of holiness.

However, this is a false comparison; nothing more than a hill of beans. No matter who we are or where we are in life, there is always someone on a lower rung of the ladder. Since we are always more generous with ourselves than we are with others, our self-perspective is continually skewed. God doesn't call us to compare ourselves with each other. If that were the case, rule-keeping might make sense. Instead, our measuring stick is the holiness of God Himself as seen in 1 Peter 1:14–16, "As obedient children, do not be conformed to the former lusts which were yours in your ignorance, but like the Holy One who called you, be holy yourselves also in all your behavior; because it is written, 'You shall be holy, for I am holy.'" When we realize that the pure, unadulterated holiness of God is the standard by which our lives are measured, we are more apt to fall in line with the lowly tax collector and pray, "God, be merciful to me, the sinner!" (Lk. 18:13).

Jesus contrasts the outward with the inward—that which is merely religious action and that which emanates from a genuine heart. In a world of outward pretenders and upside-down values, we always find Jesus pinpointing the real issue, the heart.

When Mr. Big But rich man approaches Jesus (Mt. 19:16–22), he does so with pride in his heart, seeking justification and vindication for all of the

> In no time, legalism can turn the tenderest of hearts into stone.

outward religious acts he has accomplished. After all, in his mind, he has kept all the commandments and feels he is lacking very little. Concerned about his soul in the afterlife, the rich man asks what other outward religious act he must do to inherit eternal life. In comparing himself to others, he realizes he is pretty good at keeping rules. For him, following God is a matter of strictly obeying the regulations and mandates from the holy legislative manual. If he can obey the right number of rules, or if he can learn the right combination of rules to keep, he has a chance to impress God. By doing one more "good thing," he will assure himself of life after death. In his judgment, attaining eternal life is merely a puzzle to be solved, a lock to be cracked, or a rule to be obeyed, not the unconditional surrender of one's heart.

He assumes it is a "good thing" God desires. He assumes God is chiefly interested in outward religious acts. If he prays harder, longer, and more fervently, God will be awestruck with his rule-keeping ability. So he jumps on his hamster wheel and runs himself ragged, giving more and doing more than everyone else. And, he keeps track of his score and compares it to the score of others. Trying hard to cross the finish line ahead of the masses, he seeks to do one more good deed that will elevate him above the crowd.

This is called legalism, and it is extremely deadly. In no time, legalism can turn the tenderest of hearts into stone. It has the power to seduce those fresh on the road of newfound faith and steer them on detour after detour until the road of Christ can no longer be found. In His reply to the rich young ruler, Jesus goes beyond the question, beyond the outward and external, beyond the religious façade, and pinpoints what is holding this man back from experiencing the fullness of God. He does what many of us are afraid to do—He points out the rich man's Big But.

The heart of Mr. Big But rich man is wrapped around his wealth. He is willing to follow rules, regulations, and mandates and engage in all sorts of "good things" for the Lord, but he is unwilling to do the *one thing* that can free his soul. Jesus responds in Matthew 19:21, "If you wish to be complete, go and sell your possessions and give to the poor, and you will have treasure in heaven; and come, follow Me."

Mr. Big But rich man is a "ninety-percenter." He is willing to follow Jesus to a certain point, but not all the way. He is willing to do that which is within his comfort zone, what he thinks is reasonable, but to give his all and follow Jesus with 100% commitment is a most unreasonable request. To release *everything*, even his precious possessions, is just too much to give up. He is unwilling to let go of that which holds his heart in bondage, and in return, forfeits the chance to be whole. In his eyes, the price is too high and the return is too little.

In essence, the Big But-speak of the Big But rich man sounds like this:

Big But Rich Man:
I will keep as many rules as you desire, *but* I will not part with my prized possessions. I can do great things for Your kingdom with them, *but* asking me to give away what I have worked so hard to attain is unreasonable. How can You ask for everything? I want to be complete, *but* I want to do it on my own terms.

Our lives are like a huge house, complete with multiple rooms, closets, a basement, and an attic. We allow Jesus to enter many rooms, but not all of the rooms. Some are just plain off limits. In the rich young ruler's case, Jesus is not allowed to enter the "possession" room. We say, "Enjoy the house Lord. Hope You relish the leather La-Z-Boy recliner, the big screen television, and the firm mattress with pillow-top padding. Feel free to get in the fridge whenever You want. What's mine is Yours. My house is Your house. So glad You are here."

With an invitation like that, Jesus begins to make Himself at home. We love seeing Him sitting in the leather La-Z-Boy recliner with His feet up. We notice Him getting in the fridge and we smile. We feel good when He enjoys a good night's rest in the plush bed we worked so hard to attain. We are happy He is in our life and love feeling the comfort and security of His presence.

Then one day, after getting the kids off to school, exhausted from a long, sleepless night, another argument with our spouse, and feeling overwhelmed with life, we collapse in a kitchen chair with our elbows on the table and our throbbing head buried in our hands. Not even the smell of fresh coffee can assuage our despair, and the spiritual exhaustion builds to the point of tears. We open our Bible and ask God to speak to our heart, to somehow meet our deepest need. And then it happens; Jesus does what He always does—pinpoints heart issues in our life. He begins opening boxes hidden deep in the storage closet of our life that haven't been opened for years. He begins opening doors to rooms we don't want Him to enter. We want to be complete and whole, but our Big But keeps getting in the way.

That's the way Big But-itis works. The very thing that can bring us wholeness is the very thing our Big But wants to squash. Feeling utterly hopeless is intolerable, *but* we certainly don't want Jesus rummaging around downstairs in those dusty, old storage boxes filled with all the junk that hinders us. Deep down inside, we know our Christian life is shallow and hollow, and if anyone really knew how thin the veneer really was, we couldn't withstand the embarrassment. We yearn to drink long and hard from the water of life, *but* that would mean allowing Jesus access to rooms that have forever been off limits. We know what skeletons live in the closet, but does He? How could we live with the embarrassment and the shame? What if people actually knew how spiritually anemic we really are? We feel the constant disconnect between what we long to be and what God wants us to become. We long to be whole and complete, to truly, deeply experience the living Christ, *but* it requires letting go, letting in, relinquishing control, admitting our many failures, and cleaning out the junk in the basement.

Big Buts get in the way of following and experiencing Jesus. Mr. Big But rich man earnestly desires God in his life and wants to please Him by doing things for Him. Yet, he is unwilling to do the one thing that God desires from him. God doesn't need us to do things *for* Him; He merely wants 100% of our heart. In order to experience His fullness, it is imperative that we deal with issues straight on rather than dancing in circles around them. With laser-like precision, Jesus walks into the rich man's basement, rummages through the stack of old boxes, pulls out the coveted "possession" item, holds it up to the light and declares, "Get rid of this and you will be free."

Mr. Big But rich man has a choice, like we all do when Jesus pinpoints heart issues. Will he make the right choice even though it is difficult, or will he take the path of least resistance? The choice is clear and keenly understood. He walks away sad, realizing that Jesus is unwilling to accommodate his Big But. It is But-ness that prevents him from experiencing wholeness and completeness and keeps him in a constant state of striving, despair, and sadness, always wondering if he has done enough "good things" to earn his way into heaven.

Big But Vineyard Workers: *Fairness*
Matthew 20:1–16

For the kingdom of heaven is like a landowner who went out early in the morning to hire laborers for his vineyard. When he had agreed with the laborers for a denarius for the day, he sent them into his vineyard. And he went out about the third hour and saw others standing idle in the market place; and to those he said, "You also go into the vineyard, and whatever is right I will give you." And so they went. Again he went out about the sixth and the ninth hour, and did the same thing. And about the eleventh hour he went out and found others standing around; and he said to them, "Why have you been standing here idle all day long?" They said to him, "Because no one hired us." He said to them, "You go into the vineyard too." When evening came, the owner of the vineyard said to his foreman, "Call the laborers and pay them their wages, beginning with the last group to the first." When those hired about the eleventh hour came, each one received a denarius. When those hired first came, they thought that they would receive more; but each of them also received a denarius. When they received it, they grumbled at the landowner, saying, "These last men have worked only one hour, and you have made them equal to us who have borne the burden and the scorching heat of the day." But he answered and said to one of them, "Friend, I am doing you no wrong; did you not agree with me for a denarius? Take what is yours and go, but I wish to give to this last man the same as to you. Is it not lawful for me to do what I wish with what is my own? Or is your eye envious because I am generous?" So the last shall be first, and the first last.

This Big But parable involves disgruntled workers who despise the generosity of the vineyard owner. Day laborers gather in the marketplace hoping to be hired for the day. They have nothing to offer but a strong back and their belief that the early bird gets the worm. Dependent upon the needs and generosity of another for their very survival, they are initially grateful for the work. The vineyard owner returns to the marketplace and hires additional workers throughout the day.

Imagine that you own a large building desperately in need of a new paint job. Over the years, the sun, wind, and rain inflict damage on the structure and the time has come to give it a fresh look. You possess the brushes, ladders, tarps, and all the necessary tools. You just need workers to apply the paint. Rather than contract an expensive firm to refresh the building, you remind yourself of those idly standing in the town square, eager to earn some cash and willing to put their muscle to work. You decide to hire them, if they are willing to accept your generous offer.

Realizing the building is large and the time on task will be significant, you hire laborers during the cool of the morning to get an early start. Gladly, they accept your offer and hop in the back of your truck. Departing for the job site, they look back upon those left behind and are grateful to be one of the lucky few chosen that day.

A couple of hours into the job, you realize the task is too big for the number of laborers you picked up in the morning, so you head back and hire a few more. You do this several times throughout the day so the project can be completed. You even go back to pick up a few more workers late in the day, realizing they will only be able to give an hour's worth of work. But, the job must get done.

With the sun setting and the workday complete, you call the workers together and beginning with the last group hired and working backwards, their wages are paid. Those who only put in an hour of work are paid as though they worked the entire day. When the laborers hired first notice the landowner's generosity, their eyes become as silver dollars, and they begin counting and spending all the money they expect to make long before they receive it. In their mind, if the last ones on the job are paid so handsomely after working only one hour, how much more will they receive having worked the entire day?

As they step forward and are paid the agreed-upon wage, surprise and anger rise up. Their grumbling Big But pops out saying, "These last men have worked only one hour, and you have made them equal to us who have borne the burden and the scorching heat of the day" (Mt. 20:12). Though paid exactly the amount stipulated, they feel cheated, believing you weren't fair. They rationalize in their mind a Big But response:

Big But Vineyard Workers:
We know you offered to pay us a day's wage for a day's worth of work, and yes, we were grateful when we were standing in the marketplace eagerly looking for work, **but** since you paid the same to those who arrived late, we want to change our agreement. It just isn't fair. We worked longer and harder than the others and we deserve more.

In all honesty, I think my Big But would have burst through the roof on this one too. This is the Big But of fairness. When we feel ripped off, cheated, taken advantage of, or ill-treated, out pops our Big But. Had we arrived to the worksite late in the day and were paid a full day's wage, we would be rejoicing at the kindness of God and look upon those grumbling and complaining as a bunch of unspiritual sissies whining about His generosity.

Fairness is a matter of perspective, isn't it? We all see life through our personal set of lenses—all different, and all biased to some degree. We rejoice at our own good fortune. In fact, when unexpected blessing comes our way we often feel worthy of it,

> We all see life through our personal set of lenses—all different, and all biased to some degree.

as though we somehow deserved it. When others experience God's blessing, we may rejoice with them outwardly, but inwardly we often despise them. After all, it should have been us, not them. We work harder, have been there longer, understand things better, and if anyone should receive more, it should be us.

I understand this Big But problem all too well and have battled the "fairness" issue in my own heart. I come from humble means. My father was a repairman, and my mother dropped out of high school to deliver three healthy kids at a young age. Church was not a part of my life until the sixth grade. My high school education was severely deficient, never bringing a textbook home, never studying, and never being expected to. After stumbling into college, I discovered such things as a syllabus, lectures, reading, and studying. During my first year of college, I studied five hours each night just to keep up with the other students. Never in my life had I done such a thing. I was behind in so many ways, and it was unfair. I had to work harder than everyone else, and it was unfair. Unfamiliar with higher education, my parents didn't prepare me for this road, and it was unfair.

While in seminary, I worked full-time at night just to pay my bills while other students were given scholarships, grants, and traveled a much easier road. Now, how is that fair?

After my ordination, I sojourned down the path of full-time ministry and began noticing that some folks in the denomination had legacy names. I was a nobody, whereas others could stand on the shoulders and reputation of their missionary parents or their pastor fathers. They seemed to have an advantage, and it was unfair.

My first two full-time churches were the most difficult congregations in the entire district. Why in the world did I get stuck with these churches? It was unfair. I was a good preacher and dedicated myself wholeheartedly. I pursued education in order to better serve others. Certainly I deserved more than what I received. How is it that others not nearly so dedicated, not nearly so educated, not nearly so "Terry-esque" obtained better, stable churches with flourishing ministries?

My capacious But was interfering with my perspective. I saw myself as a victim and defiantly remained faithful to the Lord even though I perceived Him to be unfaithful and unfair to me. When I think back upon my own sizeable But, I am extremely embarrassed. Although my Big But attitude was silent and locked in the inner chambers of my mind, I knew deep inside that I was wrong. Yet, I firmly clutched the key, unwilling to open the door so God's Spirit could sweep the room clean. I wanted to keep my Big But hidden in the prison of my mind where it was safe, protected, and unnoticed by others. Like a fly ridiculously standing firm against the fly swatter, I was saving my Big Buts as ammunition against a holy God who treated me unfairly.

> I was nothing but a piece of clay on the Potter's wheel complaining and grumbling because the Potter wasn't shaping me the way I desired.

How childish and infantile was my thinking. How selfish, biased, and self-serving was my perspective. How limited was my insight and understanding. How distorted were the lenses upon my face. I was nothing but a piece of clay on the Potter's wheel complaining and grumbling because the Potter wasn't shaping me the way I desired.

Like the early vineyard workers, when things don't go the way we expect or desire, and when others experience good fortune and we don't, our Big Buts erupt with skewed perspective and vision. We miss the fact that God is generous, loving, and kind. It would have been great if the early workers said, "Boy, I can't believe it, you guys also experienced the owner's kindness. I am so happy for you. Isn't it great to be working for the vineyard owner? We could still be standing in the town square looking for work. I am so glad he called us. What a great work day it has been!"

It would have been nice if I had the maturity early on in ministry to drop to my knees and cry, "This sure is painful Lord, and I don't understand it all, yet, I am so glad You see all things, know all things, and move in my life to mold and shape me as You see fit. Help me remain strong, yield to Your will, and always trust You, even in these difficult days." But no, I took the path of least resistance, and my Big But attitude hindered my relationship with the Father and blinded my eyes to His work in my life.

Big But Peter: *Selfishness*
Matthew 16:21–23

> From that time Jesus began to show His disciples that He must go to Jerusalem, and suffer many things from the elders and chief priests and scribes, and be killed, and be raised up on the third day. Peter took Him aside and began to rebuke Him, saying, "God forbid it, Lord! This shall never happen to You." But He turned and said to Peter, "Get behind Me, Satan! You are a stumbling block to Me; for you are not setting your mind on God's interests, but man's."

Our final New Testament Big But example is Peter, an apostle known to be impetuous, impatient, intolerant, and sometimes intolerable, along with a persistent habit of sticking his foot in his mouth. He possesses a big heart and an even bigger mouth that gets him in trouble all too often. In Matthew 26:33, for instance, Big But Peter arrogantly declares, "Even though all may fall away because of You, I will never fall away." Jesus sets him straight in verse 34, "Truly I say to you that this very night, before a rooster crows, you will deny Me three times." Peter's foot-shaped mouth and self-assured Big But gets in the way again: "Even if I have to die with You, I will not deny You" (vs. 35).

This is nothing more than a Big But boast from a Big But mouth. Three short verses later, Peter falls flat on his face. With the same Big But fervor he musters in declaring undying commitment to Jesus, he vehemently denies even knowing the Lord in his next breath. Once again, his selfish Big But gets the best of him.

Jesus helps His disciples understand and prepare for his death (Mt.16:21–23). According to traditional Christianity, this is the very reason He descends to earth in the first place, to become the once-for-all, perfect, sinless, substitutionary sacrifice for humankind. His sinless blood will be shed instead of our own. He will die in our place to save us from our sins.

Obviously, the disciples don't grasp all of this even though Jesus tries to establish His identity in their hearts by asking, "Who do people say that the Son of Man is?" (Mt. 16:13). Some think He is John the Baptist, Elijah, Jeremiah, or one of the prophets. More important than what others think of Him, Jesus knows that if His message is to be planted in the hearts of men and women throughout the ages, it must first be planted in the hearts of His disciples. Peering intently into their souls, He asks one of the most penetrating questions He will ever ask them: "But who do you say that I am?" (Mt. 16:15).

At this point, impetuous Peter, big mouth and all, gets it right. In reality, he gets a lot of things right, and this is one of those times. He shines bright in stating, "You are the Christ, the Son of the living God" (Mt. 16:16), to which Jesus replies, "Blessed are you, Simon Barjona, because flesh and blood did not reveal this to you, but My Father who is in heaven" (Mt. 16:17). Peter is sensitive to the Father's insight and recognizes Jesus for who He is. It won't be long before Peter preaches a powerful Pentecost sermon with three thousand souls turning to Christ (Acts 2:41).

This is a potent reminder that God still works with, forgives, and uses people with Big Buts. Peter has his Big But moments for sure, but he also has moments where his behaviors and attitudes become sterling examples to the rest of us. We all experience the inflammation of Big But-itis from time to time, but thank God, He doesn't give up on us. During the early ministry years when my But was mighty huge, God still loved me, worked with me, and refused to give up on me. I am here today, still serving, still loving, and still following Him because He didn't write me off. Instead, He helps me identify and conquer my own Big But.

We don't want to get stuck in the rut of chronic Big But-itis; that is unbecoming and dishonoring to our Lord. We also don't want to deceive ourselves with chronic "halo-opathy," where we pride ourselves in the size of our hallowed halos. Instead, we desire to walk humbly with our God, escaping both extremes.

Though Peter had a mountain-top experience confessing the identity of our Lord, he slid right off that mountain when he heard Jesus predict His death. Dying? Why, that is entirely senseless, a complete waste of the miracles, healings, and star power Jesus has achieved. Moving from a two-bit fisherman to a member of the coveted Twelve is quite an adventure. Who wants to go back to handling smelly fish on a daily basis? He has a good thing going. He is hanging out with a popular figure, and it feels great to be aligned with a mighty movement. Dying, really? A dead Jesus will upset his applecart, and his newfound notoriety will go down the drain. No, he will not allow it.

Peter inappropriately assumes the role of teacher, pulls Jesus aside, and rebukes Him. Can you imagine that? After being celebrated for his spiritual insight, Peter now experiences an acute case of "halo-opathy." He is the Golden Retriever praised for his trick and given a scrumptious doggy treat. Feeling pretty confident about the master's praise, he now lunges for human food—leftovers on a nearby plate. Much to his chagrin, he discovers the grace of his master doesn't extend to human food.

Similarly, Peter pushes it too far. His Big But bursts upon the scene with the following But-speak:

Big But Peter:
Well, sure You are the Son of God, *but* dying is ridiculous. You have a great ministry, Jesus, and I like it a lot, *but* I forbid You from traveling to Jerusalem. I am the one who recognized You as the Son of God, *but* You better listen to me. This is not a good idea and I won't stand for it.

From mountain peak to the valley below, Peter's fall is severe. His mindset is fixated upon his own needs, goals, and desires. What will most benefit him? That is often the determining factor for Big But Christians; what's in it for me? They judge every idea, every program, every ministry, every . . . every . . . everything by what's in it for them. If it furthers their agenda, they are for it. If it furthers their cause, makes them look superior, helps them feel better, aligns with their perspective, goals, and desires, and they are seen as more spiritual because of it, then by all means they are for it. If it doesn't fit these criteria, even if it is straight from God, they are against it.

Peter loves the praise; he is *for* that. He loves traveling with Jesus from town to town where crowds gather; he is *for* that. When Jesus tells him of the Father's plan, Peter doesn't see how it advances his cause, helps him look influential, or makes him feel better, and it certainly doesn't align with his perspective, goals, and desires. Therefore, he is against it. He has the nerve to pull Jesus aside and rebuke Him. My goodness, that is one Big But!

Peter's Big But becomes so large and detrimental that Jesus does something never before seen or heard in His ministry. Recognizing Peter's But-speak as a mindset from the pit of hell, Jesus speaks startling and harsh words in Matthew 16:23: "Get behind Me, Satan! You are a stumbling block to Me; for you are not setting your mind on God's interests, but man's." Ouch! That smarts.

Once again, Jesus proceeds straight to the heart of the matter. He has heard these Big But words before, from the lips of His tempter in the wilderness. Now the deceiver is using Peter's Big But for his own purposes. Without recognizing it, Peter becomes a mouthpiece for the enemy and a stumbling block in the Lord's obedience to the Father.

The Bible doesn't reveal how Peter reacts to this reprimand, but one can easily imagine that, at least for the moment, his halo is tarnished and his star-studded ego falls back down to earth. Big But-ism always goes against the interest of God—always.

Peter's Big But prompts instruction on the cost of discipleship as Jesus states, "If anyone wishes to come after Me, he must deny himself, and take up his cross and follow Me" (Mt. 16:24). Big But-itis is nothing more than a "pit of hell" perspective—a tool used by Satan to hinder kingdom work. Peter's fall from the mountain top is a lesson to us all.

Old Testament Big Buts
Big But Adam And Eve: *Blame*
Genesis 3:8–13

> They heard the sound of the LORD God walking in the garden in the cool of the day, and the man and his wife hid themselves from the presence of the LORD God among the trees of the garden. Then the LORD God called to the man, and said to him, "Where are you?" He said, "I heard the sound of You in the garden, and I was afraid because I was naked; so I hid myself." And He said, "Who told you that you were naked? Have you eaten from the tree of which I commanded you not to eat?" The man said, "The woman whom You gave to be with me, she gave me from the tree, and I ate." Then the LORD God said to the woman, "What is this you have done?" And the woman said, "The serpent deceived me, and I ate."

We can pick our friends in this life, but unfortunately, we're stuck with our relatives. In my case, I am told a man named Ebenezer arrived from England and propagated the flat-bottom gene into a line of Wises across America.

In one sense, we are all related to one another, despite skin color, culture, geographical location, or dialect. On this floating piece of rock called Earth, we are members of the human family, and the root of our family tree can be traced all the way back to Adam and Eve. In a real sense, the first humans created by God started the whole thing. They are parents to the entire human race, the beginning of the family tree, or if you prefer, Mom and Dad.

Do you realize the first nudist camp was actually located in the Garden of Eden? Nakedness without shame was a normal state of being in this place of happiness, bliss, freedom, and joy. Honesty, openness, and direct communication with God and each other was the norm.

Now fallen from heaven, Satan activates his prowling and pouncing skills for use in God's pristine garden. He maliciously desires to corrupt this astonishing place God has created. First, he tempts Eve, who in turn tempts Adam with the disastrous result of disobeying a Creator who gave the first couple everything they could ever need. Satan lies, cheats, steals, and is willing to do whatever it takes to bring about the downfall of those who love God. In the garden, Satan works his magic with Adam and Eve who succumb to his cunning ways.

Many Bible teachers refer to Jesus as the second Adam. Like our original parents, Jesus also plays a representative role for all humankind. In traditional Christianity, Adam and Eve's fall permits sin to enter the human race, and just like I inherited the Wise flat-bottom gene, humankind inherits the ability and propensity to sin. It is a calamitous infection, a plague that negatively affects all of us.

Jesus is portrayed as miraculously born of a virgin—God's perfect plan for overcoming the dreadful plague passed on from human to human. Like Adam and Eve, Jesus is fully human, but without a sin infection. Without the sinful plague, His wilderness temptation of forty days and nights is pivotal to becoming the sinless Savior of the world. Had Jesus surrendered to the cunning ways of Big But Satan, His mission would have failed, sin would have infected Him just like it did Adam and Eve, and our hope of a cure would be dashed against the rocks.

The temptation of Jesus isn't an overnight Boy Scout trip in the woods; it is a monumental turning point in human history. Would He fail as the first parents did in the Garden of Eden, or would He prevail and deliver a cure to the human race? With all the deception, trickery, lying, and deceiving he could muster, Big But Satan, masquerading as an angel of light, threw his very best at Jesus.

The intensity level must have been off the charts. We often fall at the first inkling of inducement, but Jesus withstands the gale force winds of temptation for forty days and nights. All Satan has to do is look at us with a scowl on his face, growl a bit, and we give in. But Jesus gets in the ring with him and overcomes the tempter's blows. Jesus did it. He controls Himself. He yields to the Father's will. He is strong. He stands tall. He successfully resists the devil's tricks. He is the doctor working among plague victims, touching them, ministering to them, hugging them, all without contracting the plague Himself. It isn't an issue of luck or odds, but a determined stand against the enemy.

Successfully enduring temptation without sin meant that Jesus could begin His public ministry and we are the lucky ones, the benefactors, and the recipients of all that His success entails. He is the second Adam. The first one failed; the second one didn't.

In the garden, Satan tempts Eve with a lie. If he can get her to believe that God is withholding something good from her, he might have a chance of succeeding.

It is a jugular vein temptation for Eve, a brilliant strategy by Satan, and a moment of testing for the first couple.

The Big But lie is recorded in Genesis 3:4–5, "The serpent said to the woman, 'You surely will not die! For God knows that in the day you eat from it your eyes will be opened, and you will be like God, knowing good and evil.'" Hmmm, this idea about being like God sounds familiar, doesn't it? Isn't this the very thing Satan himself desires, the very thing that gets him booted from heaven? Satan is dissatisfied with being clay, and instead longs to be the potter. In a very real sense, whenever we believe Big But lies, we too engage in similar thinking.

Like cockroaches scurrying for darkness, lies are exposed when the light of truth is brought to bear upon a situation. God actually has Adam and Eve's best interest in mind. The only thing He is withholding from them is sin, pain, increased labor, death, and spiritual separation. Satan takes something positive from God and turns it upside down in the mind of Eve so she perceives it as negative. He tricks her into thinking that his lies are much better than God's good protection. In her deceived mind, what appears so good, so logical, so right is actually upside down, lopsided, illogical, and absolutely, totally wrong. This is how Big But Satan works, and it is why he appears as an angel of light when, in reality, he is of the darkest kind.

> Like cockroaches scurrying for darkness, lies are exposed when the light of truth is brought to bear upon a situation.

After tasting the fruit and realizing she didn't die on the spot, Eve offers it to her husband, and her Big But begins to spread and infect others. Adam is without excuse. Along with Eve, he also knows what the Lord desires, and without a second thought, he freely eats of the fruit. At least Eve ponders her decision, even though she arrives at a faulty conclusion. Adam doesn't appear to consider the enormity of his actions.

To make a long story short, the Lord discovers their far-reaching deed, evidenced by their shame and the covering of fig leaves. In the serene garden created for the first couple, there is absolutely no need to cover up. The Lord confronts them, and we see our first parents introduce Big But-ology for the entire world to experience.

God asks Adam if he has disobeyed and eaten from the forbidden tree, and out pops Adam's Big But: "The woman whom You gave to be with me, she gave me from the tree, and I ate" (Gen. 3:12). Wow, Adam, that is such a pusillanimous response! Why take responsibility for your actions when you can blame someone or something else?

I am disappointed in Adam. First, he scarfed down the forbidden fruit without consideration for God's clear directive, and second, his attempt to deceive God by shifting blame reveals a fundamental misunderstanding and disrespect for his Creator. This is not a glorious day for good ole dad!

Eve's response to the Lord's inquiry is just as lame; "The serpent deceived me, and I ate" (Gen. 3:13). At least she is truthful; the serpent did indeed deceive her. The shifting of blame, however, is still present. In her mind, the one responsible for her sin is that deplorable serpent who persuades her to disobey. Her response reminds me of comedian Flip Wilson's 1970s variety television show where he plays the character of Geraldine Jones. Dressed up as a woman, Flip's (Geraldine's) famous line is, "The devil made me do it."

Rephrasing Adam and Eve's Big But responses help us identify their But-speak:

Adam:
Sure I ate of the forbidden fruit, **but** it was that woman You gave me who coerced me. What was I to do? It isn't my fault, **but** hers for giving me the fruit when she knew better.

Eve:
Yes, I ate of the fruit, **but** it isn't my fault. How am I to withstand the serpent's deception? It isn't my blunder, **but** the serpent's for deceiving me. How can I be held responsible when I am deceived?

One sure sign of a ruinous case of Big But-itis is the loss of perspective and trust. What more could Adam and Eve want? They had it all. The Lord established a home for them filled with bliss, joy, happiness, and His very presence. All they had to do was obey one command, just one. That's it. Pretty simple, isn't it? But they couldn't do it. Our original human parents were blame-shifters, never taking responsibility for their actions.

When they lost their trust in God, they also lost their perspective. They focused on the one thing they couldn't do, rather than the many good things they could enjoy. A good father protects his children by saying "no" to certain detrimental activities. Children often don't understand this, and grasp only that they have been denied. Since they do not fathom the larger perspective, trust breaks down and out pops their Big But.

When you instruct your child to look both ways before crossing the street, you do so with their best interest in mind. You tell them *not* to do something in order to prevent harm. I didn't allow my children to stay overnight with friends we didn't know. This was a protective gesture to guard against the possible dangerous actions of strangers. Even when my children were allowed to spend the night with familiar friends, we established code words for communicating uncomfortable or dangerous situations. As a loving and caring father, I was trying to protect my precious children.

God does the same thing for His children. He knows that eating the forbidden fruit will have disastrous consequences for all humanity. The only thing He is withholding from His children is disaster. Unable to grasp the larger picture, their nearsightedness costs them dearly. Any fences erected by God along our path protect us from falling into a Big But pothole and injuring ourselves. Though Adam and Eve see the fence, they defiantly climb over it, injuring not only themselves, but the entire human race. Trusting God prevents an inflammation of Big But-itis, and exercising that trust allows us to relax in God's perspective of things rather than our own.

Big But Cain: *Anger*
Genesis 4:3–8

> So it came about in the course of time that Cain brought an offering to the LORD of the fruit of the ground. Abel, on his part also brought of the firstlings of his flock and of their fat portions. And the LORD had regard for Abel and for his offering; but for Cain and for his offering He had no regard. So Cain became very angry and his countenance fell. Then the LORD said to Cain, "Why are you angry? And why has your countenance fallen? If you do well, will not your countenance be lifted up? And if you do not do well, sin is crouching at the door; and its desire is for you, but you must master it." Cain told Abel his brother. And it came about when they were in the field, that Cain rose up against Abel his brother and killed him.

Siblings can be close confidantes and bitter enemies at the same time. There were three kids in my family: an older brother, a younger sister, and myself, the neglected middle child. Firstborn children always find themselves in a coveted and exclusive position. Parents rightfully have a special connection to the one born first, though the child had no input into their birth order. After a firstborn son, my parents desired a baby girl, and instead out popped yours truly. Finally, my sister arrived as the prized baby girl. We often joke about this aspect of our birth order and how I am the unloved black sheep of the family; while it generates some laughs, it isn't true. I can fully declare that my parents loved all of us very much, but I sure milk it for all its worth.

My brother found his way in life through music and became an accomplished trombonist and professor of music education. The looks in the family were passed down to my younger sister, who sang professionally for a time and is one of the kindest people I know. Me? Well, I took after sports and girls, and not necessarily in that order. We all turned out just fine—firstborn, middle child, and baby girl. Unfortunately, the same cannot be said of Cain and Abel.

Growing up, we certainly had our share of spats as kids, some highly memorable and embellished to this day. After chasing me at full speed from the basement to the upstairs living room, my brother shoved me so hard into the wall that my head produced a melon-sized dent in the drywall; nothing that a fake plant couldn't cover up. Yet, when a neighbor boy bullied me, he came to my rescue, offering to pulverize my tormentor if that's what it took. He must have made an impression, because I had no more bully problems. That's the way it goes with brothers and sisters growing up together. Sometimes they can't tolerate each other and bicker among themselves, and at the same time they stand up against those who threaten the familial relationship. They may despise each other for a time, but they don't kill one another.

Cain and Abel were brothers who probably played together and bickered with one another as most siblings do. As adults, however, they took different vocational paths. Cain farms the land while Abel raises flocks. Both are in the food business; one grows seeds while the other raises livestock. Both are good, honest ways to make a living.

When it comes time to present an offering to the Lord, Cain brings forth fruit while Abel presents portions of his flock. The Lord is pleased with Abel's offering, but has no regard for Cain's. The rejection doesn't appear to be a permanent, insurmountable setback for Cain since the Lord says, "Why are you angry? And why has your countenance fallen? If you do well, will not your countenance be lifted up? And if you do not do well, sin is crouching at the door; and its desire is for you, but you must master it" (Gen. 4:6–7).

Cain didn't *have* to kill Abel. He can learn from the Lord's rejection and his next offering can be pleasing to a God who is forgiving, loving, patient, and gracious. Why doesn't Cain choose this path? Instead, he travels another route, one in which anger gets the best of him, and the sin crouching at his door makes its way into his heart.

With anger coursing through his veins, Cain is not to be denied or rejected by anyone, not even God. Growing up with sibling rivalry is typical, but moving from anger to murder is not. Cain's actions reveal the degree of hatred he harbors toward his brother. Cain can please the Lord by learning from his mistake and taking steps to correct his offering. Instead, he allows anger, bitterness, and resentment to control his thoughts and behavior. Whether Cain's murder of Abel is premeditated or the result of an emotional outburst, we do not know. Either way, Abel's blood is spilled and his life is taken from him. Cain becomes world-renowned as the first murderer in human history and epitomizes the disastrous effect wrought by a mom and dad who failed to obey God.

Abel's spilled blood cries out from the ground and God inquires of Cain, "'Where is Abel your brother?' And he said, 'I do not know. Am I my brother's keeper?'" (Gen. 4:9). The Lord knows what happened to Abel, and so does Cain.

Would Cain be honest? Would he own up to his evil act, or would he disrespect his Creator in the same way his parents did?

It reminds me of an incident with my own son during a hot summer vacation. We traveled to beautiful Wyoming in my first new car to visit my elderly grandmother. The countryside stretched for miles in every direction and her place contained horses, dogs, cats, and barns. My daughter played with the scruffy, longhaired outdoor dog who happily transferred his fleas to her hair. We spent one full night taking care of that little episode while my son, silhouetted against a blazing orange sunset, was outside throwing rocks.

The next morning, I noticed a dent in the trunk of the car. Had it been a clunker with peeling paint, rust, and hail damage, it wouldn't have bothered me, but this was a brand new car. I noticed the driveway was filled with rocks the size of the dent and remembered the little tyke outside throwing rocks the night before. I put two and two together and asked him about it. "Son, did one of the rocks you were throwing last night hit the car and cause this dent?" He was now faced with a choice. Would he be honest and tell the truth, which I already knew, or would he allow the sin crouching at his door to master him. He replied much like Cain, "I do not know. Am I my dad's car keeper?" That's not quite what he said, but like Cain, he feigned ignorance.

Cain exhibited a Big But like his parents. Putting Cain's actions into Big But words might look like this:

Cain:

If You must know, I did kill Abel, *but* he deserved it. You accepted his offering, *but* You didn't accept mine. I wanted my offering to be acceptable, *but* You accepted his instead. I killed him out of anger, *but* had You accepted my offering, Abel would still be alive and I wouldn't have been angry.

While Philadelphia is known as the city of brotherly love, the church, I fear, is becoming known as the city of Big But brothers and sisters. Cain would have fit right in to our modern day Big But church culture. Cain possesses such a massive Big But of anger that it moves him to murder. Unhealthy for us in so many ways, anger raises our blood pressure, stresses us out, and causes numerous health-related issues. Not only is anger physically unhealthy, but it is also spiritually unhealthy for us.

Many Christians walk around with "spiritual road rage," or free floating anger at God, at life, at the dog, at the waitress, and at the coffee they drink. They are just angry, period. Sometimes their anger is focused on a particular person or circumstance, and other times it is generalized toward life itself. They might be cool as a cucumber on the outside but a blazing furnace on the inside. They may shake your hand with a smile on their face but internally give you the finger.

Anger, I am told, is a secondary emotion. In other words, it is triggered by something else, like a disappointment, a hurt, an unfulfilled expectation, or a loss. In Cain's case, he is disappointed in God, loses face with a rejected offering, remains unfulfilled in his expectation of receiving God's favor, and instead of moving toward God, he moves in the direction of his hurt.

Realizing that unresolved anger drives a wedge into our relationship with God, Paul remarks in Ephesians 4:26–27, "do not let the sun go down on your anger, and do not give the devil an opportunity." In Paul's mind, unchecked anger can easily lead to sinful behavior. Understanding its potential danger, we prevent a Big But foothold in our lives by dealing quickly with anger. When the treatment of a venomous snake bite is delayed, the risk of death is extremely high. In like manner, the chance of sin taking root in our lives escalates when anger is allowed to percolate. When delay occurs, we are strangled by our own Big But.

While we may not physically lash out and kill someone, our heart can become "Cainanized" when anger permeates our life. Jesus said it best in His Sermon on the Mount talk in Matthew 5:21–22: "You have heard that the ancients were told, 'You shall not commit murder' and 'Whoever commits murder shall be liable to the court.' But I say to you that everyone who is angry with his brother shall be guilty before the court." As a passenger on an unsuspecting host, leeches are annoying and uninvited bloodsuckers. Similarly, anger that is allowed to fester attaches itself to our lives, sucking from us the joy and presence of God. To prevent a severe and chronic case of Big But-itis, get rid of it, and get rid of it quickly.

Big But Abraham: *Fear*
Genesis 12:10–13

> Now there was a famine in the land; so Abram went down to Egypt to sojourn there, for the famine was severe in the land. It came about when he came near to Egypt, that he said to Sarai his wife, "See now, I know that you are a beautiful woman; and when the Egyptians see you, they will say, 'This is his wife'; and they will kill me, but they will let you live. Please say that you are my sister so that it may go well with me because of you, and that I may live on account of you."

Abraham was from Ur of the Chaldeans where he and his wife Sarah met and married. The Lord promises to exalt Abraham, make him a great nation, and bless all the families of the earth through him. Abraham leaves his home, his land, his family, and his job to pursue God's command to go forth "to the land which I will show you" (Gen. 12:1).

Put yourself in Abraham's shoes. You hear God's call upon your life to pick up your belongings and hit the road. God doesn't provide detailed instructions about the trip, only that He will direct you once you get on the road. If you obey, He will bless you. Though unsure of your final destination, you are absolutely certain that He is calling you. In faith, you obey and commence the journey.

That's like piling your family into the van, stopping to fill up the tank, and bowing your head at the gas station praying, "Everyone is here Lord and the tank is full. I am not sure which direction we should go, but I am going to start driving down the road, trusting that You will direct us to the destination of Your choice." You crank the tunes and begin driving with a smile on your face and joy in your heart. God doesn't run His plans by Abraham, seeking his opinion or approval. God's direction comes as Abraham obeys and moves forward in faith. Readying the car, loading everyone in it, and filling up the gas tank is mere preparation. It is when Abraham pulls on to the road, and only then, that God directs him right or left, up or down, north or south. We often sit in our parked car seeking direction, but God leads only when we put it in drive and actually get on the road.

To move forward one step at a time requires courage and faith. Had God asked the same of me, I bet my Big But would have erupted in opposition, "God, I will leave, *but* do I have to do it right now? I will obey, *but* what about the children, the grandparents, my job, my insurance, my plans, my goals, my doctor, my dentist, and my church? We are settled here. I want to follow You, *but* it just doesn't make much sense to move forward without knowing where I am headed." Moments like these become fertile opportunities for the blossoming of Big But-itis, yet Abraham displays no acute symptoms of the debilitating disease.

Good for you Abraham . . . you da man! Way to set a solid example for us to follow. Thanks for not giving in to But-ness, when you easily could have. Thank you for following without question. Man, that takes some faith! Yet, before we jump too quickly on Abraham's bandwagon of praise, a closer examination of his life reveals some Big But incidents.

As Abraham journeys toward the Negev, a famine arises in the land so severe that he makes his way to Egypt, accompanied by his beautiful wife Sarah, in hope of finding sustenance. She appears to be "runway" worthy and could have easily graced the cover of numerous fashion magazines. Abraham, on the other hand, is Mr. Average with an above-average wife. Traveling through unknown territory, Abraham fears that foreigners will choose her stunning beauty over his normalcy, seize her, and leave him for dead. With this scenario in mind, he addresses Sarah. "See now, I know that you are a beautiful woman; and when the Egyptians see you, they will say, 'This is his wife'; and they will kill me, but they will let you live. Please say that you are my sister so that it may go well with me because of you, and that I may live on account of you" (Gen. 12:11–13).

Essentially, Abraham asks his wife to lie in order to protect his own skin. What happened to the trusting Abraham we once knew? He was "da man" of faith, the shining example of what it means to trust in God. He fearlessly leaves his home and country to follow God to an unknown land. Now he asks his wife to lie? Now he is afraid for his life after receiving the promise of God? How can a man pile his family into the van, fill the tank, and hit the road without knowing the final destination, and not trust God to take care of him during the journey?

The very thing Abraham fears actually occurs. Foreigners do indeed notice Sarah's beauty and desire her. Apparently Abraham is a smart man, just a fearful one in this instance. Had this been the only occasion of Big But-itis, we might chalk it up to traveling jitters, but in Genesis 20 we discover a second instance of lying about his wife. In this case, Abraham lies to Abimelech, King of Gerar.

King Abimelech doesn't realize that Sarah is Abraham's wife. When the Lord discloses this to him, he calls for Abraham saying, "What have you done to us? And how have I sinned against you, that you have brought on me and on my kingdom a great sin? You have done to me things that ought not to be done." And Abimelech said to Abraham, "What have you encountered, that you have done this thing?" (Gen. 20:9–10). Abraham replies, "Because I thought, surely there is no fear of God in this place, and they will kill me because of my wife. Besides, she actually is my sister, the daughter of my father, but not the daughter of my mother, and she became my wife" (Gen. 20:11–12). Really? This was Abraham's great plan of trust? Whenever he and Sarah encounter suspicious and powerful foreigners he asks her to lie, "This is the kindness which you will show to me: everywhere we go, say of me, 'He is my brother'" (Gen. 20:13).

There is often a kernel of truth in every lie, and Abraham justifies his words as a partial truth, noting that Sarah really is his half-sister from another mother. The intent, however, is to deceive the foreigner in order to save his own skin. Unfortunately, Sarah isn't Miss Perfection either when it comes to her relationship with Abraham. Unable to conceive, Sarah presents Hagar, her handmaiden, to Abraham so there can be an heir. Sarah becomes jealous when Hagar conceives, and treats her harshly with disrespect, for Sarah longs to be the pregnant one. Is this But-ness erupting on the scene? Though God promises them a child, Sarah is taking things into her own hands.

The older Sarah becomes, the more she laughs and mocks the promise of God to bless her with a son. In Genesis 18, the Lord appears to Abraham by the oaks of Mamre. While Abraham is sitting at the tent door in the heat of the day, three men suddenly stand opposite him. Knowing that Sarah is inside the tent listening, one of them remarks to Abraham, "I will surely return to you at this time next year; and behold, Sarah your wife will have a son" (Gen. 18:10). Abraham and Sarah are well beyond childbearing years and Sarah laughs to herself saying, "After I have become old, shall I have pleasure, my lord being old also?" to which the visitors respond, "Is anything too difficult for the LORD? At the appointed time I will return to you, at this time next year, and Sarah will have a son" (Gen. 18:12, 14).

By rephrasing Abraham and Sarah's Big But behavior, we can easily recognize their But-speak:

Abraham:
I will follow God to an unknown land, **but** I have to lie about my wife so I don't get killed. Lord, I know You are big enough to protect me, lead me, and guide me, **but** Sarah is gorgeous and these foreigners will kill me if I tell them she is my wife.

Sarah:
I know You promised us a son, **but** we are way beyond childbearing years and it can't happen. I believe in You, **but** this is way too much to handle. How can I have a child when we are both so old?

Hebrews 11:8 uplifts Abraham as a great man of faith for believing God and following Him even without knowing his travel destination. Sarah is even portrayed as a woman of faith in Hebrews 11:11. Yet, each of them had their Big But moments of shame.

One thing we learn from Abraham and Sarah's Big But-itis is that they are like most of us—a mix of trust and distrust, obedience and disobedience, good days and bad days. Whenever we look to people, we discover Big But failures, even in the likes of Abraham, Noah, and Elijah. This encourages us to recognize two important facts. First, no matter how hard we try, our Big Buts pop out every now and then. Rather than being the epitome of perfection, we are instead a mix of good and bad, always striving to *become*, rather than *arriving*. While we work to control our Big Buts, God continues His good work in and through us, even when we have flare-ups. Big But-itis isn't always fatal, but it is always debilitating.

> Others always let us down; Jesus never does.

Second, the only person we should ever look to as the perfect example of living a But-less life is Jesus. Others always let us down; Jesus never does. We have hope that when a Big But flare-up occurs, God remains active in our lives rather than abandoning us. We can look to Jesus as an example to follow.

Big But Moses: *Excuse*
Exodus 4:10–16

Then Moses said to the Lord, "Please, Lord, I have never been eloquent, neither recently nor in time past, nor since You have spoken to Your servant; for
I am slow of speech and slow of tongue." The Lord said to him, "Who has
made man's mouth? Or who makes him mute or deaf, or seeing or blind? Is
it not I, the Lord? Now then go, and I, even I, will be with your mouth, and
teach you what you are to say." But he said, "Please, Lord, now send the message by whomever You will." Then the anger of the Lord burned against
Moses, and He said, "Is there not your brother Aaron the Levite? I know that
he speaks fluently. And moreover, behold, he is coming out to meet you;
when he sees you, he will be glad in his heart. You are to speak to him and
put the words in his mouth; and I, even I, will be with your mouth and his
mouth, and I will teach you what you are to do. Moreover, he shall speak for
you to the people; and he will be as a mouth for you and you will be as God
to him."

After eating a scrumptious meal at a friend's house, I jokingly remarked to the
hostess, "You sure have a lot of dirty dishes here. If you need some help cleaning
up, just ask John." The expectation is that I am offering my own services, but
in reality, I merely enjoy the fruit of her labor while nominating someone else
for cleanup. It is a funny "Moses moment" because that's pretty much what
Moses did. He basically said, "I am willing to serve you Lord, but here is Aaron,
send him."

Moses is an intriguing figure, Jewish by birth and Egyptian by training. He
would have been six feet under and pushing up daisies had it not been for the
redeeming actions of his mother. The Hebrews are becoming a large populace, and
Pharaoh views them as a potential threat. Guarding against this danger, Pharaoh
decrees that every male child born to the Hebrews be slaughtered.

His mother protects him as long as she is able, but there comes a time when
Moses' presence can no longer be hidden. His life is in danger, and possibly hers
for disobeying Pharaoh's command. She places baby Moses in his own private
yacht (a water-tight wicker basket) and floats him near the reeds along the Nile
River bank.

When Pharaoh's daughter arrives at the Nile to bathe, she spots the basket
among the reeds, takes pity on the child, and brings him into her household. As
icing on the cake, Moses' birth mother is called upon to nurse him, thus circum-
venting Pharaoh's evil decree. Moses' life is spared, his birth mother nurses him,
and he receives a first-class education in the house of the king. God's sovereign
hand is obvious.

This is one of those stories where we marvel at the timing and wisdom of God. Moses "just happens" to be born at this specific time in history and his mother "just happens" to be wise enough to devise a plan for saving his life. The Egyptian who takes him under her wings "just happens" to be Pharaoh's own daughter. The woman who nurses him with her own milk "just happens" to be his birth mother. Raised in the royal household, his education "just happens" to be the best Egypt has to offer. In short, God superintends these circumstances in preparing Moses to lead the Hebrews from Egyptian bondage. Who better to do this than a Hebrew by birth and an Egyptian by training? What Pharaoh meant for evil (killing male Hebrew newborns), God turns into a cataclysmic mass exodus from Pharaoh's grasp.

In God's game plan, it is time for Moses to step up to the plate and hit a home run for the Hebrew team. After what God has done to protect and train him for this very moment, all Moses can say is, "Here I am, send Aaron!" The Potter creates him for a specific purpose, a specific season, and a specific mission. The Potter's skilled hands save Moses from certain death and grant him an insider's understanding of Egyptian culture and thought. For the Hebrews, it is freedom time, and Moses is called up from the minor leagues to pitch in the big game. It is his moment to shine, stand on the promises of God, and be the Lord's mouthpiece.

In his debut as the key figure for this turning point in human history, Moses sticks out his Big But for all to see. Of all the times to have an oversized, conspicuous But, this is truly an embarrassing one. It proves to be a most inopportune occasion, as the entire Hebrew nation is depending on him. Their freedom is at stake. In fact, when Moses' Big But egregiously erupts, it is so offensive to the Lord that His anger burns against Moses.

Moses is commissioned to lead a people of slaves to the Promised Land so they can embrace a new national identity. Of all the people God could have enlisted for this crucial task, He chose Moses. It is a privilege, a calling, a commissioning, and a position of honor. But, like collard greens in the frying pan, Moses wilts. In his view, the assignment is overwhelming. He compares his present abilities with what is required for the job. He engages in fuzzy math, and his equation is missing a key piece of information. He forgets that it is the Lord who has called him, the Creator and Sustainer of all that is. Left to our own devices and left to waddle in our own feeble strength, we are woefully inadequate for any task assigned to us, but the ability to accomplish what our Lord commands is possible only when we rely upon His strength. When God calls, He empowers, protects, and guides. As Romans 8:31 points out, "If God is for us, who is against us?" This is the key piece of the equation which Moses neglects to give adequate weight and consideration.

> *Moses focuses on his inabilities rather than on God's capabilities.*

Responding to God's call in Exodus 4:10, Moses pleads, "Please, LORD, I have never been eloquent, neither recently nor in time past, nor since You have spoken to Your servant; for I am slow of speech and slow of tongue." To this Big But response, we observe the Lord's displeasure: "Who has made man's mouth? Or who makes him mute or deaf, or seeing or blind? Is it not I, the LORD? Now then go, and I, even I, will be with your mouth, and teach you what you are to say" (Ex. 4:11–12).

Moses focuses on *his inabilities* rather than on *God's capabilities*. God reminds Moses of His great powers by pointing out who actually created the mouth and tongue to begin with. If He can create the gift of speech, He can certainly oversee the words Moses relays to Pharaoh. In fact, the Lord gives him a command, "now then go," and promises to be with his mouth and teach him what to say. What more could Moses ask for? At the proper time, God Himself will direct his very words. Yet, instead of immediately obeying, Moses stalls, and out pops another Big But, "Please, LORD, now send the message by whomever You will" (Ex. 4:13). Like a spoiled child who doesn't want to go to bed at night, Moses challenges the Lord. After a second round of defiance, the Lord's anger burns against Moses, and Aaron is allowed into the picture.

The great Moses, the one who stands up to Pharaoh, the one who leads the Hebrew children out of Egypt, the one who causes precious water to flow from a rock in the desert, the one who delivers the Ten commandments, the one with the Shekinah glow about him, yes this great icon of Christianity, exhibited a Big But so shameful that the Lord's anger burned against him.

Moses' Big But words put in easily recognizable But-speak might sound like this:

Moses:
Yes, the Hebrew people are going through a great deal of persecution, *but* leading them out of Egypt will be very difficult. I am honored that You have called me to this important task, *but* I actually had to flee Egypt at one time and am probably not the best candidate. I think it is a good idea to free Your people, *but* I don't have the abilities and talents to do what You ask. Please send someone else; anyone else *but* me.

This is classic But-speak. Moses surrenders to his fears and shortcomings rather than embracing God's ability and calling. This happens to all of us at one time or another. God asks us to do something, go someplace, say something, give

Suggesting that following hard after God is nothing but popsicles and cotton candy, however, is a tremendous disservice to others.

something, and we engage in But-speak. We make excuses, point out why it can't be done, feel unprepared, ask that someone else be assigned for the task, and note the overreaching nature of the Lord's command in the first place. Excuses are nothing more than an inflammation of Big But-itis.

Jesus did say in Matthew 11:28–30,

> Come to Me, all who are weary and heavy-laden, and I will give you rest. Take My yoke upon you and learn from Me, for I am gentle and humble in heart, and you will find rest for your souls. For My yoke is easy and My burden is light.

Suggesting that following hard after God is nothing but popsicles and cotton candy, however, is a tremendous disservice to others. Following Jesus is a breath of fresh air compared to the legalistic, knit-picky, hypocritical focus of the Pharisees. Jesus says in Matthew 23:2–4,

> The scribes and the Pharisees have seated themselves in the chair of Moses; therefore all that they tell you, do and observe, but do not do according to their deeds; for they say things and do not do them. They tie up heavy burdens and lay them on men's shoulders, but they themselves are unwilling to move them with so much as a finger.

Aah, the old double standard song and dance routine.

When Jesus invites the weary seekers to take His yoke upon them, He is not suggesting that following Him will be a cakewalk. It doesn't get any clearer than 2 Timothy 3:12, "Indeed, all who desire to live godly in Christ Jesus will be persecuted." According to tradition, all but one of the twelve apostles is martyred. Peter, for instance, is thought to have been crucified upside down. Thomas is believed to have been stabbed with a spear. The great faith chapter of Hebrews 11:35–38 notes that:

> Others were tortured, not accepting their release, so that they might obtain a better resurrection; and others experienced mockings and scourgings, yes, also chains and imprisonment. They were stoned, they were sawn in two, they were tempted, they were put to death with the sword; they went about in sheepskins, in goatskins, being destitute, afflicted, ill-treated (men of whom the world was not worthy), wandering in deserts and mountains and caves and holes in the ground.

For some, following Christ seems more like a torture walk than a cakewalk. The torture picture doesn't align well with our understanding of what "My yoke is easy and My burden is light" entails (Mt. 11:30). If being tortured, mocked, scourged, imprisoned, sawn in half, and put to death with the sword is Jesus' understanding of an easy yoke and light burden, then I would hate to see how He defines a heavy yoke.

Not all early Christians endured such ill-treatment, but Hebrews 11 honors those that did by highlighting their faith and courage. We may not experience such inhumane treatment as the early adopters of Christianity, but there may come a day when we will. If we desire to live a godly life for Christ, we will be persecuted; it comes with the territory. Jesus Himself faced opposition and was eventually prosecuted and executed as a criminal. Let's not sugarcoat the fact that godly living sets one apart from the prevailing culture, practices, and mindset of our day.

When Jesus says His yoke is easy and His burden light, He invites weary sojourners living under the curse of legalism to come out from oppressive rules and insignificant minutia to experience a dynamic, genuine relationship with Him, the One who loves, forgives, and extends grace. In the days of Christ, the Pharisees and scribes create such an oppressive and warped understanding of what following God entails that Jesus' ministry exposes their appalling theology and untangles the mess for kingdom seekers. Following God is not about legalism or tyrannical burdens; it is about loving Him from the heart and communing with Him each and every day.

> Let's not sugarcoat the fact that godly living sets one apart from the prevailing culture, practices, and mindset of our day.

In Moses' case, God asks Him to return to the Egyptians, the people who raised him, educated him, and to whom he eventually alienated by murdering one of their own. He ran from them to safety, secured a wife, and is now part of a family community. Life is safe and predictable. But now he is asked to stand up to the Egyptians, speak forcefully, and share words from a God they do not want to know. How intimidating is that? He may have been more malleable had God asked him to minister to another people, to walk in another direction, or engage in another assignment. But God didn't. Moses is to go back to Egypt, for God has ordained him for such a moment as this.

Moses knows what God is asking and clearly grasps the nature of the assignment. He knows he is to stand before Pharaoh. He knows he is to stand in the midst of those who don't believe, follow, or respect God. He knows he is to speak unpleasant words they will not receive. It is a dangerous assignment—and one that elicits a great deal of courage and trust. It isn't a simple stroll down Broadway, silently praying for those who pass by; it is standing up to the leader of a powerful nation while guiding over a million Hebrews, the foundational workforce of the Egyptian society, out of the country to become a people for God.

The task is daunting, but the Potter has the right to mold the clay into any form He desires, and that form directly relates to the wishes and purpose of the Potter. If there is a need for bowls, the Potter forms them on His wheel—some large, some medium, some small, some normal, some ornate, all for different settings and purposes. In the sovereign plan of God, the time has come for a leader to stand up to Pharaoh and free the Hebrews from slavery. That person is Moses. His number is called. The Commander-in-Chief grants him an assignment and assures him of His support, guidance, and presence. It is a time for Moses to accept the assignment, salute his Commander-in-Chief, and go forth with vigor, pride, and a sense of protection and well-being. After all, the Creator and Sustainer of all things has commissioned him and promises to be with him.

There he is, chosen, informed, blessed, and supported. God is using Moses to set into motion His great redemptive plan. Moses' historic moment is now, and when the eyes of the world are upon him, at the worst possible time, his Big But erupts in such disgusting fashion that God becomes angry. Moses fails and stumbles. His knees buckle. He questions God's sovereignty and strategy while suggesting someone else do the work.

We understand that God calls some to high-profile ministries and others to low-profile ministries. He is the Potter and we are the clay. His creative and sovereign genius decides what role we play. Our goal is to do our best in the specific assignments for which we have been created. When our moment to be in the spotlight arrives—whether it is grand, monumental, and pivotal to the history of the world, or small and hidden from others—it is still a moment of obedience, nothing more and nothing less. For most of us, our big moment is really a collection of smaller moments. We will never get the chance to lead such a large number of people out of slavery. We will not be called upon to face the leader of a powerful nation. We will, however, be asked to obey God in whatever He calls us to do. The issue isn't so much the assignment, but the obedience and the attitude behind obeying.

God may simply ask us to speak to our neighbor, boss, or co-worker about the grace and forgiveness found in Him. No great nation is involved, and no sizable event marking a change in world history occurs. It is a small act in our own backyard, which nonetheless, is a task the Lord desires of us. The key to fulfilling our purpose is not the size of the task, but actually doing what God has asked of us. We can stand in Moses' shoes, question God, and pop out our annoying Big But, giving rise to God's anger, or we can salute our Commander-in-Chief and move forward in our created role with the assurance of His presence, support, and power. Big But Moses stumbled; we don't have to.

Big But Spies: *Negativity*
Numbers 13:25–33

> When they returned from spying out the land, at the end of forty days, they proceeded to come to Moses and Aaron and to all the congregation of the sons of Israel in the wilderness of Paran, at Kadesh; and they brought back word to them and to all the congregation and showed them the fruit of the land. Thus they told him, and said, "We went in to the land where you sent us; and it certainly does flow with milk and honey, and this is its fruit. Nevertheless, the people who live in the land are strong, and the cities are fortified and very large; and moreover, we saw the descendants of Anak there. Amalek is living in the land of the Negev and the Hittites and the Jebusites and the Amorites are living in the hill country, and the Canaanites are living by the sea and by the side of the Jordan." Then Caleb quieted the people before Moses and said, "We should by all means go up and take possession of it, for we will surely overcome it." But the men who had gone up with him said, "We are not able to go up against the people, for they are too strong for us." So they gave out to the sons of Israel a bad report of the land which they had spied out, saying, "The land through which we have gone, in spying it out, is a land that devours its inhabitants; and all the people whom we saw in it are men of great size. There also we saw the Nephilim (the sons of Anak are part of the Nephilim); and we became like grasshoppers in our own sight, and so we were in their sight."

After flashing his Big But in the Lord's face, Moses finally agrees to God's assignment as long as Aaron accompanies him. The Lord obliges this Big But demand, and Moses and Aaron become twin pillars, a one-two knockout punch for Pharaoh. The Hebrew freedom story is one for the ages. Pharaoh's stubborn heart resists the Lord's command, and with each rejected appeal for freedom, a plague falls upon the Egyptians. This is God's way of moving Pharaoh toward compliance, but it isn't until the last plague that He finally gets through. The straw that breaks the camel's back in turning Pharaoh's heart is the death of his firstborn son, the tenth and final plague.

Amazing, isn't it, how our stubbornness brings about so many of the troubles we experience. God commands something of us, we know it and understand it, but like Pharaoh, we resist. Our pride is at stake, our control is threatened, and to obey implies losing face in front of others. Since Pharaoh isn't a follower of God, his hardened heart comes as no surprise. But when God's own children engage in Pharaoh-like behavior, it is both surprising and disheartening. My invented technical term for this behavior is "pharaohsclerosis," a hardening of the heart. Often, when pharaohsclerosis sets in, God must use extreme methods to get our attention as He works to soften our heart and nudge us in the direction He desires.

> Amazing, isn't it, how our stubbornness brings about so many of the troubles we experience.

The Bible describes quite a freedom scene as more than one million Hebrews depart Egypt. I would have enjoyed sitting on a Main Street rooftop during this historical event, sipping iced tea, and devouring a pepperoni pizza while marveling at the scene unfolding in the street below. Like watching the Super Bowl on a big screen television, a front row seat provides an unprecedented view of the departing slave labor. The entire Egyptian workforce is slipping out of the country right before my eyes.

The great escape is not without incident as Pharaoh has a late change of heart and chases after the Hebrews. The drama builds, and the background music climaxes at the Red Sea. In dramatic fashion, Moses parts the water and the Hebrews cross over on dry ground. As the fast-approaching Egyptian army attempts to cross, Moses stretches his hand over the sea and the waters begin to flow again, stopping the army in its tracks. The deal is sealed. The Hebrews are safe on the other side, the Egyptian army is embarrassed, and the start of a long journey to the Promised Land begins.

Their wilderness journey is a story in and of itself, filled with the miraculous provision of God on so many occasions and also marred by frequent episodes of Big But-itis. If the wanderers aren't complaining about the food, they are complaining about the clothing. If they aren't bickering over Moses' leadership, they are reminiscing about the "good ole days" of slavery. Like kids in the back seat of the car constantly screaming, "Are we there yet?" the Hebrews were, in many ways, an annoying group of Big But individuals. Big But-itis squashes their trust in God, clouds their vision, and warps their perspective so badly that they yearn for a return to slavery. The disease is so prevalent that it even stings Aaron and Miriam, Moses' brother and sister. Smitten with leprosy for her Big But, Miriam is healed only after Moses intervenes in prayer.

The Hebrews are not freed from Egypt to squander their lives away in the wilderness, complaining and waiting to die. God has a plan for them. He calls them out of bondage to become a great nation in a land He is preparing, the Promised Land. This land will not be given to them upon a silver platter; they must take it from those who currently possess it. Conquering the Promised Land means more trust in God, more reliance on His strength, greater belief in His plan, and the melding of a new national identity for the people of God. The purpose of their great escape from Egypt will only be realized if Big But-itis can be controlled.

A singular Big But event in the book of Numbers crystalizes the Hebrews' dilemma. Will they move forward trusting the God who freed them and now leads them through the wilderness in a pillar of cloud by day and a pillar of fire by night, or will they shrink from the calling and plan of God?

The land promised to them is a terrain they have never seen. Now that the chains of Egyptian bondage are severed, it is time for a glimpse of their new home. The Lord commands Moses, "Send out for yourself men so that they may spy out the land of Canaan, which I am going to give to the sons of Israel; you shall send a man from each of their fathers' tribes, every one a leader among them" (Num. 13:2). A leader from each of the twelve tribes is chosen to examine their inheritance, and for forty days they explore the land of Canaan.

In the valley of Eshcol, the spies cut down a single cluster of grapes so large it is placed on a pole and carried between two men. They find a land flowing with milk and honey, figs, pomegranates, and the ability to sustain the Hebrew populace. They also observe the towns and armies they must conquer in order to obtain their promised inheritance.

The spies report to the entire assembly upon their return. Ten of them talk But-speak, while two spies verbalize Faith-speak. Ten view the glass as half-empty; two see it as half-full. As with so many issues in life, things boil down to a matter of perspective. These weren't Egyptians tricking unsuspecting Hebrews with negative ideas and hoping for their return to slavery. No, the negativity comes from within the Hebrew camp itself, and not only that, recognized leaders from the various tribes are the instigators. They succumb to But-speak. I suppose this should not surprise us. Negativity, resistance, glass-half-empty perspectives, and the language of But-speak always seems to be most devastating when it comes from those closest to us. So often, we stumble over our own two feet. Instead of moving forward as the great army of God accomplishing His directives, we allow negative Big-But Christians to rule the day.

The spies all agree on what they see; there is no argument there. The land is indeed filled with milk, honey, grapes, pomegranates, and enough resources to sustain a nation. The land does indeed contain large fortified cities requiring battle. The country also contains Nephilim, individuals known for their large size. They all witness the same thing.

The deception of the spies is not in their eyes, but in the interpretation of what their eyes observe. Their problematic interpretation leads to an inaccurate and faithless conclusion. Note their negative, But-speak conclusion in Numbers 13:32–33:

> So they gave out to the sons of Israel a bad report of the land which they had spied out, saying, "The land through which we have gone, in spying it out, is a land that devours its inhabitants; and all the people whom we saw in it are men of great size. There also we saw the Nephilim (the sons of Anak are part of the Nephilim); and we became like grasshoppers in our own sight, and so we were in their sight."

Wow, here are the recognized leaders from ten tribes agreeing in front of the entire assembly that the land is too much for them. In their mind, attempting to conquer what God has promised is nothing but a suicide mission, a squashing of grasshoppers by stronger and more powerful grasshopper killers. Better to remain put than risk failure and be worse off.

The eyes of Caleb and Joshua see the very same things, but they arrive at a totally different conclusion, as noted in Numbers 13:30. "We should by all means go up and take possession of it, for we will surely overcome it." Caleb and Joshua could have easily given in to the majority point of view, but they didn't. They exhibited courage, positivity, and faith in what God *was* doing, what He *could* do, and what He *would* do.

> They exhibited courage, positivity, and faith in what God *was* doing, what He *could* do, and what He *would* do.

Their perspective is bigger than fortified cities and overly large warriors. Had that been all there was to see, then yes, by all means, stay put. But their eyes see so much more. They see what God wants them to see, that He has a plan, is working His plan, and they are a part of it. Would God free an entire nation from slavery, lead them, protect them, provide for them in miraculous fashion, and give them a vision of the Promised Land only to realize at the last moment that He isn't big enough to overtake fortified cities and large warriors? Could God miraculously lead an entire nation out of slavery and be too weak to make His promises come true? Caleb and Joshua lift up their eyes to what God has done, is doing, and promises to do. Good for them!

The negative Big-But spies will have none of it. They pipe up in Numbers 13:31, "We are not able to go up against the people, for they are too strong for us." Their "can't-do" theology is infectious, spreading to all the people and inspiring the rebellious spirit seen in Numbers 14:1–4:

> Then all the congregation lifted up their voices and cried, and the people wept that night. All the sons of Israel grumbled against Moses and Aaron; and the whole congregation said to them, "Would that we had died in the land of Egypt! Or would that we had died in this wilderness! Why is the LORD bringing us into this land, to fall by the sword? Our wives and our little ones will become plunder; would it not be better for us to return to Egypt?" So they said to one another, "Let us appoint a leader and return to Egypt."

Big But talk doesn't get any larger and louder than this!

Joshua and Caleb plead with the people: "Let's trust the Lord, follow Him, obey Him, move forward in faith, and possess our inheritance." Upon hearing their plea to move forward in obedience and faith, the congregation sets out to stone them and would have succeeded had the glory of the Lord not appeared at the tent of meeting.

We have the benefit of hindsight, the ability to look back upon history. It is easy to say, "What in the world was wrong with those people? Why didn't they see what God was up to and obey? Had I been there, I wouldn't have rebelled." We give ourselves far too much credit. Most of us wouldn't have even made it out of Egypt.

It is easy to look upon the grumbling, Big But congregation of Israel, shake our head in disgust, and say, "How could they?" when in reality we do the very same thing. Even after God has done wonderful things for us, proves Himself in numerous ways and removes roadblocks, we still see giants, wilt like grasshoppers, and pop out our Big But. We experience a meltdown while repeating similar Big But words, "We can't do it!" This is Big But-itis; nothing more and nothing less.

The words of the ten negative spies put in easily recognizable But-speak might sound like this:

Ten Spies:

Sure the land flows with milk and honey, *but* did you notice the many fortified cities? Well, sure those are big grapes, *but* I don't want to die trying to take them. Yes, we have a good many men who can fight, *but* did you see the sons of Anak? My gosh, they are big boys and we are nothing *but* grasshoppers in their sight, and in our own sight. We can't possibly defeat such large warriors. Canaan would be a great place to live, *but* given the many obstacles, we would be far better off returning to Egyptian slavery. I have no idea what God was thinking in bringing us out here, *but* this isn't what I signed up for.

Like a forest fire during dry summer months, negativity fanned by the winds of glass-half-empty perspectives destroys even the healthiest of trees. It is a matter of looking through the wrong lens, of seeing only the present problem in front of us rather than the upcoming solution God has promised. Negativity, like mold in a petri dish, contaminates the entire sample. It is a highly contagious Big But problem.

Have you ever been around people with the Big But of negativity? Depressing, isn't it? They drain your energy and enthusiasm, and become like rain on a parade. Who wants to be around people who don't exude the excitement, power, and joy of following Christ? In examining the life of Jesus in the New Testament, we don't get the impression that He is a downer, or that people who come in contact with Him leave depressed and drained. Quite the opposite occurs; they are energized, touched, uplifted, and excited.

My first full-time pastorate was a very small church that struggled to survive. While we had very little in terms of human or financial resources, we possessed a great deal of love for one another. We did have, of course, our own local Mr. Negative Big But. He was a trumpet player who desired a larger church with more musicians. There was talk of our congregation merging with another congregation, but it was just talk. Church mergers rarely work well and we knew it. For him, merging wasn't about the will of God or greater ministry impact, it was about more musicians. If he could toot his horn with more horn tooters, he would finally be darn-tootin happy. But without additional horn blowers, his negative Big But was not only protruding, but also growing.

Soon he became negative toward my sermons, my ideas for growth, my family, the church, and its leaders. His mind was fixated on more musicians, and the way to get more musicians was to merge with another church. He was discontent with only a few horn tooters at his side and when we didn't agree to his solution, he became negative about everything.

> Negativity is one of the hardest Big Buts to hide because it affects our countenance.

Mr. Negative Big But called the district office. His chronic complaining was so bitter that it brought the associate district superintendent out to our little church. He was to speak with Mr. Negative during the upcoming visit though he had never met or seen him. We were conversing in the front of the sanctuary when suddenly Mr. Negative and his Big But wife walked through the church doors. The associate district superintendent turned to me and remarked, "That's him, isn't it?" Quite surprised, I responded, "Yes, how did you know?" and to this day I remember his reply, "His countenance gave him away."

Negativity is one of the hardest Big Buts to hide because it affects our countenance. When we deflate negative Big But perspectives, the very life of Christ has a chance to flow in and through us, energizing ourselves and others, and bringing excitement and joy to our lives.

Big But David: *Double Standard*
2 Samuel 12:5–7a

> Then David's anger burned greatly against the man, and he said to Nathan, "As the LORD lives, surely the man who has done this deserves to die. He must make restitution for the lamb fourfold, because he did this thing and had no compassion." Nathan then said to David, "You are the man!"

Every time I read the story of David and Bathsheba, two funny thoughts always enter my mind. I guess it's that comedic side of me wanting so badly to be set free. First, I find it interesting that the woman's name is Bathsheba and that she was on the roof taking a bath. If she were taking a shower would her name be Showersheba? If she were dipping in the Jordan River, would her name be Dipsheba? If she were merely giving herself a sponge bath would her name be Spongesheba? Ok, I will give it a rest. I am up way past my bedtime and now you know why I am not a comedian!

Second, I get a kick out of Nathan crying out, "You are the man!" I bet he couldn't wait to deliver that punch line. For some odd reason, it reminds me of a sweaty televangelist holding a white hankie in his left hand and a wireless microphone in his right. Staring directly into the camera with piercing eyes and pointing his long, bony finger toward the camera, he speaks four words that send shivers down your spine and puts the fear of God in your heart: "You are the man!" Whew! Scary! We've got to admit, it took some chutzpah for Nathan to say these words to the king.

All right, funny time is over and I must quit amusing myself at your expense. Nathan was anything but a modern televangelist and Bathsheba's name has nothing to do with whether she was bathing, showering, sponging, or dipping. Of all the things this story tells us, one thing is clear: high and mighty King David has one serious But problem that is so offensive to the Lord, Nathan the prophet is sent to confront him.

Ever meet people who have one standard for others and another for themselves? Paul addresses this very condition in the book of Romans. "But do you suppose this, O man, when you pass judgment on those who practice such things and do the same yourself, that you will escape the judgment of God?" (Rom. 2:3). He continues in Romans 2:21–23,

> You, therefore, who teach another, do you not teach yourself? You who preach that one shall not steal, do you steal? You who say that one should not commit adultery, do you commit adultery? You who abhor idols, do you rob temples? You who boast in the Law, through your breaking the Law, do you dishonor God?

We can't help but notice double standards throughout life, and it is nauseating. A politician spews forth inspirational rhetoric concerning the courage and obligation young men and women possess in entering harm's way, yet that same politician uses her influence and stature to keep her own son out of the war. That's a double standard.

My best friend in high school played the ole double standard trick on me. I invited him to play tennis one evening, and he turned me down, noting that he was studying for an important test at school the next day. Hours later I discovered that he actually did play tennis that night when invited by one of the most popular jocks in the school. Studying for a test was the standard for his best friend, but when a popular jock asked him to play tennis, the school test standard went out the window. That's a double standard.

Don't you hate it when squeaky wheels always get the grease? There is often one standard for those who play by the rules, are kind, wait in line, and try to do the right things, and a different standard for obnoxious individuals who break the rules, grumble, and criticize. They get their way simply as a means to shutting them up.

James writes of a double standard problem in the early church (Jas. 2:1–4):

> My brethren, do not hold your faith in our glorious Lord Jesus Christ with an attitude of personal favoritism. For if a man comes into your assembly with a gold ring and dressed in fine clothes, and there also comes in a poor man in dirty clothes, and you pay special attention to the one who is wearing the fine clothes, and say, "You sit here in a good place," and you say to the poor man, "You stand over there, or sit down by my footstool," have you not made distinctions among yourselves, and become judges with evil motives?

David was a king all right, but he was king of the double standard. His Big But held himself to one standard and others to a different standard. Nathan was the emissary who exposes David's Big But-itis. Reflecting upon the David and Bathsheba story, we can surmise how that Big But of his became so large.

One evening David rises from his bed and begins walking on his rooftop where he spots a woman bathing on an adjacent roof. Her stunning beauty captivates the king and he takes her into his home for the night, sleeps with her, and sends her back home in the morning. It is a one-night stand resulting in Bathsheba's pregnancy. The king had his way with her.

It is possible that David experienced acute insomnia, had a lot on his mind, and needed a stroll on the rooftop to clear his head. It is also possible that his rooftop walk was much more intentional than coincidental. Watching Bathsheba bathe may have been a "planned accident." In 2 Samuel 11:1 we are told it was spring time when kings go out to battle, but in this case, David sends Joab to the battlefield while he remains in Jerusalem. Coincidence or planned?

One can't help but wonder if "staying home" is a deliberate strategy for pleasing his carnal instincts. David went to bed but got up to walk on his roof. Was he wrestling with his own fleshly desires? Women of that day often bathed on their rooftops. David certainly knew this, just as he knew that his rooftop was taller than all the others. Did he accidently catch a glimpse of a female bather on the adjacent roof, or was there a strategy behind his "accidental" viewing? He purposefully stayed in Jerusalem when kings normally go out to battle and sent Joab in his place. Was all of this orchestrated by David for a one-night stand with Bathsheba?

In a sense, David reminds us of the Pharisees in Jesus' day who pray three times a day. Obviously, there is nothing wrong with praying three times a day, but the Pharisees ensured that when the mid-day prayer time arrived, they "accidently" happened to be at the top of the Temple stairs. They strategically planned their steps so they would be at the highest, most prominent place at just the right moment where others could observe them praying in colorful, flowing robes.

We know David is a very strategic person. He spends time on the run from King Saul and often outwits his opponent. At one point, he traps Saul in a cave and could have easily taken his life. Beyond his strategic military genius, the Bathsheba event also reveals David's cunning ways, especially in his dealings with Uriah the Hittite, Bathsheba's husband.

Once David discovers that his mistress is with child, he devises a plan to shelter his sin. Bathsheba's husband serves in David's army and is away from home. Knowing Bathsheba's belly is growing and that her husband couldn't possibly have impregnated her, David understands the problem on his hands. He devises an elaborate scheme to hide sin and creatively cover his tracks. It is nothing more than "fig-leaf" theology, like Adam and Eve in the Garden of Eden, who thought, "If I cover myself with a fig leaf, maybe God won't notice that I am naked."

First, David brings Uriah home from the battlefield hoping he will spend the night with his wife, so no one will ever suspect anyone other than Uriah as being the child's father. David's plan backfires. Instead of going home, Uriah sleeps outside David's house along with all the other servants. It isn't right, in his eyes, to enjoy the comforts of home when his comrades are still fighting a war and living in temporary quarters on the battlefield. He is dedicated to his king and to his brothers in arms.

Since David's initial strategy doesn't work, he concocts a second plan, to get Uriah drunk. Surely, with one too many in his system, he will saunter home to be with his wife. But Uriah again sleeps with the other servants outside of David's house rather than enjoying the comfort of his own bed and the warmth of his wife's body.

Enter strategy number three. David orders his army commander to place Uriah on the front line of the fiercest battle and then withdraw from him, leaving him to fight alone without support. David knows Uriah will be killed in battle and the issue will then be resolved. No more husband to notice a pregnant wife and dispute the child's legitimacy. David has strategically outwitted yet another problem situation. Now he can bring Bathsheba into his house, and no one will be the wiser, except the Lord, for "the thing that David had done was evil in the sight of the LORD," (2 Sam. 11:27).

David was a king with plenty of wine, women, and song. What more could he want when he already has everything? As is often the case with those who have all they could ever need, everything is not enough. David is a warrior at heart—strategic, gifted, strong, and cunning. In fact, the Temple is built by his son Solomon because there is too much blood on David's hands.

David's abuse of power for personal pleasure reminds me of a more recent story. In 1998, President Bill Clinton finds himself in a similar situation. The President engages in sex acts with a young intern named Monica Lewinsky. Like David, he does all that is in his power to cover up the illicit affair. He barely escapes impeachment, but what strikes the American people is his callous answer to why he did it. The most powerful man in the world did it because he could. Here was a formidable man in an influential position and because he could abuse his power for personal pleasure, he did.

President Clinton didn't get away with it, and neither did King David. While the Lord sent the prophet Nathan to address the issue with David, it was Monica Lewinsky's co-worker and friend, Linda Tripp, who opened the can of worms with Monicagate. Nathan realizes the king will be more resistant to his words if addressed directly and forthrightly, so he wisely utilizes storytelling to get his point across, and it works masterfully. David falls into the intended trap and winds up indicting himself.

Nathan describes a rich man without need who seizes the lamb of a poor man. The lamb is the poor man's only possession, and the rich man arrogantly uses it for his own pleasure (to feed a traveler). It is absolutely unthinkable for a wealthy man without want or need to snatch the only precious possession from the poor. The story infuriates David. Who does such a thing? Not yet realizing it was a set-up, David's "anger burned greatly against the man, and he said to Nathan, 'As the LORD lives, surely the man who has done this deserves to die. He must make restitution for the lamb fourfold, because he did this thing and had no compassion'" (2 Sam. 12:5–6). The trap has been sprung. David is cornered. Not only does his sin convict him, but now his very own words do as well.

It is at this point that Nathan declares, "You are the man!" (2 Sam. 12:7). The tables are turned. Strategic and cunning David didn't see this coming. I imagine his pupils dilate, his pulse rate increases, his breathing becomes labored, and he begins sweating through his kingly digs. Nathan then announces the Lord's punishment, and David takes it like a man. What else can he do? He gets caught with his hand in the cookie jar, someone else's cookie jar. The illegitimate offspring of

David and Bathsheba dies, but Bathsheba bears another child, Solomon, whom God uses greatly.

David's Big But behavior put into easily recognizable But-speak might sound like this:

David:

Wow, that woman bathing is sure beautiful. I want her. I know she is not my wife, *but* I want her. I am king so I can get her. I know she is Uriah's wife, *but* he is away in battle so I can get away with it. What? Bathsheba is pregnant. I am the father, *but* I can orchestrate events to make it look like Uriah's child. I am the father, *but* I can't be found out, so I will ensure that Uriah is killed while fighting. I can manipulate this so no one knows, *but* then I will bring Bathsheba into my house for good.

David's Big But is a double standard. It is wrong for a rich man to steal a treasured lamb from a poor man, but it is fine for David to snatch another man's wife, impregnate her, and then kill her husband. There is something wrong with that kind of logic.

I have a sneaky suspicion that we all struggle with the double-standard Big But. While it is difficult to admit, it is a real problem in our lives. It is challenging to recognize because we tend to justify our behaviors and thoughts. We easily agree to the principle that double standards are wrong, until of course, it is *our* double standard, and then it becomes a justified exception.

It is amazing how deceived we can become, and how ignorant we think God is when we want to wiggle out of a tight spot.

A husband desiring his wife's care while in bed with fever, but doesn't lift a finger for her when she is sick, has a double standard. The elder who turns a blind eye to the inappropriate behavior of a fellow churchgoer he has known for years, yet quickly raises the flag on the unbecoming actions of those less familiar has a double standard. The pastor who always visits a select group of admirers while neglecting those less affirming has a double standard. The mother who does all things for her children and neglects the needs of her husband has a double standard. You get the point.

> We easily agree to the principle that double standards are wrong, until of course, it is *our* double standard, and then it becomes a justified exception.

The double-standard Big But sneaks into our lives in subtle ways because we justify it in our minds. It becomes okay because we say it is. We bend truth to make it fit our needs. Truth that is bent isn't really truth anymore. Instead, it becomes a hard and fast principle for others, but a boiled piece of limp spaghetti for us.

When truth no longer is absolute, it becomes situational. Truth-bending is a euphemism for situational ethics and becomes nothing more than a convenient method for getting our way. Double standards produce Big But-itis. King David had the disease, as do many others. The Big But Syndrome only subsides when we stop justifying our behavior and quit bending truth to suit our desires. We are to refuse situational truth and instead, align our lives with God's absolute truth.

Big But Naaman: *Unfulfilled Expectations*
2 Kings 5:9–14

So Naaman came with his horses and his chariots and stood at the doorway of the house of Elisha. Elisha sent a messenger to him, saying, "Go and wash in the Jordan seven times, and your flesh will be restored to you and you will be clean." But Naaman was furious and went away and said, "Behold, I thought, 'He will surely come out to me and stand and call on the name of the LORD his God, and wave his hand over the place and cure the leper.' Are not Abanah and Pharpar, the rivers of Damascus, better than all the waters of Israel? Could I not wash in them and be clean?" So he turned and went away in a rage. Then his servants came near and spoke to him and said, "My father, had the prophet told you to do some great thing, would you not have done it? How much more then, when he says to you, 'Wash, and be clean'?" So he went down and dipped himself seven times in the Jordan, according to the word of the man of God; and his flesh was restored like the flesh of a little child and he was clean.

Naaman, an accomplished and highly respected army captain for the King of Aram, has a huge problem; he is afflicted with leprosy, a dreadful disease. It must have been obvious and debilitating, for the family slave, a young girl from Israel, notices the predicament and mentions to Naaman's wife, "I wish that my master were with the prophet who is in Samaria! Then he would cure him of his leprosy" (2 Kgs. 5:3).

> Truth-bending is a euphemism for situational ethics and becomes nothing more than a convenient method for getting our way.

Leprosy was an appalling disease in days of old. The word refers to various diseases of the skin with the worst resulting in severe nerve damage and disfiguration. Exactly what type Naaman contracts or how far it has progressed we do not know, but it is noticeable, and so much so that a young slave girl takes pity on him and suggests a possible cure.

As the story goes, Naaman makes his way to the prophet's house along with a cadre of horses, chariots, and servants. This must have been quite an ordeal for Naaman, not physically, for he knew how to get to the prophet's house and did so without incident, but psychologically, as it must have been humiliating for him.

Naaman is a man of power who tells people to jump and they ask how high. He commands an army and his words exact power and obedience. He is in charge of all things but his health. No matter how powerful he becomes, he cannot control this terrible disease affecting his body.

Unable to cure himself, he is forced to listen to the suggestion of the young slave girl from Israel. What else can he do? He is sick, in need of a cure, and unable in his own strength and wisdom to produce one. For those in positions of power and authority, it is disturbing to realize how little control they actually have over certain aspects of life. Used to snapping his fingers where servants and soldiers jump at his command, it is belittling to be taking a trip to Samaria and seeking the help of a mysterious prophet. But like so many with terrible diseases and hopeless situations, their last resort is to seek a miracle. Naaman finds himself in this very situation.

While Naaman is willing to travel to the prophet's house in Samaria, we get a sense that it really bothers him to do so. He arrives with a chip on his shoulder and preconceived ideas of how things should go. His entourage parks itself outside Elisha's house and waits for the prophet to appear. I wonder if a little power game ensued. Naaman refuses to dismount his chariot, and Elisha refuses to go to the door. Naaman expects Elisha to say, "Oh my goodness, the great and mighty Naaman is here. I better get out there and serve him like all of his servants and soldiers." Elisha isn't a man to be jacked around, and to him, Naaman is just a man like any other. Naaman expects to be treated with the respect and obedience he is accustomed to in his homeland. He leaves Aram with an attitude of irritation and arrives at Elisha's door with an attitude of arrogance and superiority.

> ... humility had its limits. Humility was just another tool for maintaining power. It is much easier to *pretend* to be humble than to *actually* be humble.

Naaman's disposition reminds me of an elder in my second pastorate. His standard line was, "Well, if I am the problem, I will resign right now." His calculated words are designed to portray a humble attitude willing to move out of the way if necessary, yet, with friends in high places, he knows he will never be asked to step down from his coveted post. He can feign humility while continuing to grasp power. One day, he said those words to me and I accepted his resignation, and thanked him for his service and willingness to step aside so others could lead. He didn't expect it, didn't really mean it, and was shocked that someone finally took him up on his offer. Naaman is the same way. He will travel to see the prophet but won't get out of his chariot, and instead, expects the prophet to personally greet him. A short time later, the elder's wife visited me and said of her husband, "He has been an elder all of his life. What is he to do now, clean the restrooms?" For Naaman and the elder, humility had its limits. Humility was just another tool for maintaining power. It is much easier to *pretend* to be humble than to *actually* be humble.

Elisha didn't get up to greet Naaman and instead sends his messenger saying, "Go and wash in the Jordan seven times, and your flesh will be restored to you and you will be clean" (2 Kgs. 5:10). After such a long journey, without meeting the prophet, and receiving such a simplistic message, Naaman is furious. We get a sense of his negative frame of mind and his preconceived ideas in 2 Kings 5:11–12:

> But Naaman was furious and went away and said, "Behold, I thought, 'He will surely come out to me and stand and call on the name of the Lord his God, and wave his hand over the place and cure the leper.' Are not Abanah and Pharpar, the rivers of Damascus, better than all the waters of Israel? Could I not wash in them and be clean?" So he turned and went away in a rage.

Naaman's Big But actions put into easily recognizable But-speak might sound like this:

Naaman:
What? Go to Samaria to see if a prophet can heal me? *But* that is far away, yet what choice do I have? I will go down to see him, *but* I can picture it now, him coming to greet me, praying over me, and curing me. Elisha, I am here on my chariot outside your house, *but* what is this, you send a servant to give me, a great military commander, a message. You've got to be kidding me . . . the Jordan River? I would do some great thing to be healed, *but* dipping in the dirty Jordan River is ridiculous. I came all the way from Aram to be healed, *but* this whole trip is a tremendous waste of time. I will head home.

Naaman had a good sized But before he even left Aram. Now his But is growing larger because a servant greets him instead of Elisha, his preconceived idea of the meeting doesn't occur, and dipping in a dirty river is a simplistic and stupid request. He begins to complain and grumble because things don't turn out as he expects, and his But enlarges by the minute. Full of disgust and sensing he has wasted his time, he turns his horses and chariots around to begin the long journey home—that is, until his wise servants intervene.

Isn't it funny how God uses small people to accomplish big plans? They often become keys that unlock doors to spiritual insights. In this scenario, God uses Naaman's servants to speak calm, reasonable words to their master. During one of my pastorates God gave me such a "small" person, a janitor. Every once in a while I would sit and talk with him, and during these times I gained a better sense of where I was, what I was doing, and where God was leading. His words were simple, true, and on point. He was unpretentious, open, and shared his own life as a way of helping mine. He was a godsend, and who would have thought that the church janitor would be used of the Lord to give strength and spiritual insight to the senior pastor? That is how God works. He uses everyone, regardless of rank or stature. If it hadn't been for Naaman's servants talking some sense into him, there is a good chance Naaman would have returned home without a cure. The servants challenge his flawed thinking and reason that if he were asked to fulfill some grand request he would do it without question, so why won't he do something simple like dip in the Jordan River?

Naaman gives in, dips himself in the filthy Jordan River and "his flesh was restored like the flesh of a little child and he was clean" (2 Kgs. 5:14). The word of the Lord through the prophet Elisha rings true. This is quite an anti-aging routine. You know you're getting old when you stand up, but your skin doesn't. I would dip in the Jordan River seven times so my skin could be restored to that of a little child! In fact, I would swim in it all day long to turn back the hands of time.

How close was Naaman to heading back home without a healing? After his little dip in the water, I wonder if he is kicking himself for being such an arrogant and obstinate mule of a man. Well, at least we can say of Naaman that once dipped, he corrects his response to one of gratitude.

He returns to thank Elisha and offers to pay for the healing. Unlike many unscrupulous ministers, Elisha turns him down. He will have nothing to do with it. The healing miracle is the work of the Lord; Elisha is merely the medium by which the message flows. He refuses to undermine God's glory. We shall see shortly that Elisha's servant will not let this financial opportunity pass, but Elisha did not yield to such greed.

Naaman becomes a worshipper of the Lord, saying, "Behold now, I know that there is no God in all the earth, but in Israel" (2 Kgs. 5:15). In fact, transformed Naaman requests to return home with two mule loads of dirt so he can worship the God of Israel with burnt offerings. Elisha blesses Naaman and sends him on his way.

Do you ever wonder what it would be like to receive a special award or for the first time meet someone you have always longed to see? We play the event over and over in our mind, grasping for a mental picture of how things will go. But when the big event arrives, things don't unfold as we expect. The reality is far different than our puffed up imagination. This often leads to disappointment and unful-filled expectations. It can trigger Big But-itis.

Naaman conceives in his mind how things should go. Elisha would come out to meet him, be impressed with his accomplishments, do some ritual dance, pray loudly, wave his magic hands, and poof—he would be healed. That's not how the events unfold. While Naaman's expectations are being deflated, his But is becoming inflated.

Not only do unfulfilled and unrealistic expectations lead to But enlargement, a poor attitude is also a contributing factor. In Naaman's case, he resents traveling to Samaria for a cure. He is forced to embark on the journey out of desperation. He is miffed that Elisha doesn't greet him. He is miffed that healing instructions come by messenger rather than Elisha himself. He is miffed at the simplicity of the instructions. He complains about dipping in the dirty Jordan River. In a huff, he turns his caravan around to head home. In his mind, it is another fruitless journey and another unfulfilled expectation in his life. This kind of attitude leads to But-ness. By now his But is so large, I am surprised he doesn't just float away when he finally does enter the Jordan River!

As a teenager in the church, I remember a white-haired gentleman leading congregational singing. He always wore a suit and tie, and he went off singing harmonies while supposedly leading the congregation in the melody. I was confused, thinking, "Am I supposed to follow him or stay with the melody?"

When I became older, my father told me a story about this white-haired song leader. He was pouring concrete one day when heavy rains descended and washed away all of his hard work. His driveway was ruined and his money flushed down the drain. He was so disappointed and upset with God that he walked away from the church, disgusted and disappointed with the Lord. He was a modern Naaman. While he isn't sitting atop a beautiful chariot, he is just as proud, refusing to get off that high-horse of his. He perceives in his mind how things will go, and when they don't turn out the way he imagines, he blames God. Here is an opportunity to show humility, to show friends and family how a man of God reacts in these types of situations, but instead of listening to sage counsel around him, he chucks it all and turns his back on God. His Big But blinds him from feeling the love of God again in his life for quite some time.

A friend of mine is called to a ministry that involves a great deal of emotional investment and attack from the enemy. It is frontline warfare activity with a heavy outlay of physical, mental, and emotional resources. God gave her a gift and called her to exercise it. In one sense, the Lord is calling her to a "dip in the river" experience. His words aren't really about dipping, but about obeying. The more she runs from His directive, the more miserable she becomes; when she finally obeys, she feels His presence in ways never experienced before. Yes, it is taxing, but she experiences God in ways most of us never will. In a sense, she dips in her Jordan River, and because of her obedience, she walks with God, talks with God, and ministers for God with a closeness I have yet to experience.

Do we really think that God bends to our will, yields to our daydreaming, or walks on rice paper to meet our every desire and expectation, no matter how childish they are? Naaman has a severe skin condition, and still his proud, self-centered mindset almost did him in. Our self-serving Big But often blinds us to God's moving in our lives and causes us to turn our horse toward home instead of discovering new vistas along the journey. Sometimes God asks us to dip seven times in a river. Sometimes He asks us not to get wet, and sometimes He is silent for a time. Whatever God is asking of you in this season of your life, whether dipping or drying, the question remains, are you obeying or is your Big But blinding you to all that He wants you to experience?

Big But Gehazi: *Greed*
2 Kings 5:20–27

> But Gehazi, the servant of Elisha the man of God, thought, "Behold, my master has spared this Naaman the Aramean, by not receiving from his hands what he brought. As the Lord lives, I will run after him and take something from him." So Gehazi pursued Naaman. When Naaman saw one running after him, he came down from the chariot to meet him and said, "Is all well?" He said, "All is well. My master has sent me, saying, 'Behold, just now two young men of the sons of the prophets have come to me from the hill country of Ephraim. Please give them a talent of silver and two changes of clothes.'" Naaman said, "Be pleased to take two talents." And he urged him, and bound two talents of silver in two bags with two changes of clothes and gave them to two of his servants; and they carried them before him. When he came to the hill, he took them from their hand and deposited them in the house, and he sent the men away, and they departed. But he went in and stood before his master. And Elisha said to him, "Where have you been, Gehazi?" And he said, "Your servant went nowhere." Then he said to him, "Did not my heart go with you, when the man turned from his chariot to meet you? Is it a time to receive money and to receive clothes and olive groves and vineyards and sheep and oxen and male and female servants? Therefore, the leprosy of Naaman shall cling to you and to your descendants forever." So he went out from his presence a leper as white as snow.

Gehazi represents a sad note to the river dipping saga. Naaman arrives in Samaria with a Big But, decides to obey, and returns home cured of leprosy. Elisha's servant Gehazi, on the other hand, decides to disobey and returns home with Naaman's leprosy. Gehazi's Big But is one of greed.

Elisha is a man on the straight and narrow, who follows the Lord no matter what. He appears to be a matter-of-fact kind of guy who tells it like it is and simply does what is right. He doesn't play fast and loose with the things of God.

If God tells him to go to a certain town, take certain food, and do certain things, he does it without complaint and without expectation of personal enrichment. The same cannot be said of Gehazi.

You have heard it said, "Once a thief, always a thief." True or not, the statement reflects a streak of larceny running through our hearts. Once there is a bent, or inclination in a certain direction, it only takes the right set of circumstances to turn that inclination into a reality. Law enforcement officials often set up sting operations to catch criminals. An individual thinks he is pressing the button to detonate a bomb when it is merely a fake. He is arrested and his attorney cries, "Entrapment!" but the law looks to the intent of the criminal and his propensity to commit the crime. Is he pushing the detonator because he is coerced by undercover law enforcement, or because in his mind he actually intends to detonate a bomb?

Gehazi isn't entrapped in any way; he sees an opportunity for personal financial gain. He intends to engage in sinful activity as seen through 1) his lying to Naaman and Elisha, 2) following after Naaman to seek money, 3) actually taking money and clothing, and 4) storing the goods in his home. That's not entrapment, but a streak of larceny in his heart.

I haven't had much luck with youth pastors over the years. In fact, the last one I hired might as well have been named Gehazi for all the lying and stealing he practiced. This is not a diatribe against youth ministers, as I am grateful for their ministry. In my case, however, I just haven't had good luck with the ones I've hired. But then again, I am the guy who gets in the shortest checkout line at the store, and low and behold, it ends up being the longest line. I can sure pick them! God seems to even use grocery shopping to test my Christianity! At Christmas time I simply stay away from the stores, otherwise it becomes merely a season to ask for forgiveness.

This youth minister stole funds from the church and lied his way through a cover up. He is found out, takes no responsibility for his actions, and when the law and his lies catch up with him, he winds up in jail for a time while his wife initiates divorce proceedings. He saw opportunity for personal enrichment at the expense of the kingdom. While it taught the church a lesson on tighter financial accountability, it cost this youth pastor his job, his family, and his reputation. His greedy actions defamed the cause of Christ. He was a nice guy, extremely talented, a go-getter, and kids loved him, but he flew by the seat of his magnetic personality and utilized his energies to concoct lies in efforts to secure financial gain. Like Gehazi, he gets caught.

A tainted heart can corrupt the whole heart. It only takes a little leaven to raise the whole lump of dough. Vigilance in maintaining a pure heart is an effort worth pursuing, because opening the door to a little corruption is disastrous. It can lead to Big But-itis.

Earlier I shared that I was asked to leave a senior pastor position and how demoralizing that was in my life. My departure was not for moral or doctrinal reasons, but for growth and personality reasons. Growth threatens those holding power, and it is easier to vilify one individual than deal with larger Big But issues. While I was broken, I was not crushed, and the pastors that followed me should have been a lesson to the church. One was released for allegedly using church computers to fulfill his pornographic lust, and the other was terminated for embezzling thousands of dollars from the church coffers. They were Gehazis with tainted hearts, just waiting for opportunities to ripen. When they saw a crack in the doorway, they busted it down to pursue their greed.

Gehazi's Big But actions put into easily recognizable But-speak might look something like this:

Gehazi:
Naaman brought gifts for my master, **but** Elisha never makes use of these kinds of opportunities. I know Elisha is trying to honor the Lord, **but** there is no reason why I shouldn't take advantage of this bounty. Elisha passed on this wonderful opportunity, **but** I am not about to miss out on it. Elisha told Namaan one thing, **but** I will lie to him so I can be remunerated properly. Elisha wouldn't like what I am doing, **but** what Elisha doesn't know won't hurt him.

Judas sold Jesus down the river for thirty pieces of silver. My youth pastor sold out his ministry for the sake of greed. Two pastors followed the streak of larceny in their tainted hearts to ruinous ends. A streak of larceny leads to all kinds of Big But symptoms and greed can taint the holiest of hearts.

Protecting our hearts from the taint of sin is an important theme in the Bible. Jeremiah 17:9 declares, "The heart is more deceitful than all else, and is desperately sick." Realizing how the stain of sin can destroy a relationship with the LORD, King David writes in Psalm 51:10, "Create in me a clean heart, O God, and renew a steadfast spirit within me." The wisdom of Proverbs 4:23 advises, "Watch over your heart with all diligence, for from it flow the springs of life."

It is the heart that is important to God, as 1 Samuel 16:7 notes, "for God sees not as man sees, for man looks at the outward appearance, but the LORD looks at the heart." When Jesus is asked to identify the greatest commandment, He replies in Mark 12:30, "And you shall love the LORD your God with all your heart, and with all your soul, and with all your mind, and with all your strength." Loving God with all that we are is the core of all biblical teaching.

If God looks at the heart and desires that we love Him with single-minded devotion, we benefit by quickly discovering and removing any blemish before it has opportunity to blossom. This is the "firecracker" principle. As a kid, firecrackers became the main staple of our July Independence Day celebration. They are fun, noisy, and can blow up mounds of dirt, plastic cars, and all sorts of things. If you aren't careful, they can also blow off fingers, damage eyes, and blow out eardrums. We didn't think much about that as kids; we just thought it was cool to blow things up, not blow ourselves up. We lit a firecracker, cocked our arm, aimed for the intended target, and gave it a heave. Most of the time this worked well, but on rare occasions, the firecracker blew up in our hand before we could release it. Man, that smarts. I still have all my fingers, but I think that is because luck outwitted my stupidity.

My point is this: once the fuse is lit, there is only a small window of time to stop the explosive event from occurring. To sit and stare, ponder, or waiver back and forth means certain detonation. To stop the fuse from igniting the gunpowder while in our hand, we had to act quickly and decisively. Wholehearted devotion entails diligence on our part. We can't be couch potato Christians. When we sense sin crouching at our door and attention is turned toward the streak of larceny in our heart, it is time to act quickly, decisively, and in so doing, prevent the destructive explosion in our life.

Seeing an opportunity for personal financial gain, Gehazi's greedy Big But springs to life, causing him to receive the leprosy Naaman has just been cured of. This story is absolutely incredible. Gehazi is in the presence of a holy man. He not only serves Elisha, but he watches him do wondrous things for the Lord. What would cause a man in this situation to risk it all for two pieces of silver and some clothing? Why would he lie and scheme to pursue financial gain when his master demonstrates what is proper? Greed will cause a person to do that. Greed will taint a heart. Greed will produce Big Buts with disastrous and long-lasting inflammation. Gehazi sowed greed and reaped leprosy. We do not sow the seeds of greed without reaping a harvest of negative side effects.

Big But Jonah: *Disappointment*
Jonah 1:1–3

The word of the Lord came to Jonah the son of Amittai saying, "Arise, go to Nineveh the great city and cry against it, for their wickedness has come up before Me." But Jonah rose up to flee to Tarshish from the presence of the Lord. So he went down to Joppa, found a ship which was going to Tarshish, paid the fare and went down into it to go with them to Tarshish from the presence of the Lord.

Jonah is a runner—not a sprinter or a marathoner, but an internal runner. His heart runs away from God. As he runs he complains, and the more he complains, the more he runs. His Big But condition is of a critical nature; so much so, that he erroneously believes he can outrun God and His sovereign will. How foolish!

Francis Thompson, author of the English poem "Hound of Heaven" discovers this for himself. Thompson's father wants him to study at Oxford University. Underneath Francis' miserable failure at Oxford and his addiction to drugs lies a hibernating genius, soon to be awakened by the Heavenly Father. Eeking out a woeful existence by sleeping on the streets of London, Francis is chased by Christ Himself, the hound of heaven. Even in his abysmal state, Francis cannot hide, nor run from the heavenly hound. Christ has picked up his scent and is chasing him down, rescuing him from his feeble, despicable condition, to become the instrument of God he is destined to be. The short version of his poem goes like this:

I fled Him down the nights and down the days.
I fled Him down the arches of the years,
I fled Him down the labyrinthine ways
of my own mind: And in the mist of tears
I hid from Him, and under running laughter
Up vistaed hopes I sped;
Down titanic glooms of chasmed fears
From those strong feet that followed, that followed after
For though I knew His love that followed
Yet I was sore adread
Lest having Him I have naught else beside.
All that I took from thee I did but take
Not for thy harms
But just that thou might'st seek it in my arms.
All which thy child's mistake fancies are lost
I have stored for thee at home:
"Rise, clasp my hand, and come."
Halts by me that footfall:
is my gloom after all,
shade of His hand, outstretched caressingly.
Ah, fondest, blindest, weakest,
I am he whom thou seekest!
Thou dravest love from thee, that dravest me. [1]

God has the right, as Commander-in-Chief, to direct His army. As the Father, He has the right to oversee His children. As the Great Shepherd, He has the right to lead His sheep. As the Potter, He has the right to mold the clay. Our role is not to dictate, interfere, or run, but simply follow. Like Francis Thompson, no matter where we go, how fast we run, or how deep our reprobation, we can never outrun God. Jonah is about to learn this very lesson.

Matthew 18:10 is an interesting runner verse: "See that you do not despise one of these little ones, for I say to you that their angels in heaven continually see the face of My Father who is in heaven." Why would angels in heaven continually behold the face of the Father? Were they stunned by His glory? Possibly, but most often a glimpse of God's glory causes deep knee bending into prostrate positions of worship. In this case, the angels don't bow or bend; they behold. Could the reason be that they are ever attentive to God's directives? In other words, angels are messengers and ministering spirits who move at the direction and command of the Father. Here they are in heaven, looking intently at the Heavenly Father (beholding), waiting for a signal, a nod of the head, a verbal command, or a hand gesture, so they can quickly move to implement His will.

> . . . no matter where we go, how fast we run, or how deep our reprobation, we can never outrun God.

For example, little Amy with her blonde hair and blue eyes is in need of protection from a stranger, and at just the right time, the Father says, "My little Amy needs protection, go now," and in a moment's notice the angels run to protect her. Angels continually behold the face of God so they can move quickly and decisively toward implementing the Father's will. While angels in heaven are ready, willing, and anxious to obey God, Jonah, on the other hand, is not. He will obey, as long as the directive fits within the confines of his personal preferences. He's like the person called to missions who is willing to serve as long as the assignment is in the Virgin Islands and the accommodations are at the Marriott. Jonah is a Big But runner, yet, instead of running to obey God, he tries to run from God. It is an effort in futility.

But-ness begins in the heart, springs to life when conditions are ripe, and upon manifestation, relegates God's role to that of spiritual advisor, not Lord of our life. When the directive of the Lord comes to Jonah, son of Amittai, instructing him to cry against Nineveh's wickedness, we realize that Jonah doesn't have a hearing problem. He not only hears with precision and clarity, he completely understands the instructions. He knows without a doubt that it is God speaking to him, and he knows without a doubt the nature of the assignment. He just doesn't want to do it. So he runs to Joppa, boards a ship to Tarshish, and waddles in his Big But.

Sometimes our Big But erupts like a volcano and we simply don't recognize it as such. God has to work with us and over time, as we mature and grow, not only are we able to identify But-ness, we are actually able to overcome it. At other times our Big But explodes by design. We know it, encourage it, and don't find its presence particularly bothersome. It is one thing to have a soft heart with a few streaks of But-ness skimming the surface and quite another to have a rock solid Big But heart with only a few streaks of softness. In Jonah's case, he is not only aware of his Big But, he embraces and nurtures it. He exhibits clear disdain for the instruction and desire of the Lord.

> But-ness begins in the heart, springs to life when conditions are ripe, and upon manifestation, relegates God's role to that of spiritual advisor, not Lord of our life.

One easily detects a sense of sarcasm and cynicism from Jonah in 4:1–3,

> But it greatly displeased Jonah and he became angry. He prayed to the LORD and said, "Please LORD, was not this what I said while I was still in my own country? Therefore in order to forestall this I fled to Tarshish, for I knew that You are a gracious and compassionate God, slow to anger and abundant in lovingkindness, and one who relents concerning calamity. Therefore now, O LORD, please take my life from me, for death is better to me than life."

In 1:1, Jonah receives clear instructions for traveling to Nineveh and preaching against its wickedness. In an attempt to flee from God's presence and circumvent the Nineveh preaching endeavor, he boards a ship heading in the opposite direction (1:2). The Lord brews up a turbulent storm to get Jonah's attention, and the ship is about to break into a thousand pieces. Sailors seek explanation as to this calamity and discover that Jonah is fleeing from the Lord in 1:10: "For the men knew that he was fleeing from the presence of the LORD, because he had told them." Jonah's disobedience is the cause of this perilous storm, and his Big But put the lives of others in danger.

With his But still large and uncontrollable, he asks to be thrown into the raging sea. In his feeble mind, it is better to die in the sea than obey the Lord. The raging storm ends when his body hits the water and is swallowed by a big fish. The fish thinks it captures a tasty meal, and Jonah can't believe this is happening to him.

Who wants to be in the smelly belly of a fish? Though there must have been an air pocket for breathing, the belly must have also been stinky, dark, and extremely tight quarters. Unfortunately, God often has to bring disobedient individuals through fish-belly experiences so they shut up, listen, and get their mind right. There is only one thing to do in a fish belly, and that is to pray. Jonah does just that in chapter two, where he acknowledges the sovereignty of God. It is the prayer of someone in a tight situation needing help. The underwater cruise is over when, "the LORD commanded the fish, and it vomited Jonah up onto the dry land"

(2:10). His life is spared, he is now on dry land breathing fresh air again, and the call of God upon his life remains. The words of the Lord come to Jonah a second time, instructing him to preach against the wickedness of Nineveh. This time Jonah obeys, although reluctantly.

Upon hearing Jonah's message, the city of Nineveh repents of their wicked ways. Even the king removes his royal robe, replaces it with sackcloth and ashes, and issues a decree for repentance. He leads by example, and humility spreads from the top down. Repentance moves the heart of God and in 3:10, forgiveness is disbursed rather than judgment, "When God saw their deeds, that they turned from their wicked way, then God relented concerning the calamity which He had declared He would bring upon them. And He did not do it."

> Unfortunately, God often has to bring disobedient individuals through fish-belly experiences so they shut up, listen, and get their mind right.

The dispensing of grace disturbs Jonah. This is exactly what he feared would happen. Here he is proclaiming words of judgment, and God goes and forgives these wicked people. We read in 4:1 that the Lord's act of grace to the city of Nineveh "greatly displeased Jonah and he became angry." Jonah desired judgment for Nineveh rather than forgiveness. Stated in modern lingo, 4:1 might read like this, "Jonah didn't like it that God dispensed grace rather than judgment and his Big But became exceedingly large, so large that it caused him to lose all sense of perspective." In 4:3 Jonah pleads to die: "Therefore now, O Lord, please take my life from me, for death is better to me than life."

Really? Death is better than life? That's not what you were saying when you were in the belly of the fish? There you were crying like a baby for God to save you. Now you want to die because He doesn't do what you want Him to do?

Jonah's Big But actions put into easily recognizable But-speak might sound like this:

Jonah:

What Lord? You want me to go where? Nineveh? Sure, I will go to Nineveh, *but* only when hell freezes over. I am out of here. God wants me to preach to those filthy Ninevites, *but* I will jump a ship to Tarshish and flee His presence. I will go anywhere You want, *but* not Nineveh. This sea is getting very choppy and dangerous. Just throw me overboard. I will die, *but* I am not going to Nineveh. Well, I just preached in Nineveh for You Lord, are You happy now? I preach judgment, *but* You bring forgiveness. That is just not right. I obeyed You, *but* look where it got me. I would rather die than live.

GOD AND JONAH

Text	God's Saving	Jonah's Disobedience
Jonah 1:1	God gives a command to Jonah.	
Jonah 1:2–3		Jonah disobeys and flees on a ship.
Jonah 1:4	God sends a great storm.	
Jonah 1:5–16		Jonah seeks to die by being thrown overboard.
Jonah 1:17	God saves Jonah by sending a big fish to swallow him.	
Jonah 2:1–9		Jonah offers a remorseful prayer in the fish belly.
Jonah 2:10	God saves Jonah as the fish vomits him on dry land.	
Jonah 3:1–2	God commands Jonah a second time.	
Jonah 3:3–9		Jonah finally obeys and preaches to Nineveh: the city repents.
Jonah 3:10	God saves the city of Nineveh from destruction.	
Jonah 4:1–3		Jonah is upset and pleads to die.
Jonah 4:4–11	God teaches Jonah a lesson.	

Jonah's story is similar to Israel's history as a nation and their cycle of sin: 1) God commands, 2) Israel disobeys, 3) God intervenes, 4) Israel obeys, 5) good comes of obedience, 6) Israel disobeys, and the cycle repeats itself. The same cycle is seen with Jonah. Every time he disobeys, God intervenes, until obedience is finally forthcoming. Things go well until disobedience raises its ugly head and God has to intervene again. It is the cycle of commandment, disobedience, repentance, salvation, obedience.

When Jonah finally does travel to Nineveh, he does so with drudgery and acquiescence rather than enthusiastic submission. He obeys, but he does so reluctantly, and with his bottom lip protruding. He realizes that Nineveh is certainly preferred to a wind-tossed sea and a smelly fish belly. Rather than full and complete compliance, in his mind, he is choosing the lesser of two evils. He doesn't want to be on a boat about to break apart or in the darkness of a fish belly; yet, he doesn't want to be in Nineveh either. Of the three alternatives, the latter one seems to be his best option. At least he will be on dry ground.

Does your Big But ever cause you to make similar decisions? You know precisely what God is calling you to do, but instead of obeying, you run in a different direction. Had the Lord asked you to do something amenable to your personal desires and comfort, you would gladly obey in a heartbeat . . . but Nineveh? What is your personal Nineveh? Where is God asking you to go in your own life that you are unwilling? In what ways is God intervening in your life to draw you to His commands and desires? What is your "seasick boat" story and your "fish-belly" tale where God has to get your attention? And, does He finally get your attention, or are you still running? When God vomits you up on dry land, again presents His instructions, do you obey willingly or begrudgingly? Is there a smile on your face or a protruding bottom lip, the proud sign of poutiness?

> Obedience brings blessing—not only to us, but to others.

Like Jonah, our Big But of disappointment can override the many ways God desires to use us in His kingdom. Nineveh is spared because Jonah obeys. Nineveh experiences the grace and forgiveness of God because Jonah obeys. The lives of countless people are influenced for the kingdom because Jonah obeys. Obedience brings blessing—not only to us, but to others. Our Big Buts cause us to run *from* God instead of running to Him. Had Jonah obeyed immediately, he could have avoided the nasty boat trip, the plunge into a shaking sea, coach class travel accommodations in a fish belly, the thrill of being vomited up with stomach contents, and the disappointment and anger at the Lord's loving, kind, and forgiving heart. Big But-itis leads to disobedience.

Big But Elijah: *Self-Pity*
1 Kings 19:1–4

Now Ahab told Jezebel all that Elijah had done, and how he had killed all the prophets with the sword. Then Jezebel sent a messenger to Elijah, saying, "So may the gods do to me and even more, if I do not make your life as the life of one of them by tomorrow about this time." And he was afraid and arose and ran for his life and came to Beersheba, which belongs to Judah, and left his servant there. But he himself went a day's journey into the wilderness, and came and sat down under a juniper tree; and he requested for himself that he might die, and said, "It is enough; now, O LORD, take my life, for I am not better than my fathers."

Our final Bible Big But to be examined is the prophet Elijah, another Old Testament heavyweight. His shameful moment takes place soon after defeating the prophets of Baal on Mt. Carmel, when the very next day, Queen Jezebel threatens to take his life.

Our world is rocked when we realize that even the biblical heavyweights struggle with Big But-itis. Innately, we seek convincing examples of how we ought to be and live. Unfortunately, whenever we focus on fallen human beings, whether it's Elijah, Elisha, Moses, Abraham, Peter, Paul, etc., we always unearth flaws and failures. We hunger to find someone who actually does it right, lives for God wholeheartedly, and overcomes the flaws and failures we ourselves know and experience so intimately. But, alas, there is no one, not even giants of the faith. Once again, we are disappointed.

Our hearts are uneasy until we fix our eyes on the only human being ever to fulfill the law and the prophets, exemplify what living for the Father looks like, and reflect the very nature of God to us. His name is Jesus. Realizing this dilemma early on in my life, I wrote a little poem titled "I Must" soon after graduating from high school reflecting my need to focus on the cross:

> *I must*
> *press on and not give up*
> *though many times I fail.*
> *My weaknesses are many,*
> *by His strength I will prevail.*
>
> *I must*
> *keep my focus on the cross,*
> *and not look above or beyond;*
> *for if I look anywhere else,*
> *my guiding light is gone.*
>
> *I must*
> *dear Lord, be filled with Your Spirit.*
> *Help me now to start anew.*
> *Not only to worship, pray, and serve,*
> *but in everything, to do it for You.* [2]

I struggled to find my stellar example until I understood that I was looking in the wrong place. Finally, I set my eyes upon a man who was nailed to a cross, realizing that to look anywhere else merely invites disillusionment. When my eyes are fixed on the crucified One, I find the example I long for.

Elijah lived an interesting and exciting life. He serves as a mentor to Elisha, who picks up the prophetic mantle once Elijah is absent from the scene. Elijah lives in a time when Israel's state of affairs is in serious decline. King Ahab marries Jezebel, a Canaanite woman who uses her regal influence to suppress the worship of Yahweh and establish devotion to Baal, a false God from her homeland. Jezebel is so venomous that King Ahab wilts in her presence and prophets of Yahweh hide

> Finally, I set my eyes upon a man who was nailed to a cross, realizing that to look anywhere else merely invites disillusionment.

in caves to survive her vicious persecutions and killings. It is not a good time to be a representative of Yahweh.

Fortunately, we don't find Elijah hiding in a cave like the other prophets. Instead, he confronts Ahab face-to-face. He plants his feet firmly in the strength of the Lord and warns Ahab of disastrous consequences if things don't change. In light of Jezebel's influence and deathly demeanor, it takes a great amount of courage to meet with Ahab. Elijah is risking his life.

A few years later, Elijah returns to the king. Nothing has changed. In fact, things have gotten worse. The land has not experienced rain for three and a half years, and instead of heeding Elijah's warning, the king languishes in front of Jezebel like a flower enduring its first frost.

This time, Elijah challenges Ahab to a duel. Enough spiritual decay has occurred, and it is time to put an end to such sinful practices. In essence, Elijah is saying, "Ok, you call on your God and I will call on mine, and the one that answers, we will follow." The challenge is issued, and King Ahab falls head on into the trap.

The meeting occurs in a place familiar to King Ahab and the prophets of Baal. Mt. Carmel is a sacred place for worshiping the Canaanite god. Elijah challenges them in their own back yard. And so they gather, 450 prophets of Baal, and one prophet of Yahweh. Can you imagine the scene? The odds seem stacked against Elijah—like Muhammad Ali fighting against Pee-wee Herman! The crowd must have wagered their bets on Baal if only because of the sheer number of prophets. But in God's economy, 450, 4,500, or 45,000 false prophets makes little difference to Him. The challenge is over before it begins, because one faithful follower of Yahweh, trusting and obeying Him, is unconquerable. Elijah knows what the outcome will be, but he has to go through the motions in proving to others that Yahweh is alive and well.

Elijah wisely uses the gathering as an opportunity to challenge the gawking crowd. "How long will you hesitate between two opinions? If the LORD is God, follow Him; but if Baal, follow him" (1 Kgs. 18:21). Each side places their animal offering on wood with no fire underneath it. The god that consumes the sacrifice will be the winner. Baal's prophets call upon their god with dancing, prancing, prodding, praying, and great theatre, but with no response. There is no fire and no consumption of the offering. Nothing. Nada. Not a thing. In fact, Elijah mocks them recognizing the doom their insolence and false religion will bring upon them.

Now it is Elijah's turn and in dramatic fashion, he repairs the broken altar of the Lord, digs a trench around it, lays down his wood with offering, and asks that water be poured on the offering and the wood. This is done three times until water flows into the trench surrounding the altar. Without a doubt, Elijah intends to make a statement, "Yahweh, the God of Israel, is the true living God, so powerful that He will consume the offering even though it is soaked in water."

Fire and water do not mix. In fact, water is the very thing that can put out fire. Try starting a bonfire by dousing the wood with water prior to lighting the match. It won't catch on fire. If a water-soaked animal carcass and drenched wood is consumed by fire, then surely it must be because of Yahweh. And this is exactly why Elijah did it.

Elijah prays to God and fire falls from heaven consuming the wet offering, the soaked wood, the stones, and the water in the trench. Poof! It is all gone, licked up with fire slung from heaven. The event is so powerful, the curious crowd falls on their faces crying, "The LORD, He is God; the LORD, He is God" (1 Kgs. 18:39).

> The challenge is over before it begins, because one faithful follower of Yahweh, trusting and obeying Him, is unconquerable.

At the end of the day, the crowd acknowledges Yahweh, Baal's prophets are seized and killed, and Elijah stops the drought by praying for and receiving rain. As you might suspect, Ahab runs home to Jezebel like a whipped puppy and spills his guts. Jezebel, a control freak with a zeal for promoting false religion, must have been furious. I bet even wimpy Ahab paid a heavy price for his unsuccessful endeavor upon returning home to a wife whose blood is boiling. In her mind, Elijah must pay dearly for defying her. How dare he challenge her control, topple her religious regime, and cause such embarrassment. Who would dare come against her prophets, her religion, her power and control? Who would dare have the courage to kill her prophets? She was, after all, the Queen, and had worked hard to establish her stern reputation.

Spiritual giant or not, we are all prone to Big But-itis, especially after a great spiritual victory or a time of spiritual exhaustion. Mountain-top experiences are often followed by steep spiritual downfalls. On the mountain top, Peter acknowledges Jesus as the Christ, the Son of the living God, and turns right around and rebukes Him for traveling to Jerusalem in fulfillment of God's divine plan. On the mountain top, Gehazi, servant of Elisha, watches the miraculous healing of Naaman and turns right around seeking personal financial gain. On the mountain top, Elijah overcomes 450 prophets of Baal and leads the crowd to acknowledge the Lord, and then turns right around begging to die because Jezebel is after him.

Elijah goes from the crowd to the wilderness, from jubilant success to the gutter, from the mountain top to the valley. I have seen it happen numerous times in the lives of so many, and quite frankly, I have seen it in my own life. One of the most dangerous mountain-top experiences for ministers occurs right after a successful building project. So much time and energy goes into initiating and sustaining the project that by the time it is completed, ministers experience exhaustion and congregations begin wondering if new leadership is necessary for the next phase of ministry growth.

As kids, my sister and I attended church camp and had a blast. It was a spiritual high for us, with emotionally charged "come to Jesus" campfire meetings and late-night talks about the faith. Upon arriving home, however, our mountain-top experience made life miserable for everyone else. My father threatened never to send us to church camp again. Our fall from the mountain top to the valley was too hard on him. We had Big Buts, and our Big Buts were of a spiritual nature. In other words, Big Buts don't have to be Buts of greed, selfishness, disbelief and all those negative things. Big Buts can also be dressed in nice religious clothing. A Big But is *a perspective or behavior that conditions, justifies, or excuses our conduct and thinking, or reveals discontentment with God.* Good things, spiritual things, and even mountain-top experiences can lead to Big But-itis if they are used to condition, justify, or excuse our behavior. In my case, church camp was a great experience, but I went home using the mountain top to justify and excuse my "holier than thou" attitude. No wonder my parents scratched their heads in disbelief.

> But life is not about being on the mountain top or being in the valley; it is about the journey.

Lollipop Christians promote mountain-top experiences as the norm, and anything less than 18,000-foot living is nothing more than flirting with failure. Do you see what is happening? This in itself is a form of Big But-itis. If I lift up the mountain top as the norm for living, down you as a failure, uplift myself for being at 18,000 feet, then my Big But justifies my behavior of downing you and promoting myself as spiritually superior.

Mountain-top experiences are wonderful. I love them. But expecting to always live on the mountain top is unrealistic, unbiblical, and sets us up for failure. We don't hit a home run every time it's our turn to bat. Instead, life is a series of singles, strikeouts, doubles, triples, and homeruns. Single hits and strikeouts seem to be the norm. Every once in a while we hit doubles, triples, and homeruns. Sometimes they are well placed and drive in runs; when that happens, we feel good.

But life is not about being on the mountain top or being in the valley; it is about the journey. It is a process, not a result; a journey, not a destination. This is an important point to remember. We are strangers and aliens in this life, just passing through as "our citizenship is in heaven," according to Philippians 3:20. This life is merely a training ground filled with ups and downs, joys and sorrows, sickness and health, love and hate, mountain tops and valleys, strikeouts, singles, doubles, triples, and homeruns. That's just the way it is. The final, eternal mountain-top experience will be in heaven. Until then, life is a journey. The question is not so much where you are, but how you are traveling. Carrying the extra baggage of a Big But slows you down and makes the journey more grueling than it needs to be.

> We don't get to a mountain top without climbing the mountain, and it is the climbing that tests us, shapes us, and helps us grow and mature.

Be grateful for the mountain tops and enjoy their beauty. Breathe them in deeply and carry the experience in your heart. But remember: there are more mountains to climb. We don't get to a mountain top without climbing the mountain, and it is the climbing that tests us, shapes us, and helps us grow and mature. If life is about the journey, then we should be checking out our gear and ridding ourselves of useless loads of sin, guilt, and Big Buts so we can easily and readily journey to where God is leading us, whether mountain top or valley. Big Buts and long journeys don't travel well together. Get rid of the Big But, and your journey will be much more enjoyable.

Bible Big But Summary

If anything ought to confirm that life is a journey rather than a continuous mountain-top experience, it is the Bible itself. We easily recognize Big But-itis in others because we often bear the brunt of their disease. We know deep down inside, whether we admit it or not, that we have our own problem with the Big But Syndrome. Our own Big Buts are just as devastating to others as theirs is to us. We all have issues with acute and chronic But-ness. Since we haven't yet arrived at our final destination, our journey continues.

Evidenced in both the Old and New Testaments, we are surprised to discover that many characters in the Bible experienced Big Buts too. In fact, But-ness appears to be a human problem, a condition needing the help of God to overcome. Giants of the faith wrestle with the disease, including such heavyweights as Adam, Abraham, Noah, David, Elijah, Elisha, Peter, and the rest of the disciples. They experience the mountain top, but more often than not, they are either in the valley or climbing the mountain. They are human. They are like us. They are on their own journey. They too wrestle with the Big But problem in their own lives.

One of the reasons Jesus walked among us is to model a life free from But-ness. When we look at others, ourselves, and even giants of the faith, we can easily become discouraged and overwhelmed at the degree of But-ness in the human condition. When we look to Christ alone, however, hope and courage take root in our hearts. He becomes an example to follow as we sojourn through this life. Though perfection and ultimate freedom from the effects of Big But-itis won't be fully realized until we reach heaven, we find comfort in this life by the example of Christ and the power of the Holy Spirit to guide, empower, and sustain us during a journey filled with mountain climbing.

BIG BUT CLUSTERS

A flare-up of Big But-itis can be triggered by just about anything, and often without a moment's notice. You can exhibit a Big But about life, children, God, church, job, grocery shopping, which version of the Bible to study—anything at all. What matters most is not the object of our But-ness, but how our perspective and behavior regarding that object is being used to condition, justify, or excuse godly behavior and thinking.

Realizing the depth and breadth of all possible objects of But-ness, it becomes nearly impossible to list them all. It may be feasible, however, to cluster the recurring troublesome spots seen in the life of Christians. A similar clustering occurs in marriage counseling. Although couples experience various relationship problems, most issues seem to revolve around communication, sex, money, kids, and religion. Big But clustering acts like a magnet attracting like issues and helps us better understand and manage Big But flare-ups. While the following list certainly isn't official or exhaustive by any means, it does reflect, from my own experience, key areas that seem to cluster together:

Big But Cluster List

- Fear and Worry
- Doubt and Unbelief
- Control
- Misconception of God and the Bible
- Less Than Total Commitment
- Myopic Vision of God's Plan
- Misconception of Ourselves
- Pain, Disappointment, and Anger

Big But Cluster 1: *Fear and Worry*

While scholars may promote technical distinctions between fear and worry, for me, they are like heads and tails, two sides of the same coin. Fear produces worry, and worry produces fear; a vicious and destructive cycle feeding off each other. Both point to a lack of courage, and both zap strength from our ability to live in the present.

In her book *Clippings From My Notebook*, Corrie ten Boom writes, "Worry does not empty tomorrow of its sorrow. It empties today of its strength." [3] If anyone understands the gripping effects of fear and worry, it is Corrie ten Boom, a Holocaust survivor under Nazi Germany. Enduring the cruelties of a corrupt and tortuous regime, she recognizes firsthand the mental prison fear and worry can lock people into.

My father, whom I loved and respected, was a chronic worrier, fearful of what *could* happen, and what *might* go wrong. Being cautious and gathering all the facts prior to making significant decisions is a wise thing to do, but incessant worst-case scenario and doomsday thinking extracts so much mental and emotional energy that nothing remains for present living.

In sharing a particular worry with a friend, I was told the following story. During the days when pioneers traveled west, there was a large river to be crossed along the route. Worried travelers spoke of this river on numerous occasions, allowing their fears to enlarge, spreading rumors of calamity, and interrogating the guide on his plans for getting them across the terrifying roadblock. As an experienced pioneer, the guide uttered to the assembly, "I don't cross the river until I get there." What sage advice. His present strength was not stolen from him by worrying about a future event.

Had we been there and heard those words, some of us may have responded, "But I wasn't worrying. I was simply planning. I was thinking ahead. Me, worry? Never!" Call it what you want, but when your focus is either on the past or the future, and your present energy is consumed in a negative manner, it is fear and worry.

Some folks are gifted in being cautious and deliberative. I know several individuals, chief financial officers, medical personnel, pastors, lawyers, and students who have a real aptitude in cautiously sifting through information and producing careful analysis of various options and alternatives. There is nothing wrong with this. In fact, their gift helps balance out those personality types with a tendency to move quickly without all the facts. Being cautious and deliberative isn't fear and worry in my book; sometimes it is being smart.

It is when "cautious" and "deliberative" become euphemisms for "worry" and "fear" that things become problematic. It is okay to realize a river must be crossed along the western route, seek the shallowest portion of the river for crossing, strategically pack to lighten your load, or even bring along your speedos. That may be cautious and deliberative. But incessant conversation, constantly thinking about it, losing sleep and appetite, and allowing the river to ruin the trip is worry and fear.

The fear and worry I experience in my own life seems to put me in "freeze mode." It locks me down so I can't move forward. Enjoying the present is difficult because I am worried about some action or event in the past, or some unknown future.

In introducing my son to water, we led him into the shallow end of the swimming pool. He clung to me as though his very life depended on it. His death grip reminded me of how I feel in a dentist's chair. I laid him out flat, allowed him to float, and all the while he whimpered like a baby; half crying, half shuttering at the same time. My arms cradled him, he wore arm floaties to prevent sinking, he was in shallow water with mom watching from the side, and yet, fear and worry got the better of him.

What I remember most about the event is his "freeze mode." Gripped with fear, he couldn't let go, couldn't process what I was saying, and couldn't grasp his surroundings. Fear and worry paralyzed his mind so he was unable to accurately assess the reality of his situation. I get that way myself sometimes. Fear and worry lock me in, freezing me into a constant whirlwind of cognitive and emotional dysfunction. I can't go forward, backward, or sideways. Trapped in the chains of fear and worry, I can't seem to find the key to free myself.

I suppose there is a good kind of fear, like the fear of the Lord, or the fear of having to kiss a rattlesnake on the lips, but that's not the kind of fear I am referring to. I am talking about the kind of fear that hinders our relationship and trust in a loving God; the freezing kind of fear that promotes cognitive and emotional dysfunction. Many Bible references assure us that fearing God is healthy, producing a sense of awe in His marvelous works, character, and nature, "The fear of the LORD is the beginning of knowledge" (Prov. 1:7). But any other kind of fear in the Bible is never positive. In fact, it acts as a hindrance to experiencing God.

Abraham, for example, fears the Lord in a good way when he is commanded to leave Ur of the Chaldeans and follow God's leading to a new land. His awe of God allows him to move forward in faith. On the other hand, he fears for his own life along the journey when he worries that strangers will seize his beautiful wife and leave him for dead. This fear causes him to lie and distrust God.

Peter experiences positive fear of the Lord (great awe) when he steps out of the boat and onto the water trying to reach Jesus (Mt. 14:22–33). What is a little thing like walking on water when the One you are going to see raises dead people, turns water into wine, commands storms to cease, heals various diseases, and casts out demons? That kind of awe leads Peter to begin his walk on water. But after a few steps, fear and worry turn his focus toward current surroundings instead of the splendor of his Lord. He quickly begins to sink. That pretty much sums up how fear and worry work in our life. Exhibit great awe of the Lord, and we experience Him in wonderful ways. Live in fear and worry, take our focus off the Lord, and we get locked into an energy draining, visionless existence that sinks us from experiencing the abundant life.

People like consistency and routine. It brings them security and stability, like a rock to stand upon or an anchor in rough seas. The problem, however, is that our formula for stability and security is often inverted. In reality, we already possess stability and security through Christ, and yet, we search for it in other venues. Let me explain.

This life is uncertain, unstable, and filled with constant change. More change has occurred in the last fifty years, many believe, than in all the previous years combined. Because the rate of change is constantly accelerating, it becomes difficult to keep up. Technology, for instance, has taken dramatic leaps forward in size, speed, ability, and use. Older folks feel they are so far behind that any effort to learn is futile. The world they knew no longer exists. They think social media is visiting with friends during a church potluck, and a CD Rom drive is actually a cup holder.

When my father died, I purchased a cell phone for my mother to help her feel safe and easily keep in touch with her children from anywhere at any time. She didn't use it at all. It was too much change for her to grasp. I would have experienced far greater success had I simply purchased a used rotary dial phone for her use!

The stock market is extremely volatile, natural disasters frequently occur, climate is morphing, the color and religion of our nation is shifting, and the country's moral climate is drifting. I once bought a home that increased in value by nearly $150,000. I felt pretty good about the investment until the housing market crashed and I sold the home for $50,000 less than what I originally paid for it. One day you can be healthy, breathing, and living life to the fullest, and the next day brought to your knees with a severe medical condition or life calamity. Life is anything but predictable and stable. Any security we find on this earth is temporal at best.

But God, on the other hand, is absolutely stable and secure. He is changeless. Malachi 3:6 states, "For I, the LORD, do not change." Similarly, Hebrews 13:8 indicates that "Jesus Christ is the same yesterday and today and forever." God's character, nature, attributes, and promises are sure as the setting sun. No matter what happens in this life, good or bad, He remains. In a sea of instability, God is the lighthouse; the foundation stone and guiding light we look to for strength, security, and stability. He is ours and we are His.

But here is the problem: we don't want it to be that way. We believe stability and security come from the Lord, but to live out that belief requires a level of faith and trust we don't want to exert. So we take the easy route and invert the formula. By doing so we experience fear and worry and wonder why God doesn't act the way we think He should. We prefer that this life be stable and secure instead of God, and we want God to change instead of this precious life we hold so dear. It doesn't work that way.

Correct Security Formula:

God is a stable, secure, and firm foundation,
while this life is insecure, unstable, and unpredictable.
Therefore, I will trust Him as I walk through this changing life.

Incorrect Security Formula:

This life **should** be secure, stable, and a firm foundation,
while God **should** constantly change to meet my every want and desire.
Therefore, I will trust in this life as I walk with a changing God.

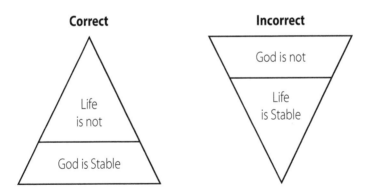

Fear and worry come into play when we invert the correct formula. We want the stock market to be stable and guarantee that our investments will be there for us when we retire. We don't care for unpredictable natural disasters that destroy lives, property, and landscapes. We want our homes to appreciate, not depreciate. We don't want to get sick or experience pain. We want to live to be ninety years old and die quietly in our sleep. We want this life to be secure, stable, and predictable, and we want a God who changes to meet our every want and desire.

This is a devastating outlook and one that warps our view of reality. It leads to constant fear and worry, not to mention high doses of disappointment from unrealistic expectations. It is about as crazy as riding a behemoth incoming wave off Ocean Beach and expecting it to be as stable and secure as the ground in front of it. This life is not our home; we are citizens of another country, subjects of another king, merely sojourning through this life. Even Jesus recognizes life's instability when He says, "In the world you have tribulation, but take courage; I have overcome the world" (Jn. 16:33).

God Himself is the path to security and stability. When we expect life to provide security for us, the groundwork is laid for major Big But popping episodes. We are constantly tempted to take things into our own hands, focus on the temporal rather than the eternal, and find ourselves stuck out in the open with a ghastly Big But. When this happens, our energy is quickly depleted and our sojourn becomes drudgery rather than a thrilling adventure.

I am not a psychologist, counselor, or psychiatrist, but here is what I discern about the negative twins of fear and worry:

Fear and worry are a complete waste of time and accomplish absolutely nothing of value.

The Bible puts it this way: "And who of you by being worried can add a single hour to his life?" (Mt. 6:27). Worry doesn't change a thing; it only drains you of the present. Living in fear doesn't enhance courage; it holds you in its powerful "freeze mode" grip, preventing you from accomplishing great things for the Lord.

Fear and worry affect our health in negative ways.

Numerous studies reveal substantial negative consequences fear and worry place upon our physical and mental health. These destructive twins deposit a heavy load upon our mind, contribute to sleep deprivation, diarrhea, anxiety, phobias, breakdowns in coping mechanisms, and all sorts of health issues. As Proverbs 12:25 notes, "Anxiety in a man's heart weighs it down."

Fear and worry erode our trust in God.

Some activities are good for us and some aren't. Exercising and eating right are good for us. Smoking isn't. Meditating upon Scripture is good for us. Pleading ignorance and unfamiliarity with the holy text isn't. Trusting that the Creator and Sustainer of the universe will take care of us is good. Engaging in fear and worry isn't. Notice the little sentence about faith at the end of Matthew 6:30: "But if God so clothes the grass of the field, which is alive today and tomorrow is thrown into the furnace, will He not much more clothe you? You of little faith!" Fear and worry erode our faith in God to the point where we become people of "little faith."

Fear and worry prevent kingdom seeking.

As noted in Matthew 6:31–34, God takes care of us when we first and foremost seek His kingdom:

> Do not worry then, saying, "What will we eat?" or "What will we drink?" or "What will we wear for clothing?" For the Gentiles eagerly seek all these things; for your heavenly Father knows that you need all these things. But seek first His kingdom and His righteousness, and all these things will be added to you. So do not worry about tomorrow; for tomorrow will care for itself. Each day has enough trouble of its own.

Correct seeking equals competent caring. Fear and worry prevent us from experiencing the Lord's personal care. He desires that we lean on Him, as noted in I Peter 5:6–7, "Therefore humble yourselves under the mighty hand of God, that He may exalt you at the proper time, casting all your anxiety on Him, because He cares for you." We experience His care when we first seek His kingdom. Where fear and worry prevail, there is never a shortage of Big But opportunities for Big But explosions to create Big But problems.

Big But Cluster 2: *Doubt and Unbelief*

In addition to fear and worry, another common Big But cluster congregates around doubt and unbelief. Faith, the opposite of doubt and unbelief, is an essential ingredient to Christianity. In fact, the great faith chapter of Hebrews 11 declares, "And without faith it is impossible to please Him, for he who comes to God must believe that He is and that He is a rewarder of those who seek Him" (Heb. 11:6). Even John 3:16, a well-known verse of Scripture, reveals the importance of belief: "For God so loved the world, that He gave His only begotten Son, that whoever believes in Him shall not perish, but have eternal life." Woven into the tapestry of vibrant communion with God are words like "believe," "trust," and "faith," while doubt and unbelief are never exalted as positive spiritual attributes.

Realizing the centrality of faith to Christian living, we are not surprised that doubt and unbelief become attractive neighborhoods where But-ness takes up residence. Smugly sitting in our comfortable, regular Sunday church seat, we suppose that

> Sometimes we make faith and belief to be some deep and difficult concept to grasp, when in reality it is very simple to understand.

Jesus' teaching on doubt and unbelief refers to those outside the faith—those in need of conversion. We believe His words are directed to someone other than ourselves. In reality, when Jesus speaks of doubt and unbelief, He is mostly referring to believers— those who should exhibit trust and confidence in the Lord, but who allow doubt and unbelief to hinder their Christian walk. When it comes to doubt and unbelief, Jesus isn't speaking to "them," He is speaking to "us."

Sometimes we make faith and belief to be some deep and difficult concept to grasp, when in reality it is very simple to understand. We operate by faith every day, even in the little things. When we invest in the stock market, we believe that by doing so, our nest egg will grow over time. When we board an airplane, we believe it will arrive at its destination faster and safer than other modes of transportation. When our children receive immunization shots, we believe it will protect them from dreaded diseases. On the more exciting end of the spectrum, if we jump out of an airplane with a parachute on our back, we believe it will open when we pull the cord. If we scuba dive in pristine Bahamian waters, we trust that our oxygen tanks will help us breathe underwater.

No analogy is perfect, and I realize mine break down, too. Airplanes sometimes crash, parachutes sometimes fail, and immunizations sometimes backfire. I am not comparing God, who never fails, to a parachute that sometimes does. I am illustrating that in this life we understand what it means to believe and we exercise faith all the time and in many different ways, even when things don't work out perfectly. Faith is nothing more than belief with conviction; a belief that causes us to act. If we don't believe God can rescue humankind, we are doomed. If we don't believe airplanes arrive safely at their destination, we will not board. The substance of belief propels us toward actions in furtherance of our convictions.

> Faith is nothing more than belief with conviction; a belief that causes us to act.

There is no deep secret to believing God. Just believe. Any Christian, young or old, recent convert or longtime follower, can trust God. It is nothing more than trusting God, taking Him at His word, and acting upon those convictions. It is that simple.

The issue for many is that they are asked to believe in someone they cannot see, touch, smell, taste, or hear. While the Holy Spirit resides within to lead, teach, and empower us, it is a different dynamic than having someone physically present. As you lay in bed speaking with your spouse about the day, you can hear each other softly speaking, sense the warmth of each other's body, hold hands, smell the lingering scent of perfume, and kiss each other goodnight. Our senses experience the person physically lying next to us. But with God, it is different. We don't visibly see Him, audibly hear His voice, touch Him, smell Him, or taste Him. It is a relationship unlike any other. I am not suggesting that because He is not tangibly present like you and I are, that He cannot be known or experienced; He certainly can be, and in deeper ways than we might ever imagine. Yet, the relationship is indeed like no other we have experienced.

Success in this kind of relationship requires faith on our part; faith that the nudging we sense in our soul is the whisper of God speaking to our heart. We may not audibly hear His voice, but we know when He is speaking, convicting, leading, urging, encouraging, and providing. We must hear with something other than our ears and go beyond our five senses to the inner chambers of our spirit. Communicating and experiencing our Lord extends further and deeper than our five senses, and that requires faith.

Little faith is required when everything is laid out perfectly in front of us ahead of time. Faith is moving forward, trusting, and believing as we sense His leading moment by moment and step by step. Faith most often requires multiple little steps rather than one giant leap.

Faith unlocks doors; doubt and unbelief shut them tight. Faith opens our hearts and minds to the wondrous work of God; doubt and unbelief focus on what *can't* be done. Faith and belief allow us to experience God; doubt and unbelief perceive Him to be distant, untouchable, and unconcerned.

Abraham moves forward in faith as he travels from Ur of the Chaldeans to a land God promised him. Keep in mind that Abraham has no clue where he is going. He has no idea what hardships await him along the journey. He simply packs his belongings and hits the road in obedience. He acts upon his belief and moves forward one step at a time—one action of belief after another which finally leads to his destination.

In Matthew 9:20–22, we find a desperate woman suffering twelve years from a bleeding disorder who simply believes that Jesus can heal her. Although she is ceremonially unclean and a social outcast, she makes her way through the crowd with unwavering faith and touches the hem of Jesus' garment, believing she will receive a healing. Her faith is extraordinary, and she receives her healing.

A Roman centurion also comes to Jesus seeking healing for his servant who is home suffering and paralyzed (Mt. 8:5–10). Jesus agrees to return to the centurion's home and heal his servant, but the soldier doesn't think it is necessary. In his mind, Jesus is so powerful that all He has to do is say the word and the servant will be healed. What great faith. Jesus recognizes it as such and marvels.

Doubt and unbelief prevent us from experiencing God's moving in our lives. It stunts our spiritual growth, debilitates us, and removes faith and belief from the experiential world to the theoretical and abstract domain. This is unfortunate because faith is real; it is something to be exercised and experienced in the world of everyday living.

Faith and belief trigger action, as seen in examples like Abraham, the bleeding woman, and the centurion. Faith is active. Doubt and unbelief are passive and cause us to stop in our tracks and remain stuck; like a big ole freight train sitting on the track and going nowhere. A relationship with God is not merely intellectual or abstract, but real and experiential. He fancies that we experience abundant life in Him, and that abundant life is only experienced through believing and acting in faith. When doubt and unbelief seize the reins, we end up knowing *about* God, but we don't know *Him* or experience Him personally. Religion becomes a pointless mental exercise without any concrete experiential connection to our lives. Religion without practical experience is worthless.

> When doubt and unbelief seize the reins, we end up knowing *about* God, but we don't know *Him* or experience Him personally.

I am a canine lover. I grew up with little yappy ones, but now I enjoy medium-sized dogs with some meat on their bones and enough girth to become my pillow while lying on the floor. My children grew up with Coaster, our beautiful and well-trained Golden Retriever, who has since gone to the land of big bones in the sky. He was a wonderful pet and we hold dear the memories of his time with our family. Several years had passed since Coaster died, and one day I happened to see a beautiful dog online for adoption. Many non-profit organizations work hard to foster abandoned or relinquished dogs, link them to a good home, and provide a happy and wholesome future for both dog and owner. Lottie was one of those dogs, and we couldn't be happier.

She was timid and fearful upon arriving to our home. Would I harm her? She didn't know what to expect when I left the house. Would I come back? Was there a secondary escape route for her should things turn sour? It has now been several years since we adopted Lottie, and the experience has been absolutely wonderful for all of us. She trusts me completely and unreservedly. I now leave the house and she sprawls out on the floor, dreaming and snoring, trusting that I will return. She no longer worries about her next meal, believing that I will feed her.

My Lottie story reminds me of our relationship with Christ. Over time, our trust and belief seem to grow deeper and stronger, the result of little acts of trust. Sometimes we think faith involves a one-time gigantic leap, when it is most often the little things that build up over time that strengthen us. Little acts of conviction and small items of trust allow us to engage in bigger acts of belief. Exercising faith in the small things enables us to grow into larger acts of belief, and the more we act on our belief, the larger our faith grows. Like a muscle, the more we exercise it, the bigger and stronger it becomes.

The following chart may be helpful in distinguishing faith and belief from doubt and unbelief:

FAITH AND DOUBT

Category	Faith & Belief	Doubt & Unbelief
Object of our faith	What God can do	What God can't do
Subject of our faith	We exercise faith	We exercise unbelief
Substance of our faith	Complete trust	Lack of trust
Fruit of our faith	Obedience	Disobedience
Consequence of our faith	Spiritual growth & experiencing God	Stunted growth & no experience of God

The object of our faith is all important. For those who believe, trust is placed in the Creator and Sustainer of all things; the one who keep His promises, honors His word, and meets our needs. Unbelief isn't faith at all, but a belief in doubt. Faith uplifts what God can do, while doubt and unbelief promote uncertainty. The object of faith is the all-powerful, all-knowing God who cares for us; the object of doubt and unbelief is a God who is weak, absent, unable and unwilling to help us.

In reality, a God who isn't able to fully care for us, protect us, or meet our needs, isn't much of a God at all. Why believe in Him in the first place if that is the way He is? If He cannot be trusted or lacks the ability or desire to help, then why follow Him? We would be far better off putting our faith in ourselves, science, or other humans. At least we know they have a chance to occasionally come through. You see, this is the crucial difference between belief and unbelief. The object of our faith is absolutely critical. Faith places all hope, all trust, all confidence in the simple knowledge that God is able and worthy of our trust. Doubt and unbelief mock the living God as nothing more than a boat ride on the Titanic, about to hit a spiritual iceberg from which no recovery is available.

> Unbelief isn't faith at all, but a belief in doubt.

When we exercise faith, our Buts remain tiny and our view of God is enlarged. Faith is an enabler. It enables us to experience the living God and grow in our spiritual walk. Doubt and unbelief are disablers. When there is no confidence in God, volcanic eruptions of But-ness explode on the scene. If you can't trust in the God of the Bible, then who can you trust? When there is no faith, it is impossible to please Him. When doubt and unbelief prevail, we are disadvantaged and over time, our garden becomes overrun by the weeds of But-ness and our ability to produce pleasing fruit unto the Lord is severely diminished. A lack of trust in God is predicated upon an incorrect view of the object of our faith, God Himself.

Big But Cluster 3: *Control*

A third cluster attracting enormous Big But issues is an inherent trait in human nature—our desire for control. Like many others, I wrestle with this aspect of my Christian walk. To help myself feel better, I label it something different in my mind, something more palatable and less convicting than it really is. It sounds less damning if I call it "being strategic" or "being responsible" than to actually use the C-word, control.

Control is an inner desire to manage, direct, and command our own life rather than submit to the management, direction, and commands of God. Our inner desire for control manifests itself in diverse ways. We stereotype control freaks as wildly unconstrained, ranting and raving when things don't go their way. As non-verbal behaviors surface and aggressive anger escalates, the desire for control becomes obvious even to the casual observer. This is merely one way Big But control issues rise to the surface.

Others, however meek and mild they may appear, express control through guilt-tripping others, playing the victim, passive-aggressive behavior, and subtle manipulation. The issue is not so much how a controlling desire manifests itself; rather, the greater disturbance is that we long to usurp God's control in the first place. Our craving to manage, direct, and command our own life rather than submit to the management, direction, and commands of God touches every facet of our lives. We seek to control our spouse, our children, and our destiny. We thirst for control over our schools, our friends, our health, and our finances. Let's face it, we like it when things go our way and others do what we expect of them. When people or circumstances fail to align with our demands, we can become frustrated, depressed, aggressive, outspoken, and angry.

> The issue is not so much how a controlling desire manifests itself; rather, the greater disturbance is that we long to usurp God's control in the first place.

Is control always negative, or can it sometimes be positive? After all, if the ship is going down, we want someone shouting orders and communicating direction to save as many as possible. In God's holy order, He has ordained submission, authority, order, and control. By submitting, we acknowledge that someone with greater control, authority, and responsibility is above us.

According to Scripture, slaves submit to their masters, Christ submits to the Father, the church submits to Christ, local church members submit to elders, children submit to parents, young men submit to older men, citizens submit to governments, wives submit to husbands, and Christians engage in mutual submission to one another. Voluminous books have been written on the meaning and manner of submission in relationship to these categories, but our purpose here is to merely indicate that God has established both the role of authority and submission. Dysfunction prevails where there is a lack of order and control, and the Bible simply does not promote such anarchy.

In and of itself, control is not evil. God's control is good. Authority structures are good. Self-control is good. Harnessing our thoughts and behaviors is positive and helpful for good and godly living. Exercising oversight within the church as an elder or holding a secular administrative position overseeing large sums of money and numerous employees is not immoral by any means. In fact, some possess a gift for such things. There are those who hold leadership positions, engage in controlling responsibilities, and organize chaotic situations in a good and God-honoring manner. Their very role is to be in charge.

> There can be only one captain of the ship, and it isn't us!

The Big But of control isn't a structural problem, for God has established orders of authority. The Big But of control isn't an issue of utilizing leadership gifts for bringing organization out of chaos or exercising control on a ship about to capsize. The Big But of control certainly isn't engaging in the positive discipline of self-control that is so helpful to our lives. These aren't the kind of controlling desires that get us into trouble. We can't do away with control simply because of its abuse. We don't throw away all traffic laws because some drivers run stop lights. It is entirely possible to be in a position of authority and exercise that responsibility in complete submission to the Father.

The control that is so destructive to our lives is the inner desire to manage, direct, and command our own life rather than submit to the management, direction, and commands of God. This is the dark side of control, and nothing good comes of it. There can be only one captain of the ship, and it isn't us! I can't think of one Bible character who ignores God's directives, casts aside His commands, rebuffs His guidance, and is congratulated for such behavior. While God is certainly able to clean up our miserable mistakes and create beauty out of the stain, He does so as a testimony of His grace and mercy, not as the result of our flawed wisdom and self-serving ambition.

Our quest to dispense with God's management, direction, and commands for our life is nothing more than a self-conceived back-up plan to cover God in case He fails or doesn't deliver on our expectations. Imagine that, God needing a back-up plan! But that is exactly what control is—taking into our own hands what God won't do, or what we think He should do. It is an arrogant approach to our Lord, like the greasy-fingered child desperately clutching her fast-food French fries and screaming, "No!" when mommy asks to taste one. This haughtiness believes the creature knows more than the Creator; that we are more powerful than the all-powerful One; that we possess greater authority than our Lord; that we are able to discern and judge in more accurate ways than our all-wise and all-knowing Father; that we know what is best for our lives instead of Him.

We want control of all things without the attributes needed for such a role and without the weight of responsibility that God Himself shoulders. In essence, why do we even need God? If we want to control things, don't believe that He can or will, and see ourselves as His back-up plan, why go to all the trouble pretending that we want nothing but His perfect will for our lives? What a mindless game we play. Under such deception, our Buts can grow to epic proportions.

The issue with control is simple. We want it. We don't mind the *concept* of submission, but not at the expense of control. We often desire the *appearance* of submissive behavior, yet seek to maintain control on the inside. It is entirely possible to be humbly sitting on the outside and arrogantly standing on the inside.

> We don't mind the *concept* of submission, but not at the expense of control. We often desire the *appearance* of submissive behavior, yet seek to maintain control on the inside.

To conquer the unpleasant Big But explosions our deep desire for control produces, we must deal with the inner desire for such control. Jesus has a penchant for pinpointing the heart of a problem. It is not enough to merely control an explosive outward act; we also must deal with the inner desire prompting the eruption in the first place. Control is a heart issue. Overcoming such vile aspiration involves voluntarily yielding ourselves to the will of God and recognizing that He directs our lives with His glory and our good in mind. By submitting to Him in all things, we rightfully acknowledge His nature, attributes, and abilities. Submission to God brings blessing upon our lives.

My own understanding of control and submission has changed over the years, but only because of the hard knocks I have endured. It would have been so much easier had I just submitted to the Lord, but no, my hard head wouldn't allow such clarity of thought. Though pain is a tremendous teacher and has a way of grabbing our attention, it is often an unnecessary tutor.

I wonder how much ministry occurs in our own strength, our own wisdom, our own strategic thinking, and our own control. Oh I know, we call it the "leading of the Lord," when in reality, God is relegated to back-seat driving and only asked for occasional directions. Much of what occurs on any given Sunday morning drips with selfish ambition and is little more than a bunch of like-minded individuals gathering together to exercise human endeavors. While that statement may come across as harsh and sarcastic, it is not intended to be such a reflection. In fact, I readily include myself in such biased and humble analysis. I desired the leading of the Lord, but I didn't really know how to ascertain it, understand it, or implement it, and so I dripped with human effort, human strategy, human wisdom, and in the end, obtained human results.

I am not suggesting that a lack of planning, preparation, and study, or a laissez-faire approach to ministry equates to the leading of the Lord. In fact, I would argue they equate to laziness and shoddy Christian living. But I am sending a clarion call for freedom—freedom from merely engaging in our own best human effort and asking God to bless it. Instead, my exhortation is to strip ourselves of trying to accomplish spiritual ends through human effort alone. My freedom trumpet sounds to follow God's leading, trust His ways, and yield to His management, direction, and commands for our life as the way to live. Stop asking God to jump on your bandwagon and instead, jump on His.

Big But Cluster 4: *Misconception of God and the Bible*

Have you ever experienced serious consequences for misjudging a person or event? I have, on numerous occasions, and often to my own ruin. As a teenager, my friend and I decided to go skiing after he discovered old-fashioned cross-country skis in his garage. We climbed a hill behind the house, strapped on those long, uncontrollable wooden toothpicks and began making our way down the snowy hill. This was a brand new experience for me. The only thing I knew about skiing was what I saw on television during the Winter Olympics. How hard could it be? I soon discovered that strapping six-foot-long wooden boards to my feet and controlling them wasn't as easy as it appears on television.

At the bottom of the hill we built a small bridge across a stream rumbling with icy cold water. The goal was to ski down the hill, over the homemade bridge, and through the woods on the other side. This was wishful thinking on my part. I misjudged the bridge, my speed, and the proper way to control skis. As a result, one ski slid off the bridge and into the creek as I tried to cross. The rest of my body followed. There I was in the middle of winter, sitting in a creek with ice cold water up to my waist, unable to move my mangled legs since the six-foot-long timbers were stuck in the mud. Misjudgment cost me.

Have you ever stereotyped an individual and had your socks blown off because they turned out to be totally different than you imagined? We think funeral directors are long, skinny, boney individuals with a scary Alfred Hitchcock feel about them. We erroneously believe all overweight people are lazy and that those living on the streets are homeless because of their own putrid choices. We think all politicians are greedy power mongers and attorneys are vultures who prey off the defenseless public. In most cases, we couldn't be more wrong.

While teaching a graduate course on legal issues in the business environment, I noticed two African-American students in the class who seemed to be marginalized by other students. I invited them out to dinner one night before class. At first, they thought they were in trouble, or that somehow I was using the event as a pretext for something else. I assured them that I had no agenda, no ulterior motive, and just wanted to get to know them.

Well, let me tell you, those boys could eat. Good thing I took them to a buffet, or I would have had to find a part-time job just to pay their food bill. We began to talk about their degree program, how they were treated by the school, their hopes and dreams, and their challenges. We spoke about our experiences with racism, and I shared with them some stories about myself and my past. It was a great night, relational walls were broken down, and new friendships begun. When I left the school, one of the fellows wrote me an email thanking me for my investment in him. However, it was his closing statement that touched the sweet spot in my heart, "Dr. Wise, when I first saw you, I assumed you were racist, had an easy life, and would treat us like everyone else has. After meeting you and spending time with you, I realized I was the racist one." He initially stereotyped me, but once he got to know me, he realized his initial judgment was inaccurate.

Our misjudgments also extend to our understanding of God. All too often we misjudge His motives and methods. We conceive of Him as someone totally opposite of His true nature. In stereotyping Him, we misunderstand His ways and His work in our life and occasionally our socks get blown off when we realize how much our limited perspective is off the mark.

Judge/Friend

There is a tendency to view God through our present or past circumstances. If you grew up poor with little hope of advancement in life, you may be inclined to see God as someone who rescues and frees the oppressed. Every aspect of the Bible is filtered through this interpretive lens. If you are a linear, logical, and sequential thinker, you may see God as some great mastermind exemplifying logical consistency. If you have experienced deep suffering, then God may be viewed as someone who cares deeply for those experiencing physical, emotional, and spiritual wounds.

Big But-itis can quickly overtake us when our conception of God doesn't align with the reality we experience. God is certainly concerned about the oppressed, but He is much more than that. The Creator is indeed a mastermind who far exceeds our own limits of logic, but He is much more than that. His heart is big and we see Him caring for the wounded, but He is much more than that.

Misconceptions about God may have also been a problem for the recipients of Peter's first letter. "If you address as Father the One who impartially judges according to each one's work, conduct yourselves in fear during the time of your stay on earth (I Pet. 1:17). Experiencing persecution for their faith in Christ, Peter's readers perceive God as their loving Father who cares for them, watches over them, provides for them, and comforts them. The truth of the matter is that God is indeed all that they believe Him to be, but He is so much more. Peter reminds them that stereotyping God can be detrimental and one-sided. Not only is God their Father who cares for them as a virtuous human father cares for His own children, but He is also the One who will judge them impartially according to their work and conduct.

> Focusing on one aspect of God's attributes to the exclusion of all others creates an unbalanced and unhealthy view of God.

Focusing on one aspect of God's attributes to the exclusion of all others creates an unbalanced and unhealthy view of God. We become so fixated on His love, for instance, that we forget about His justice. A lopsided perspective may lead to Big But meltdowns.

Slot Machine Theology

Another common misconception concerns God's role in our lives. For many, He is an add-on, a safety valve, or a celestial genie in a bottle. We are the center of the universe, and God exists for the sole purpose of catering to our every need. He is the eternal cosmic slot machine. We pull the lever and expect goodies to fall from the sky. We wouldn't state it in such stark terms, but that is exactly how we feel. Life revolves around us and God owes us one.

We expect to be the center of *His* world because we are the center of our own world. He is like a lover we try to manipulate with a sexy smile or the flash of our eyelashes. We want and we take, and we expect God to give. After all, that is what He is there for, to be a forever Santa Claus and pass out candy and gifts. Satan advances these half-truths and exploits them for his purposes. Yes, God is concerned about us, loves us, desires the best for us, and longs to meet our needs, but that is only half of the truth.

This is an exceedingly childish and fundamentally flawed understanding of God that leads to epic explosions of But-ness. Rather than a thing to be used or a celestial genie to be manipulated, God is the Creator of the universe—so powerful that He merely speaks its existence into being and His power continues to hold it all together. Yes, we are part of the universe, for God created us, but we are certainly not the center of it. The universe revolves around the One who created and sustains it. We are but dust in this world. Or, as my friends often say, "We are butt dust" in this world. Life revolves around God, not us.

Rather than being a forever Santa Clause, God is a king and ruler. Rather than Him living His life for us, we live our lives for Him. We worship Him; He does not worship us. He rules our lives, we do not rule His. He is the Commander-in-Chief, and we are the soldiers in His vast army.

How easily we misjudge God's role, power, authority, and right to lead, guide, and oversee our lives. We fall so easily into the trap of treating our Lord as though He is some impersonal object designed solely to meet our every desire. We want to use Him for personal gain, and He wants to use us for significant kingdom work. We want to transform Him to be like us, and He wants to transform us to be like Him. We believe if He does what we think He should it will be best for us, but God wants to actually do what is best for us whether we think it is or not.

White, Republican, American

Another misconception of God is that He aligns Himself with our ethnicity and political beliefs. Any race, political party, or geographical location could be used to illustrate this point, but in America many consider God to be aligned with white, Republican, Americans. There is nothing at all wrong with being white, Republican, or American, but labeling our personal perspective as that of God's is a prevalent mistake, and an exceptionally shallow one at that.

Think about the absurdity of such sentiment. Jesus wasn't a Republican or American. The prophets weren't, either. The Apostles don't match these criteria. Has God really chosen a political party? If so, are Republican and Democrat the only options available to Him? Can one be a Democrat, interested in social agendas, expecting government to provide greater assistance for the people it governs, and still be a solid Christian? Or, is God really behind smaller government, reduced social involvement, lower taxes, and limited fiscal spending?

> Just because one is a white Republican from America doesn't mean that God is too.

Believing that God agrees with our personal political view, our personal perspective on how government should spend and tax, and to what extent government should be involved in caring for the governed, is a matter of personal preference, not a mandate from Scripture. Somehow it makes us feel better about ourselves if we believe God aligns Himself with our perspective on life. Therein lies the problem. God is not like us and when we make Him out to be just like one of the boys down at the club, a severe case of Big But inflammation can set in.

One's skin color is absolutely irrelevant to who God is. Whether one is from Africa, America, South America, Europe, Middle East, or Far East is irrelevant. The pigment level in our skin merely brings about certain tones and colors. Our country of origin is merely a geographical location. No doubt these things influence our experiences on this earth and determine many things, like access to education, the type of government we live under, and what religious expressions inundate our culture, but they really don't dictate much about who God is. Just because one is a white Republican from America doesn't mean that God is too.

It is true that we are created in God's image, but that doesn't mean we are little gods or that God is a great big us. We are material; He is immaterial. Our knowledge is finite; His is infinite. Our power is limited; His is limitless. We are sinful; He is sinless. We are created; He is the Creator. God certainly understands our plight and created each of us with a particular skin color in a particular geographic location and culture, but He is unlike us.

We are unable to cure ourselves and need outside assistance from our Creator. We are saved by someone "wholly other" than ourselves. Scripture attributes human characteristics to God (anthropomorphisms) as a way to shed light upon His nature and character. For instance, we are told that God hears our prayers. God doesn't literally have an ear, for He is spirit according to John 4:24, but the human-like description does its job in emphasizing the point that God actually hears and listens to our prayers. In Exodus 7:5 we read, "The Egyptians shall know that I am the LORD, when I stretch out My hand on Egypt and bring out the sons of Israel from their midst." Does God literally have a hand that He stretches out? No, for He is spirit. But the anthropomorphism helps us understand His power and authority.

While God is above and beyond us in so many ways, that doesn't mean He is uninvolved in our lives or that He can't intimately be known. Lowering God down to the level of our personal preferences brings Him far too low, and elevating Him to unreachable heights makes Him distant and uninvolved in our lives. But-ness occurs when we travel the extreme paths in either direction. The key is not to bring God down to our personal views or elevate Him to inaccessible heights, but to maintain a balanced perspective.

Legalism

Our Big But misconceptions about God may also stem from a legalistic view of the Bible. Many see Scripture as Grand Central Station for the collection of rules, regulations, and decrees that if broken, will land us in God's jail. This perspective seeks a rule for every situation and when circumstances arise where no applicable rules are found in the Bible, legalistic Bible teachers feel it their godly duty to create them.

How disheartening is this outlook? This view turns God's love letters to humankind into statutory laws. God becomes the great policeman in the sky who hides behind the highway to heaven billboard, just waiting to catch us speeding past His laws. Those with the least number of tickets at the end of life get into heaven, while the rest of us spend time in an underworld jail. This view is completely discouraging and doesn't propel us toward goodness or bring out the best in us. Instead, it sucks the very life and joy out of us and establishes a twisted conception of the God we serve. With this outlook, Big But tsunamis crash into our lives in the form of pride and self-righteousness. I don't want to play spiritual cops and robbers with God; I want to live with freedom and joy. I want to serve God from the deep wells within me stocked with gratitude for the kindness, grace, and mercy He has shown in my life. But-ness often congregates around the chains of legalism.

Inspiration

Citing 2 Timothy 3:16, traditional Christians believe that Scripture originates from God. "All Scripture is inspired by God and profitable for teaching, for reproof, for correction, for training in righteousness." In fact, inspiration literally means "God-breathed."

Though many Christians seem to agree on biblical inspiration, it is the implication of that belief that is often problematic. If the Bible were merely a collection of sixty-six books written by human authors sharing their opinions on life, religion, and personal dogma, then we have nothing more than a collection of human thoughts. We might be better off choosing a different collection of human writers to read and admire. But the fact that Scripture is "God-breathed" adds an element not found in other writings and elevates the words to a new status.

If Scripture is indeed inspired, it must also, by necessity, be authoritative over our life. The two go hand-in-hand. We are under no obligation to submit ourselves to the teachings of Plato, Homer, Shakespeare, or any other great human writer. But we are obligated to rank ourselves under the writings emanating directly from God's breath. When we are unwilling to place ourselves under the authority of Scripture, the Big But Syndrome slithers into our life.

We readily accept the *benefits* of inspired Scripture as authoritative for our life. After all, we are banking on such things as heaven, forgiveness, and God's comfort in this life. Yet, when it comes to such challenging items as guarding our minds, putting others first, or turning the other cheek, we are slow adopters. We believe our specific situation differs from the circumstances of others, thereby entitling us to exemptions from such authority. We want to pick and choose what to obey, what to believe, what to apply to our life. No one, not even God, is going to tell us what to do, how to do it, and when to do it. This misconception ignores the implication of inspiration and creates a fertile environment for growing large Buts.

> When we are unwilling to place ourselves under the authority of Scripture, the Big But Syndrome slithers into our life.

Paul experiences a similar situation with the church in Corinth (1 Cor. 6:1–8). Fellow believers bring their disputes before secular courts. For Paul, this is shameful. The spiritual family has become so dysfunctional that they are unable to find amicable ways of settling disputes even though Christ Himself is the great mediator. Instead of following the Lord's teaching, they air their dirty laundry before unbelievers. Was there not one wise individual among the brethren who could provide help and guidance?

The issue isn't that outsiders cannot know of our dirty laundry, for we all know the church has a clothesline full for public view. The disparity, however, is an obvious oxymoron, a glaring contradiction. On the one hand, believers claim a life transformed by the living Christ, and on the other hand, they are unable to get along with one another. It's like claiming you drive a brand new red Corvette convertible as you pull out of your driveway in a rusted out Buick station wagon. There is something wrong with that picture—people certainly notice the difference between what you claim and what you drive. Reality is a hard thing to cover up.

Here is the point I want you to catch. The Corinthians were willing to follow the way of Christ as long as it didn't entail giving up rights or losing to fellow Christians in secular courts of law. In Corinth, the Lord's teaching wasn't absolute authority, but rather, a first stab at resolving conflict. If things didn't go their way, they could always appeal to a higher authority, secular law courts and tribunals overseen by those with mere human wisdom and no regard for God. Their view of authority is inverted. In their mind, Scripture is subservient to the secular courts of law, whereas for many Christians, Scripture holds greater authority.

Our view of Scripture is reflected in our obedience to it. What good does it do to elevate Scripture on a pedestal, extol its virtues, and claim inspiration, if it has no authority over our lives and we are unwilling to submit to its teaching? Many toy with Scripture and feign allegiance, but when that allegiance runs into difficult terrain requiring commitment and stamina, it quickly gives way to pragmatism. Inspiration implies authority much like heat implies warmth. When we refuse to place ourselves under the authoritative teaching of Scripture, we experience Big But explosions on a regular basis.

Study and Learning

Not only do misperceptions arise from viewing Scripture as a collection of codi-fied statutes, a lack of Bible knowledge and study habits can also add fuel to the fire. It is one thing to read the Bible and quite another to actually study it. Modern Bible studies are often nothing more than the collective sharing of ignorant opinions by well-meaning people. We ask the question of those present, "What do you think it means?" and the most convincing outlook is adopted as the bibli-cal meaning.

We aren't seeking what one *thinks* a passage means, but rather, what it *actually* means, and that takes study. Even after hours of serious study, all we can do with certain passages is provide an informed opinion.

> Modern Bible studies are often nothing more than the collective sharing of ignorant opinions by well-meaning people.

My point is not that we cannot ever have opin-ions on various interpretive elements of Scripture; my point is that merely giving willy-nilly opinions on the meaning of a given text without serious study is nothing more than a blithering uninformed statement. If the Bible really is "God-breathed" words from the heart of God, understanding its meaning seems to be rather important, and understanding its meaning entails actually studying the Bible, not just randomly flipping through its pages. Reading the Bible is a good thing, but studying the Bible is a better thing. There will always be areas of ambiguity, even after earnest study; however, that shouldn't dampen the spirit of increasing our knowledge and understanding.

We habitually bring our contextual situations to the Bible, and that affects how we interpret it. For instance, if we've had a bad day at work, feel depressed, or just fought with the children, we may read the Bible by picking out sparkling verses that seem to assuage our problems. Verses pulled out of context to make us feel better may not even be applied to our lives in a correct manner. Rather than read-ing our twenty-first century context into the Bible, the proper study of Scripture is to first discern the context of the Bible. Rather than force our own theological perspective upon a particular passage, an understanding of how the original hear-ers of the text understood the words is necessary if we seek to appropriately apply its meaning to our twenty-first century environment.

Misinterpreting or misapplying Scripture is devastating, because we put forth as truth that which is false. Without actually studying the Bible, it is easy to begin with the wrong starting point; when that happens, we arrive at faulty conclusions. If I gave directions on how to get from Kansas City to Sacramento, but mistakenly thought that Cleveland was Kansas City, my directions would be entirely off the mark and lead to an incorrect destination. Studying Scripture is like starting at the right point so we can actually arrive at the intended destination. Incorrect starting points lead to Big But-itis, an unintended destination.

> Misinterpreting or misapplying Scripture is devastating, because we put forth as truth that which is false.

I am not suggesting that we all earn a Ph.D. in theology or read Greek, Hebrew, and Aramaic in order to understand the Bible. I am suggesting that to grow in our knowledge and understanding of Scripture, we must invest time and energy in sincere study. Studying the Bible is serious business, and we harvest nuggets of golden truth as we dig from its goldmine of teaching.

While teaching a class on leadership, I asked ministry students to keep a log of everything they did for two weeks. After assessing their two-week time logs, many were amazed at what consumed precious minutes in their day and what important items were squeezed out. The exercise was taught from a time-management perspective, but I imagine it would be good for all of us to do. Most of us would discover that though we read the Bible, we do not allocate time to actually studying it. Learning how to study the Bible is a worthwhile investment that will serve us well. Increasing our understanding of Scripture decreases the number of seismic Big But eruptions we experience.

Big But Cluster 5: *Less Than Total Commitment*

Some time ago, I purchased a workout program advertised on a late-night infomercial. I am not prone to such impulse buys, but since I needed to lose weight, I gave in, opened up my wallet, and anxiously awaited the delivery of this wonder program that was going to whip me into shape. Enthusiastically, I began the program and instead of whipping me into shape, it nearly killed me. A vast chasm stood between how out of shape I *thought* I was and how out of shape I *actually* was.

My intentions were the best. I really did desire a rock-hard body, but it wasn't long until my commitment to the program waned. There was no defect in the product. It was excellent, and I am glad I purchased it. The problem was me. I allowed excuses to undermine my commitment level. After all, I was tired from a draining day at the office. Working the program was painful, and I convinced myself to skip a workout, "just this once." My stockpile of excuses became extensive. I failed because my commitment to the program only went so far. I had a bailout point, like most of us do. I failed, and I confused my lack of commitment with an excuse.

This next Big But cluster involves our lack of 100%, sold out, total commitment to God. Even the best of intentions won't prevent Big But-itis. Fully embracing the cause of Christ acts as a Big But preventative, and when our commitment level begins to fade, But-ness creeps into our lives. We start out so well, but as time passes we become wounded by other Christians, disillusioned with politics in the church, and we experience the disappointments of life. Instead of being sold out to Jesus, we fade away, anxious to sell our faith for cheap at the spring garage sale. What good is it to us?

There are many issues surrounding this cluster of But-ness, but three prominent reasons why our commitment waivers come to mind: 1) lack of communion with God, 2) impatience with His work and way in our life, and 3) disparity between head and heart.

Communion with God

Life seems like a merry-go-round, spinning faster and faster until we eventually fall off. The dizzying tempo of life is killing us. We have progressed from walking, to riding a horse, to riding a train, to riding in a car, to flying in a plane. Outpacing us, technology connects us anywhere and anytime with just about anyone. We can't even eat a meal in a restaurant without listening to the maddening, loud-mouthed individual with a fork in one hand and a cell phone in the other, interrupting everyone's meal with an annoying public conversation no one wants to hear.

If the past is represented by a Model T Ford, the present is a space shuttle, and who knows the speed of the future? Simply put, we are going so fast that we don't have time for God. You don't pop this kind of relationship into the microwave for thirty seconds to reheat it; a relationship with our Creator is something to be cultivated, nurtured, and treasured. An investment of time is essential.

> As we sprint through contemporary culture, creating space for God is difficult, but certainly not impossible.

Our commitment waivers like cattails in the wind. As we sprint through contemporary culture, creating space for God is difficult, but certainly not impossible. In many respects, we wouldn't know how to commune with Him even if we did make the time. We know what it is like to use Him and ask Him to do things for us, but that is not communion. We may experience emotional euphoria listening to some theatrical preacher, but that may only be the fleeting exhilaration of a momentary roller coaster ride. Communion, on the other hand, is a deep, abiding sense of God's presence and guidance in our lives. It is talking *with* Him, not *to* Him. It is seeking to please Him, not to use Him. It is hearing and listening to His still, small voice. It is confirmation and affirmation of His presence in our life. It is being in alignment with the will and pleasure of our Creator.

We allow the merry-go-round of life to steal away precious minutes in our day as we engage in meaningless endeavors, become idiotized in front of the television, and squeeze God into the few leftover minutes we can spare. Instead of keeping the main thing the main thing, we struggle to slow down. We want to keep God on our priority list because He is important, and after all, we might actually need Him some day.

Sometimes we confuse being involved in church, volunteering for non-profits, teaching Sunday school, etc. for communing with God. He may indeed ask us to do such things, but that isn't communing with Him—that's obeying Him. Once again, instead of actually spending time cultivating the relationship, we get busy doing things for Him, believing that busyness in the kingdom is next to godliness. Stop it! We would be far better off backing away from all church involvement if it meant replacing those activities with actually spending time with God. Yet, when the pressures of the day come calling, the main thing never gets done and we engage in religious busy work all the while pretending that it replaces communion with our beloved. When all is said and done, we have done everything but the main thing, cultivating a relationship with our Creator.

I fight this "time creep" issue every day and have come to realize that it matters little whether you are a retired grandmother, a factory worker, or a Wall Street broker—life seems to get in the way of spending time with God. People's priorities are seen by what they love, what they spend their money on, and what consumes their time. When God does take primacy in our life, commitment begins to blossom and the truth of Matthew 6:33 becomes real, "But seek first His kingdom and His righteousness, and all these things will be added to you."

Often I find myself pondering the life of Jesus as a busy man with crowds clamoring for His attention. At times, we find Him stealing away in an effort to be alone with the Father. Jesus knows when to heal, whom to heal, where to go, what to say, and when to leave. How does He know all of this? He certainly has no instructional manual on how to be a proper Messiah. Instead, His life is guided by the Father Himself. Jesus knows what the Father desires because He spends time with Him. Though He is busy, His one objective in life is to know and do the will of the Father. He is totally committed to it, and because of that, He takes the time to cultivate and nurture a deep, abiding relationship.

We are often more dedicated to drumming up excuses than we are at following our Lord. Deep down inside, we realize the primacy of God. Instead of making the necessary adjustments for a life of total commitment, we convince ourselves that we don't have enough time in the day for devotion with Him. Life happens! In reality, we have just as much time in a day as everyone else. The question isn't how much time did our busy schedule allow for God, but rather, am I willing to adjust my schedule so I make time to commune with the Father?

Our amazing Lord aspires to commune with us. He desires that we know Him, sense Him, experience Him, and that we know and do His will. He is not a distant

God, so aloof that it is impossible to commune with Him even if we wanted to. No, He is a God who is real, who loves us, and who yearns to share with us in ways that affirm His presence and inspire our souls.

Addressing the Jewish exiles, prophets, and priests taken to Babylon after Nebuchadnezzar conquered Jerusalem, Jeremiah writes in 29:11–14,

> "For I know the plans that I have for you," declares the LORD, "plans for welfare and not for calamity to give you a future and a hope. Then you will call upon Me and come and pray to Me, and I will listen to you. You will seek Me and find Me when you search for Me with all your heart. I will be found by you," declares the LORD."

What has carried us away is not a physical exile to a foreign land, but the swift undercurrent of life's busyness that prevents devotion with God. We drown in a raging river of frenzied activity and discover that God is absent. Our merry-go-round life hinders communion and encourages Big But-itis. Frustration mounts until destructive Big But bangs are heard by those around us. We really do want a dynamic relationship with God and become frustrated when it is not forthcoming. Yet, we won't change our ways to obtain what we so desperately need and desire.

Like the Jewish exiles, the kind of deep, personal relationship we long for with God won't be found until we heed the words of the Lord in Jeremiah 29:13–14: "You will seek Me and find Me when you search for Me with all your heart. I will be found by you." Those who find God are those who seek Him with sold-out, total abandon.

Impatience with God

The speed at which we live our lives has brought on an unintended consequence: impatience with God. We like things to be done without delay, and if the checkout line is too long we roll our eyes and sigh. The first microwave oven was invented by Percy Spencer after WWII and later introduced as a countertop model to the American public in the late 1960s. During my teenage years, our family traveled from small-town Iowa to my cousin's home near the big city of Dallas, Texas. Much to my delight, sitting on their kitchen counter was a microwave oven. I had never seen such an inventive gadget. My introduction to this new contraption arrived with hot ham and cheese sandwiches ready to eat in only seconds. In a world of high-tech gadgetry and microwave mentalities, we know what we want, and we want it this instant. Waiting is a pain, a waste of time, and out of line with our expectations.

As newlyweds, my wife and I owned virtually nothing, let alone anything new. With few exceptions, our furniture and vehicles were hand-me-downs. We realized that it would take time, especially on a pastor's salary, for us to accumulate the necessary funds to secure a few upgraded items for our home. Combining credit card access with an insatiable appetite for instant gratification, younger generations struggle with excessive debt in their quest to accumulate instantly what took my generation years to obtain.

> In our mind, waiting means something is wrong, a process is flawed, or incompetence is lurking. It never occurs to us that waiting is a good thing . . .

Our fast-food mindset has permeated the church and our relationship with God. What takes time to cultivate, we want to harvest immediately. We desire the gap between what we want, and when we get it, to be abridged as much as possible. We don't like to wait, not even on God. We have become ADHD Christians—restless, hyper, inattentive, and anxious for our instant and impulsive cravings. Waiting on God only exacerbates the issue.

In our mind, waiting means something is wrong, a process is flawed, or incompetence is lurking. It never occurs to us that waiting is a good thing, or that it has absolutely nothing to do with incompetence, a flawed process, or an overworked God who struggles to keep all the balls in the air. Unlike a large hospital where there is never a lack of "hurry up and wait" experiences, Christians wait upon the Lord for His perfect timing with the events and experiences of their life.

God's perfect timing is seen throughout both testaments of the Bible. For instance, the coming of Jesus isn't a chance happening, but the perfect timing of God as noted in Galatians 4:4–5, "But when the fullness of the time came, God sent forth His Son, born of a woman, born under the Law, so that He might redeem those who were under the Law, that we might receive the adoption as sons." God sends Jesus at just the right time. Generations upon generations anxiously awaited His coming, and it arrives on schedule and in God's perfect timeline.

Joshua is required to march around Jericho for six days prior to attacking the city. His obedience and patience leads to conquering the city in God's perfect timing (Josh. 6:1–21). While Jesus is teaching in His home town of Nazareth, irate townsfolk lead Him up a hill intending to throw Him down the cliff, but they are unable to fulfill their objective as Jesus walks away (Lk. 4:14–30). In God's schedule of events, it is not yet time for Jesus to die. When Mary's brother Lazarus becomes sick, she sends for Jesus, thinking that if He comes quickly Lazarus will be spared. Upon hearing the news, Jesus lingers for two days before going to the burial site. Mary is upset by this. Jesus' delay is costly for her. In her mind, had she not waited on Jesus, Lazarus' death could have been prevented, but in the mind of God, Mary waits for God's perfect timing so a resurrection miracle can occur (Jn. 11:1–15). Story after story abounds of God's perfect timing, not only in the Bible, but also in our lives as well.

Big But-itis can flare up in surprising ways when we become impatient with God's timeline. We question His abilities, His resources, His concern, and His competence. Waiting means that we are not in the driver's seat, and that bothers us immensely.

While overseeing the development of university courses in the context of higher education, every new program aspires to be fully functional with short notice. The process of instructional designers working alongside faculty takes time. Sure, there are templates and processes in place, but well-designed courses entail thought and creativity. In order to deliver programs to the marketplace faster, pressure arises for "just in time" curriculum. In other words, launch the program and build it as you go so the courses are prepared "just in time."

This model might work with a small number of programs, but when this philosophy becomes the predominant mentality for all new programs, the making of a perfect storm emerges. When there are too many planes circling in the air waiting to land on a busy runway, "just in time" really means "nothing is on time." As expected, the "just in time" mentality ran into problems because of work delays, lack of personnel and funding, communication problems, equipment and software failures, etc.

In God's perfectly timed economy where there are no process or resource issues, "just in time" actually means "always on time." There are never failures with God, no system process issues, and no lack of resources. The One delivering His promises, leading us step-by-step, is none other than the all-knowing, all-powerful, all-loving God. We can wait on His timing with perfect peace, knowing that He always comes through. According to Isaiah 40:31, waiting on the Lord is a necessary and positive endeavor, "Yet those who wait for the LORD will gain new strength; they will mount up with wings like eagles, they will run and not get tired, they will walk and not become weary." But-ness that erupts during periods of waiting always stands on the back of impatience.

Head and Heart

Not only does our commitment waiver as we fail to commune with Him and we become impatient with His way in our life, our commitment also falters when there is imbalance between our heart and our head.

Loving God entails our whole being, according to Mark 12:30. "And you shall love the LORD your God with all your heart, and with all your soul, and with all your mind, and with all your strength." In its simplest terms, loving God with our heart, soul, mind, and strength means loving Him with every fiber of our being, with everything we have and everything we are. We give Him our all, without reserve or hesitation. It's kind of like the difference in a ham and egg breakfast. The chicken contributes an egg to the meal, but the slice of ham on the plate is only there because of the pig's total commitment. He gave everything, while the chicken only gave a portion.

While we are complex creatures made up of many parts, the head and heart concept is something most folks readily grasp. While scholars lament my simplicity, we actually know people with a bent toward the head and those with a bent toward the heart. Head folks tend to be logical thinkers who love to analyze, evaluate cause and effect, and ponder things deeply. Heart folks tend to exude feeling, compassion, empathy, and care for others. It's not that head folks are devoid of feelings or heart folks don't reason, it's just that one is more prominent, preferred, and comfortable than the other. A solid commitment to God entails balance between the two.

One day I heard loud, clunking noises emanating from the laundry room. As I stuck my head in the doorway to see what was happening, I saw the wash machine shaking violently, rocking back and forth, and slowly scooting across the floor. The cause of such commotion was an imbalanced load. Even the washing machine understands the need for balance. Without a balance between our heart and our head, we can easily spin out of control and scoot through life producing annoying Big But noises.

In many ways, life is like walking a tightrope. At times our life is easy, we are happy, and all is well. The tightrope is only two feet off the ground. We don't worry too much about balance, because if we fall, we can just hop right back on without much damage. At other times, life's tightrope seems to stretch from Niagara Falls to the Canadian border. Balance now soars to elevated importance as the winds and rain increase above the raging waters below. Falling now takes on heightened significance with life or death consequences.

Tightrope walkers carry a long balancing pole that helps counter external forces and changing conditions. As the winds of life constantly shift, adjusting the balancing pole offsets the force trying to push us off the tightrope. If our weight begins to move too far in one direction, the pole acts to counterbalance the load. The higher the rope, the greater appreciation we have for balance.

In walking the tightrope of life, our head and our heart act as a balancing pole. In many ways life is a constant balancing act. One day we are healthy, the next we may be near death. One day we are happily married, and the next we are widowed or divorced. One day our children love and value us, and the next day they are on their own believing we are irrelevant. One day we are employed and secure, and the next we are without income. One day we feel God's presence and love Him deeply, and the next we question His very existence. These are the forces that act upon us as we walk life's tightrope.

There will be days when we don't feel much like following God. Our emotions are charred and raw. Life has been hard on us, and the warm fuzzies are all but gone. There is little emotional energy left in the tank, and like the noisy washing machine violently scooting across the floor, we are out of balance. The balancing pole needs to shift and reallocate trust to the head until our emotions have time to heal and catch up. It is a time to think, ponder, and stand on God's promises.

King David experiences this very thing. Prior to becoming the King of Israel, he was a shepherd boy whose life was simple and easy. He watches a flock of sheep and loves God with all of his heart. He is filled with passion. I can see him under the light of a full moon, stars fading in the background, sheep resting in peace, and David sitting on a rock with outstretched arms praising God. Life is good and filled with passion.

David's passion is seen in I Samuel 17:1–58 when he kills Goliath, who is taunting the chosen people of God. David hears that someone is challenging Israel and mocking God. His passion is aroused and his emotions are inflamed. He proceeds to the battlefield seeking to defend God's reputation and put the boastful giant in his place. King Saul takes one look at the scrawny, youthful shepherd and says, "You are not able to go against this Philistine to fight with him; for you are but a youth while he has been a warrior from his youth" (I Sam. 17:33). To prove his fighting ability David replies in verses 34–37,

> Your servant was tending his father's sheep. When a lion or a bear came and took a lamb from the flock, I went out after him and attacked him, and rescued it from his mouth; and when he rose up against me, I seized him by his beard and struck him and killed him. Your servant has killed both the lion and the bear; and this uncircumcised Philistine will be like one of them, since he has taunted the armies of the living God . . . The LORD who delivered me from the paw of the lion and from the paw of the bear, He will deliver me from the hand of this Philistine.

Fueled by intense passion and powerful devotion to the Lord, he runs to the battle line and with a sling and a stone, downs the arrogant Philistine. His response to the lion, the bear, and the Philistine giant isn't the result of long nights of strategic planning or logically laying out the pros and cons of such action; David's response is pure heart.

As David grows older, life isn't as simple as it had once been while tending sheep in the fields. He now has to use his head to maintain balance. Passion is good and profitable. It moves us to action, quickly and forcefully when needed, but it may be the head that sustains us for the long haul.

King Saul, whose army David has just saved, becomes jealous of David and desires to kill him. For years David is on the run, fleeing the crazed wrath of King Saul. The circumstances in David's life have changed, and the winds are blowing from a new direction. Now is the time to utilize his head, to think, to plan, and outwit his opponent. On one occasion, King Saul gathers three thousand men to pursue David in the wilderness of Engedi (1 Sam. 24:1–22). Along the way, King Saul privately enters a cave to relieve himself, not realizing that David and his men are inside. Had David relied merely on passion, he could have easily killed the man who was making life so miserable for him. Instead, he uses his head, spares Saul's life, and does not touch the Lord's anointed.

David, we are told, penned many of the Psalms, of which two stand out in revealing him as a man of reflection and meditation. Psalm 77:11–12 says, "I shall remember the deeds of the LORD; surely I will remember Your wonders of old. I will meditate on all Your work and muse on Your deeds." Psalm 63:6–7 is similar: "When I remember You on my bed, I meditate on You in the night watches, for You have been my help, and in the shadow of Your wings I sing for joy."

What sustains David over the long haul is his head. He takes time to meditate on Scripture and remembers God's work in his life. In the challenging times of life when emotions are spent and the grip of depression sets in, it is time to use our head to think upon and remember the promises of God. Balance requires both head and heart. At times we move the balancing pole to emphasize more care, love, and concern for others, and at other times, we adjust the pole to think and reason through God's promises, even when we don't feel like it.

The Apostle Paul is another example of head and heart balance. Early on in his life, he demonstrates unbridled zeal for God in misdirected fashion as he persecutes Christians with vigor and delight. The Lord meets him on the Damascus Road, and his life forever changes. Now he has to learn about The Way. It is head time. He becomes a chief spokesman for Christ in the early church and eloquently and accurately defends the faith. Sometimes appearing rough and gruff in his thought-provoking letters to the churches, Paul's heart is also touched with compassion and care as he remembers those whom God sends his way in service and ministry. They become the ministering hands of Jesus in his life.

Heart people are wonderful. Head people are wonderful. Total commitment to Christ involves both. Too much heart, and we fizzle out like a rocket using up all its fuel before leaving the atmosphere, only to tumble out of control back to earth. Passion's ability to withstand the gale force winds of life may be short-lived. Too much head, and we become cold, unloving, and sometimes unlovable, always thinking but never displaying emotional fervor or tender care. Imbalance leads to a wash machine condition, scooting out of control across the floor exhibiting numerous annoying Big But explosions. Total commitment for the long haul involves balancing the head and the heart.

Big But Cluster 6: *Myopic Vision of God's Plan*
In junior high school things got a little blurry for me, literally. Not that I paid much attention in class anyway, but I couldn't make out the writing on the chalkboard near the front of the room. It wasn't long before I became the proud owner of a brand new pair of glasses.

My condition, known as myopia, is commonly referred to as nearsightedness. Rays of light entering my cornea focus just in front of my retina instead of directly upon it. This means that objects at a distance are out of focus. Corrective lenses bend entering rays of light so they focus in the right spot with the pleasant result of no longer seeing people as walking trees. I absolutely need my glasses to view things clearly; otherwise, everything is one big blur.

Without corrective lenses, life is lived dangerously. By the time a hitter in the batter's box sees the 90 mph fastball blazing directly at him; it is too late to duck. A driver may notice a blurry blob in front of her but miss the fact that it is a large diesel truck swerving into her lane. Without corrective lenses, our sight is always out of focus and our view is always inaccurate, resulting in a hazardous propensity toward danger.

This Big But cluster occurs when our spiritual eyesight becomes myopic just like our physical eyesight. When God's work in our lives is viewed without clarity and acuity, our perception of spiritual realities becomes blurred and dulled. Off-kilter spiritual vision increases the odds of Big But-itis becoming a real distraction in our spiritual walk. We become like those with hearing problems who constantly complain that others should speak up and quit mumbling, when all the while the issue is with their very own ears. They refuse hearing tests, dismiss the possibility of hearing loss, and scoff at the very idea of wearing hearing aids. Instead, they turn the television up even louder, disgustingly shake their head at the perceived insolence of others, and live in their own quiet world with a garish Big But.

Because of His unique vantage point and powerful attributes, the Grand Designer sees the beginning from the end, directs our paths, and weaves a beautiful pattern into our lives. We crave to make ultimate decisions and judgments about our lives and our experiences. We seek control. We desire God in our lives, but in reality, we want to control Him too. The idea of subjecting ourselves to the master plan of a Grand Designer is often problematic, for we don't know what path He will ask us to travel. While we desperately salivate to design our own lives, the fact remains that the Christian life doesn't work that way. There is only one Grand Designer, and it isn't you!

The bottom line is really a matter of trust and control, isn't it? Either God is the all-powerful Master Weaver who knows what He is doing and who has our best interest in mind, or He isn't. We either trust Him with our life, or we trust in ourselves. One is the mouse in the maze trying to discover an escape route, while the other created the maze to begin with. We either quit trying to micromanage our lives or we allow God to direct our steps, no matter where they lead.

I suppose I should just say it and get it off my chest right now—God is smarter than you. In fact, this may be the biggest understatement of the year. I am not demeaning your intelligence, but I *am* elevating His brilliance. He knows more than we do. He knows all things, while we know some things. He is more powerful than we are. He created all things while we are the created ones. He sees past, present, and future while our vision is fuzzy at best. He knows the hearts and motivations of all people, while we can only guess, and even at that we are wrong most of the time. He combines justice with mercy in perfect timing and in perfect proportion. Ours is a far cry from the unadulterated, genuine justice and mercy of God. He is holy and untouched by sin, while we are not immune from the dreadful disease. He is the One who saves us. We are unable to save ourselves.

Is the picture becoming clearer? We simply don't have what it takes to be the grand designer of our own lives, let alone anyone else's. However, we can be encouraged that 1) God promises to lead us, 2) the Bible provides examples of His leading, and 3) we, along with many others, have personally experienced walking with Him.

God Promises to Lead Us

God takes great care in His love letters to remind us of His tender guidance throughout our Christian walk. A sampling of verses reveals His desire and promise to direct our steps.

Psalm 23:2–3
He makes me lie down in green pastures;
He leads me beside quiet waters.
He restores my soul;
He guides me in the paths of righteousness
For His name's sake.

Psalm 25:9
He leads the humble in justice,
And He teaches the humble His way.

Psalm 31:3
For You are my rock and my fortress;
For Your name's sake You will lead me and guide me.

Psalm 32:8
I will instruct you and teach you in the way which you should go;
I will counsel you with My eye upon you.

Psalm 37:23
The steps of a man are established by the LORD,
And He delights in his way.

Psalm 48:14
For such is God,
Our God forever and ever;
He will guide us until death.

Psalm 73:24
With Your counsel You will guide me,
And afterward receive me to glory.

Psalm 78:52
But He led forth His own people like sheep
And guided them in the wilderness like a flock.

Psalm 78:72
So he shepherded them according to the integrity of his heart,
And guided them with his skillful hands.

Isaiah 48:17
I am the LORD your God, who teaches you to profit,
Who leads you in the way you should go.

John 10:3
To him the doorkeeper opens, and the sheep hear his voice, and he calls his own sheep by name and leads them out.

John 10:27
My sheep hear My voice, and I know them, and they follow Me.

Romans 8:28
And we know that God causes all things to work together for good to those who love God, to those who are called according to His purpose.

The consummate reference to God's promised guidance in our lives is Proverbs 3:5–6. "Trust in the LORD with all your heart and do not lean on your own understanding. In all your ways acknowledge Him, and He will make your paths straight." Early on in my Christian life, I memorized this passage, and throughout my many seasons of doubt, I refer to it as a precious reminder of God's adept skills in weaving a marvelous pattern into my life.

This comforting passage asks us to 1) trust in the Lord with all of our heart (this is what our spiritual journey is all about), 2) lean not on our own understanding (He is smarter than us), and 3) acknowledge Him in all that we do (recognize Him as the Grand Designer), and He will indeed direct our steps.

Biblical Examples of God's Leading

It is one thing to hold on to a promise and quite another to possess an historical record of God actually fulfilling promises. No doubt, we have experienced those who promise the moon and deliver nothing, who overpromise and under-deliver. Our Heavenly Father can be trusted to fulfill His pledge to lead and guide us, not only because He is able and willing, but because He has been leading and guiding His beloved sons and daughters throughout the ages. The historical record alone should bolster our faith in His nurturing abilities.

Christian history swarms with story after story of God's leading. He leads Noah to build an ark that saves humankind from a devastating flood. He leads Abraham from Ur of the Chaldeans to become a great nation. He leads Joseph to save his family from starvation during a famine. He leads Abraham's servant in finding a wife for Isaac. He leads the Hebrew nation from Egyptian slavery and into the Promised Land. He leads Jesus into the wilderness to look temptation in the eye. He leads Paul to conversion on the road to Damascus. The list could go on and on.

Acts 16:7–10 records the leading of God during Paul's second missionary journey:

> And after they came to Mysia, they were trying to go into Bithynia, and the Spirit of Jesus did not permit them; and passing by Mysia, they came down to Troas. A vision appeared to Paul in the night: a man of Macedonia was standing and appealing to him, and saying, "Come over to Macedonia and help us." When he had seen the vision, immediately we sought to go into Macedonia, concluding that God had called us to preach the gospel to them.

In his quest to spread the gospel and encourage local congregations, Paul seeks to enter a province called Bithynia, but the Spirit of God does not permit it. Instead, Paul bypasses Bithynia and travels to Macedonia in response to the Lord's guidance.

Not only does Scripture promise that God will lead us, but we also encounter countless examples of such guidance throughout the annals of Christian history. An additional pillar of support is the internal witness we share with many others who experience His leading on a daily basis.

As is often the case, we may best perceive God's leading in our lives by looking back and reflecting. While traversing through dangerous rapids, we are busy navigating the difficult terrain, avoiding protruding boulders, and keeping the raft afloat. It is only as we reach smooth water that we find time to wipe the sweat from our brow, sit back, and say, "Thank you Father. I couldn't have made it without Your guidance and protection." When we trust Him, He leads us. Pretty simple, isn't it? We may not hear an audible voice or encounter a Damascus Road episode like Paul, but nonetheless, we know that He is directing our path.

Jesus knows He is being led into the wilderness for a time of intense testing. Paul knows he is not permitted to enter Bithynia, and realizes God is calling him to Macedonia. In wrestling with the essential requirements for salvation, the Jerusalem Council arrives at a decision they recognize as the leading of God's spirit: "For it seemed good to the Holy Spirit and to us to lay upon you no greater burden than these essentials" (Acts 15:28).

A radical missionary in his day, 21-year-old Hudson Taylor sailed across a vast ocean on a small clipper to share his faith with the Chinese people. China was a distant frontier at the time, newly emerging in the consciousness of American missionaries. During his teenage years, Hudson experienced a powerful encounter with the Lord, which eventually prompted his lifelong service to China. Though often criticized by fellow Christians for wearing Chinese clothing and putting his hair in a pigtail, he senses the leading of God upon his life and obeys with trust.

Blazing a pioneering trail teaches you a lot about God. In several of Hudson Taylor's famous quotes, we catch a glimpse of his experience in following the Grand Designer's lead:

- I am no longer anxious about anything, as I realize this; for He, I know, is able to carry out His will, and His will is mine. It makes no matter where He places me, or how. That is rather for Him to consider than for me; for in the easiest positions He must give me His grace, and in the most difficult, His grace is sufficient. [4]

- It does not matter how great the pressure is. What really matters is where the pressure lies— whether it comes between you and God, or whether it presses you nearer His heart. [5]

- When I cannot read, when I cannot think, when I cannot even pray, I can trust.[6]

- God's work done in God's way will never lack God's supplies. [7]

- I have never passed a more anxious or trying month in my life, but I never felt God so present with me. [8]

- Christ is either Lord of all, or is not Lord at all. [9]

But-ness increases when trust decreases. Are you willing to live with His leading no matter where the path takes you? Will you trust in His grand design for your life, in fact, for all of life? The more we believe our fuzzy view is accurate, the more myopic we become.

Our limited perspective is like viewing the world through a straw. There is so much more that we miss, and so much more that God sees. Scripture teaches that in this life our understanding is limited. "For now we see in a mirror dimly, but then face to face; now I know in part, but then I will know fully just as I also have been fully known" (1 Cor. 13:12).

I envision squealing with delight upon entering heaven and filling in the gaps of my present finite knowledge. I am excited to know fully what I now see only dimly. Though I bear the ambiguities of life without fully grasping all the various twists and turns I am about to encounter, I am content to give my heart in full trust to the Grand Designer who leads my every step. I still have many questions, wonder why He turns me left instead of right, and experience struggle and pain in my journey, but I find comfort in knowing that He is with me, and that He leads with my best interest and His glory in mind. I am fully cognizant of how much I don't know, don't see, and don't understand as I live out my time on this planet. And that is just the way it is. My full understanding awaits a time when I "will know fully just as I also have been fully known." Until that day, I obey, I trust, and I stand on the promises of God. In so doing, I keep my view of God large and my But small.

Big But Cluster 7: *Misconception of Ourselves*

While myopic vision fails to grasp the pattern woven into our lives by the Master Weaver, this particular Big But cluster fails to comprehend our role in His plan. Ever met a cocky little boy fancifully strutting about like he has the world by the tail, yet, you realize he knows absolutely nothing? His bravado is merely ignorance cloaked in that little puffed up chest of his.

Groveling in worm theology and disregarding our status as God's beloved children is not only theology amiss, but also a critical case of Big But-itis. On the other hand, progressing in the extreme opposite direction where we think more highly of ourselves than we ought is equally mistaken. Like the cocky little adolescent, we arrogantly puff out our chests and fancifully strut around while giving God a piece of our Little Napoleon attitude.

Many of the problems we experience are rooted in an incorrect understanding of ourselves, an overestimation of our abilities, and an attitude of independence that falsely believes we can stand on our own two feet without the Lord. Observing the twinkling stars on a moonless night reminds us just how small we are in God's vast creative handiwork. We are but a speck in the universe, or in more visual language, we are the size of a pea rolling down an eight-lane highway!

Don't get me wrong—we are *somebody* in Christ, but our *"somebody-ness"* is largely due to our connection with Him (Jn. 15:4–5).

> Abide in Me, and I in you. As the branch cannot bear fruit of itself unless it abides in the vine, so neither can you unless you abide in Me. I am the vine, you are the branches; he who abides in Me and I in him, he bears much fruit, for apart from Me you can do nothing.

God has indeed freed us from the marketplace of sin. He then cleans us up, furnishes a new identity, and calls us to serve Him. Nothing should detract from such central truths.

Yet, this distinct Big But cluster encompasses haughtiness of spirit, arrogance, self-confidence, and false bravado cloaked in ignorance. This perilous cluster took deep root in the heart of Lucifer, a magnificent angel created to protect the glory of God. Unfortunately, a Little Napoleon attitude snuck in and stole away the beauty of his innocence. He puffed up his chest, popped out his Big But, and thought more highly of himself than he should have. It cost him dearly.

In many ways, we just can't seem to get it through our dense skulls that God is the Potter and we are the clay (Rom. 9:20–21).

> On the contrary, who are you, O man, who answers back to God? The thing molded will not say to the molder, "Why did you make me like this," will it? Or does not the potter have a right over the clay, to make from the same lump one vessel for honorable use and another for common use?

Clearly, Paul indicates the Potter has a right to do what He wants with the lump of clay. And that is exactly what irritates us. The potter/clay concept is not difficult to grasp, it is difficult to accept, and we resist and resent our expectation to acquiesce.

In the Old Testament, the potter/clay concept is used as an example to Jeremiah of God's work with Israel (Jer. 18:1–10).

> The word which came to Jeremiah from the LORD saying, "Arise and go down to the potter's house, and there I will announce My words to you." Then I went down to the potter's house, and there he was, making something on the wheel. But the vessel that he was making of clay was spoiled in the hand of the potter; so he remade it into another vessel, as it pleased the potter to make. Then the word of the LORD came to me saying, "Can I not, O house of Israel, deal with you as this potter does?" declares the LORD. "Behold, like the clay in the potter's hand, so are you in My hand, O house of Israel. At one moment I might speak concerning a nation or concerning a kingdom to uproot, to pull down, or to destroy it; if that nation against which I have spoken turns from its evil, I will relent concerning the calamity I planned to bring on it. Or at another moment I might speak concerning a nation or concerning a kingdom to build up or to plant it; if it does evil in My sight by not obeying My voice, then I will think better of the good with which I had promised to bless it."

The Lord's dealing with Israel didn't set well with some Israelites as they wondered how He could do this or that. The attitude is much like our thinking today. "How can God allow this? How can God do such a thing?" In asking such questions, we reveal our own heart perspective. What we really mean is, "I certainly wouldn't do it that way." In essence, we take offense that God disagrees with our idea of what is right, proper, and acceptable. And that, my good friend, is exactly the heart of the issue. We misjudge our role and our place. We don't mold the clump of clay; we *are* the clump of clay. God is the Potter who has the right to mold as He pleases. We know someone has to have final authority on things; we just don't like that it isn't us. And in this, we have to trust the good nature and positive attributes of a just and loving Heavenly Father.

I have many questions about God; why He allows certain events or circumstances to occur, and the manner and timing of His leading often escapes my logic. But I am reminded of Isaiah 55:8–9, "'For My thoughts are not your thoughts, nor are your ways My ways,' declares the LORD. 'For as the heavens are higher than the earth, so are My ways higher than your ways and My thoughts than your thoughts.'"

Is it wrong to even ask such questions, or to wonder why God does what He does? Questioning can become a powerful reminder that His ways are not our ways and His thoughts are not our thoughts. He is the Potter, we are the clay. He is the eight-lane highway, we are the tiny pea. Instead of groveling, we begin to yield, trust, move forward in faith, and discover a companion who is closer than a brother.

But when the questioning leads to bulging Big Buts, we veer into trouble. This accusatory tone reminds me of the young men and women competing for singing fame on popular national television shows. Everyone thinks they have the vocal chops to become a star. In reality, some do, most don't. What amazes me is the depth and level of self-deception among competitors. Bless their hearts, they have the guts to get off the couch and compete, but they are often sorely unrealistic about their abilities. They think their voice is God's gift to the world and can't figure out why they don't already have a recording contract in hand. When competition judges point out their deprivation of talent, many contestants become angry and downright aggressive. In their mind, they are America's next rock star, but everyone else in America sees it differently. It is comical and sad at the same time.

We do the same thing, except in other venues and in other ways. Satan aspired to be God and forgot he was a lump of clay. His self-deception led to a heavenly rebellion, banishment from a lofty position, and will eventually lead to his total ruinous defeat. The Pharisees in Jesus' day thought more highly of themselves than they should have. They looked down on others, judged them to be inferior, and neglected the darkness of their own hearts. Jesus said of them, "Woe to you, scribes and Pharisees, hypocrites! For you are like whitewashed tombs which on the outside appear beautiful, but inside they are full of dead men's bones and all uncleanness" (Mt. 23:27). Clearly, they perceived themselves to be the Potter, when they were merely clumps of clay.

Two of Jesus' followers ask a special favor of Him revealing an overestimation of themselves in Mark 9:33–35,

> James and John, the two sons of Zebedee, came up to Jesus, saying, "Teacher, we want You to do for us whatever we ask of You." And He said to them, "What do you want Me to do for you?" They said to Him, "Grant that we may sit, one on Your right and one on Your left, in Your glory."

Wow, what chutzpah—the nerve of these two! Earlier in Mark, Jesus uses the Pharisees as an example to His disciples that evil springs from the heart (Mk. 7:14–23). He then teaches them about humility, noting that if they want to be first they must become the least (Mk. 9:33–35). And now, the brothers' audacious request comes immediately on the heels of Jesus sharing with them His upcoming suffering and death.

These two fellows didn't get it. All they thought about was their own wants and desires. It is like a co-worker standing on the fourteenth floor window ledge about to jump, and two of his office friends yell out to him, "Hey, can we have your chair and desk when you are gone?" It is bad timing, a selfish request, and certainly misses the gravity of the situation.

Jesus informs John and James that they do not know what they are asking. They seek for something only the Potter decides, not the clay. They want the glory, honor, and prestige of being near Jesus in His future kingdom without understanding the difficult path required to get there. They view themselves as worthy of such an honor and desire to make Potter-like decisions when they are merely clumps of clay.

Every time we try to be the Potter, we reveal our displeasure with our own clay status. This is a colossal failure of judgment and results in epic Big But eruptions. I have noticed something else about Christians—many are uncomfortable in their own skin. They realize God is the Master Designer with power and authority to craft the clay, but they despise the outcome. They see Him as a great painter; they just don't like His paintings. They are not challenging His right to be the Potter, only His decision to make them what they are. If He makes them a bowl, they want to be a cup. If He makes them a cup, they want to be a bowl.

I suspect the disciples wrestled with this as well. It could be that James and John felt a little intimidated by the other disciples. I wonder if they ask to sit next to Jesus in order to elevate themselves above their brothers, dissatisfied with their status in the group. Peter is an outspoken, up-front kind of individual, while his brother Andrew is quiet and shy. I wonder if Andrew ever thought to himself, "I wish I were more like my brother Peter. He is so outgoing, so brave, so ready and willing to speak his mind." I wonder if Peter ever said to himself, "I wish I were more like my brother Andrew. All I ever do is open my giant mouth and get myself in trouble while Andrew quietly befriends people and leads them Jesus."

Everybody wants to be like somebody else. It is true that others may have qualities worth emulating, like patience. However, it is untrue that when the Potter crafted us, He made a mistake, or we are somehow flawed.

Don't like your nose? Is it too big, or too long? Don't like your body shape? Not tall enough? Wish your face looked differently? Are your ankles too thick? Get over it. Embrace yourself. Love what God has created, thank Him for His intelligent and beautiful design, and move on. He has the right to create you as He desires,

> If you are dissatisfied with you, then you are dissatisfied with God. In essence, you disagree with what the Potter has created leading you to misperceive your role and response to Him.

and His design is without flaw or misstep. If you are dissatisfied with you, then you are dissatisfied with God. In essence, you disagree with what the Potter has created leading you to misperceive your role and response to Him.

I can relate to this aspect of misperception. It wasn't until age thirty-five or so that I began feeling comfortable in my own skin. I was pretty self-conscious in junior and senior high school. Who was I, in light of the good-looking, popular kids and athletes, to be going anywhere, doing things, or participating in anything? Rarely did I attend high school football or basketball games. To get up from my seat and walk in front of all those people just to get some popcorn was extremely uncomfortable. Would they notice my fears, my flaws, and that I didn't measure up?

With my lack of confidence now behind me, I couldn't care less what others think. It means nothing to me. Now I go to football games, concerts, and interact with all sorts of people. But I made a common mistake along the way to accepting the Potter's design for me. The more success I enjoyed, the more confident I became. You have one doctorate? I have more than you. You've written how many books? I've written more. You make how much money? I make more. Your job title is that, well mine is this.

It wasn't that my successes were achieved without the Lord; for I knew the Master Weaver was at work in my life, and I was grateful for it. But I placed undue emphasis on accomplishments, thinking that they somehow justified my existence on this earth, that I was okay because I had progressed and advanced far beyond others. With my successes in hand, I could now get out of my seat during a basketball game, walk in front of thousands while making my way to the popcorn stand, knowing that I had nothing to fear because I had accomplished more than the lot of them.

Pretty arrogant attitude, wouldn't you say? My security came not from the Lord, but from my accomplishments. But even that mistaken attitude reveals my own misunderstanding of myself. In reality, my successes and accomplishments are nothing. In other words, the Potter made me who I am and since He makes no mistakes, I could have started accepting His intricate design of me way back in junior and senior high school. I could have bypassed all the needless off-roading to find out who I was in Christ and became comfortable in my own skin long ago.

Of all people, the Apostle Paul has much to boast about. He is educated, articulate, zealous, and possesses an impressive resume. Yet, he doesn't boast in these things. Instead, he boasts of his weaknesses as a way to show forth God's wondrous work in his life. In essence, his boasting is in the Lord (2 Cor. 10:17). In fact, Paul is willing to give up everything for the sake of knowing Christ more intimately:

> But whatever things were gain to me, those things I have counted as loss for the sake of Christ. More than that, I count all things to be loss in view of the surpassing value of knowing Christ Jesus my Lord, for whom I have suffered the loss of all things, and count them but rubbish so that I may gain Christ, and may be found in Him, not having a righteousness of my own derived from the Law, but that which is through faith in Christ, the righteousness which comes from God on the basis of faith, that I may know Him and the power of His resurrection and the fellowship of His sufferings, being conformed to His death; in order that I may attain to the resurrection from the dead (Phil. 3:7–11).

Jesus also has plenty of reason to puff Himself up. He changes water into wine, miraculously feeds five thousand with a scant amount of bread and fish, heals many diseases, raises people from the dead, and draws large crowds. He teaches in the synagogues without formal education and outsmarts the smartest rabbis. Impressive!

Yet, Scripture is clear that "the Son of Man did not come to be served, but to serve, and to give His life a ransom for many" (Mt. 20:28). Philippians 2:5–8 encourages us,

> Have this attitude in yourselves which was also in Christ Jesus, who, although He existed in the form of God, did not regard equality with God a thing to be grasped, but emptied Himself, taking the form of a bond-servant, and being made in the likeness of men. Being found in appearance as a man, He humbled Himself by becoming obedient to the point of death, even death on a cross.

You have to be pretty comfortable in your own skin, with how God made you, His call upon your life, and embrace utter contentment with the Potter's grand design to do what Jesus did. With such comfort in His role and task, Jesus, in John 13:1–17, humbles Himself to that of a rank and file servant washing the feet of dinner guests. No one else is willing to serve in this capacity, so Jesus wraps a towel about his waist and begins washing His disciples' feet. He displays majestic humility and is an example of comfort and contentment with the Potter's will and right in His life.

We don't engage in enough joy, appreciation, thanksgiving, and contentment with how the Potter designed us. We need to do more of that. In the privacy of your own home, I dare you to stand naked before a full-length mirror one day and with full voice proclaim the beautiful words of Psalm 139:14, "I will give thanks to You, for I am fearfully and wonderfully made; wonderful are Your works, and my soul knows it very well."

We are valuable not because of what we accomplish, the possessions we own, or the amount of money we earn. We are valuable solely because we are made by the Potter, designed specifically and intimately to reflect His intentions and become fruitful in His kingdom. It doesn't get any better than that. He possesses both the right to be the Potter and to mold the clay as He desires. He makes no mistakes, only beauty.

But alas, the seed of But-ness seeks constant vivication in our lives. Misperceiving our role keeps us from experiencing abundant life, serving with contentment, following with joy and gladness, and faithfully trusting His good pleasure throughout the journey.

Big But Cluster 8: *Pain, Disappointment, and Anger*

This final Big But cluster is the one we may be most familiar with and involves issues of pain, disappointment, and anger with God, people, circumstances, and events. When our expectations are unfulfilled, we can experience pain, disappointment, and anger. This produces a jaded perspective which triggers further pain, disappointment, and anger.

Expectation ⟶ Letdown ⟶ Jaded Perspective ⟶ Further Pain Triggered

"Of all the problems you see in your practice," I asked a counselor friend of mine, "how much is directly related to issues of pain, disappointment, and anger?" The answer didn't surprise me, since nearly every problem involves each of these items to some degree. They are not separate, disparate, and ancillary topics, but issues intricately connected to, and triggered by, so many other things. The counselor noted an additional necessary item for exploration in these situations, the need for, and process of, forgiveness.

In one sense, there is a positive side to pain, disappointment, and anger. Pain, for instance, has a protective nature about it. Once our hand is burned in the flame, we learn about fire. It would be difficult to protect ourselves from dangerous situations if we could feel no pain. Disappointment can be a motivator. If your goal is to run a five-minute mile and you time out at six minutes, the disappointment may spur you to keep practicing until the five-minute goal is reached. As an emotion created by God, anger is a precious gift to us. Jesus Himself became angry at times, even overturning the moneychanger's tables in the Temple. Angry? Yes. Loss of control? No. There is a time and place for anger guided by the Spirit of God.

But more often than not, we experience the negative and destructive side of pain, disappointment, and anger. People come to church to experience God, and then, with the best of intentions, they become involved. They join a committee, serve on the leadership board, or volunteer in some capacity. From that moment on, their eyes are forever opened to the adverse and harmful side of church life, something they were hoping to avoid, or didn't know existed. They become wounded and experience buyer's remorse, often berating themselves for volunteering in the first place. Had they simply remained in the pew, things would have been much easier. In their mind, they naively expected people changed by the grace of God to actually behave differently. Their desire to serve is dulled, their expectations are lowered of what church is and could be, and their jaded perspective can easily turn into suppressed anger just waiting for the damn to burst.

Make no mistake about it—this is a major stronghold of the enemy. Pain, disappointment, and anger is a Big But minefield. If we don't carefully watch our step, we will be blown to smithereens. Think about your own Big But explosions. Do they erupt when you are content, happy, and in right alignment with God? Of course not! They occur when you are angry, disappointed, or hurt. If your life were a garden, the miracle fertilizer for growing large Buts is pain, disappointment, and anger.

My first ten years of full-time pastoral ministry were the most challenging. Inflicted by co-workers in the kingdom, pain, disappointment, and anger was something I experienced on a regular basis. While there were no fist fights or body blows, the emotional pain I endured within the church through backstabbing, false accusations, judgment of motives, being cheated out of money, etc. was overwhelming.

I found myself being disappointed in others. Is it really too much to ask that church leaders actually honor their word? Is it too much for leaders to be honest, rise beyond their own personal agendas, and seek the Lord's voice rather than engage in manipulative power plays? It was so disheartening to me.

While I controlled my anger outwardly, I was dry kindle on the inside primed for a match. I kept it bottled up, fed up with unscrupulous power moves by religious, legalistic, judgmental, hypocritical Christians. In fact, if someone remarked how they were cheated, ill-treated, manipulated, or ran over by a power-monger, my response at the time was, "Oh, they must be a Christian."

This is what pain, disappointment, and anger does to people. It can rot us from the inside out. Thinking becomes skewed, corrupted, and sarcastic. My heart longed to find just one person whose life was truly transformed by Christ, but I could find no such example. At the same time, I knew that I wasn't an example myself. What I vehemently disliked in others, I had become.

Pain, disappointment, and anger become fertile breeding grounds for the blossoming of Big Buts. Paul realizes this very thing in Ephesians 4:26: "Be angry, and yet do not sin; do not let the sun go down on your anger." Dealing quickly with anger prevents the emergence of Big But-itis. To let pain, disappointment, and anger fester is like handing your house key to a burglar. It is an invitation to steal, plunder, and pillage.

I can't count the number of times I have been knocked down in one way or another—bruised in battle, and so often wanting to cry "uncle," but I haven't. If pain, disappointment, and anger were going to kick me in the backside, I was determined that they kick me forward. I would use these experiences to better myself, grow in Christ, and empathize more with others. Then it dawned on me that I wasn't the only one experiencing such difficulties; I was in the company of many committed followers of God.

One cannot read Psalms without noticing the angst and desperation of the writers. Many plead for help as they experience difficulties. Wrestling with matters of justice, the prophet Jeremiah says, "Righteous are You, O LORD, that I would plead my case with You; indeed I would discuss matters of justice with You: Why has the way of the wicked prospered? Why are all those who deal in treachery at ease?" (Jer. 12:1). Even Job, who experiences tremendous suffering says, "Why do the wicked still live, continue on, also become very powerful? Their descendants are established with them in their sight, and their offspring before their eyes, their houses are safe from fear, and the rod of God is not on them" (Job 21:7–9). Jeremiah and Job wrestle with what is, and what ought to be.

On one hand, the writer declares, "As the deer pants for the water brooks, so my soul pants for You, O God. My soul thirsts for God, for the living God," and in the next breath, "Why are you in despair, O my soul? And why have you become disturbed within me?" (Ps. 42:1–2, 5). Finally, we read of further desperation in verses 9–11,

> I will say to God my rock, "Why have You forgotten me? Why do I go mourning because of the oppression of the enemy?" As a shattering of my bones, my adversaries revile me, while they say to me all day long, "Where is your God?" Why are you in despair, O my soul? And why have you become disturbed within me?

Plenty of psalms reveal pain, desperation, attitude struggles, and the questioning of God. Just take a look at Psalm 88, 116, and 146. It's pretty clear the writers wrestled with the same Big But attitudes we struggle with.

"Well," you say, "we all wrestle with things." Yes, we do, and some more than others. But before we downplay their struggles, a look at some imprecatory psalms may convince us just how intense their struggles were. An imprecatory psalm is one that calls for judgment, calamity, curses, or punishment upon enemies. They aren't pretty and we are often embarrassed of them. We much prefer the happy, praise passages like Psalm 145. Do you sense pain, disappointment, and anger in the following imprecatory Psalms?

Psalm 69: 22–28
May their table before them become a snare;
And when they are in peace, may it become a trap.
May their eyes grow dim so that they cannot see,
And make their loins shake continually.
Pour out Your indignation on them,
And may Your burning anger overtake them.
May their camp be desolate;
May none dwell in their tents.
For they have persecuted him whom You Yourself have smitten,
And they tell of the pain of those whom You have wounded.
Add iniquity to their iniquity,
And may they not come into Your righteousness.
May they be blotted out of the book of life
And may they not be recorded with the righteous.

Psalm 109:6–15
Appoint a wicked man over him,
And let an accuser stand at his right hand.
When he is judged, let him come forth guilty,
And let his prayer become sin.
Let his days be few;
Let another take his office.
Let his children be fatherless
And his wife a widow.
Let his children wander about and beg;
And let them seek sustenance far from their ruined homes.
Let the creditor seize all that he has,
And let strangers plunder the product of his labor.
Let there be none to extend lovingkindness to him,
Nor any to be gracious to his fatherless children.
Let his posterity be cut off;
In a following generation let their name be blotted out.
Let the iniquity of his fathers be remembered before the Lord,
And do not let the sin of his mother be blotted out.
Let them be before the Lord continually,
That He may cut off their memory from the earth;

Such harsh words are also displayed in the New Testament. With strong language, Jesus blasts the Pharisees and scribes by calling them fools, blind guides, serpents, vipers, hypocrites, and whitewashed tombs in Matthew 23:13–32. Tell us how you really feel about them Jesus!

Paul declares in I Corinthians 16:22, "If anyone does not love the Lord, he is to be accursed." We see his anger in Galatians 1:8–9,

> But even if we, or an angel from heaven, should preach to you a gospel contrary to what we have preached to you, he is to be accursed! As we have said before, so I say again now, if any man is preaching to you a gospel contrary to what you received, he is to be accursed!

Pain, disappointment, and anger daily seek to enter our lives, and we often rationalize their presence when they succeed. The Psalmists, on the other hand, take their concerns directly to the Lord and cry out to Him in genuine and authentic ways. Crying out to God is a good thing, but when pain, disappointment, and anger fester in our life, major Big But explosions transpire.

Big But Cluster Summary

Big But clusters simply group similar issues together. Though not exhaustive, the list helps us grasp But-ness in our lives and reveals the fact that most Christians deal with similar problems. Just because an issue is similar doesn't mean it is identical. There are nuances with each issue as applied to different individuals in diverse circumstances. The list, however, does what it is intended to do—help us discover Big But infections in our lives so that we can identify and acknowledge their presence and begin seeking relief.

BIBLE TINY BUTS

ust all Buts be the result of Big But-itis? Are all Buts bad, or are there some respectable ones out there? Yes, there are virtuous Buts for us to examine, and before we explore them, it is a good time to pause and reflect upon what has been presented so far.

THE BIG BUT PROBLEM

Big But Definition:	Big But-itis is a perspective or behavior that conditions, justifies, or excuses our conduct and thinking, or reveals discontentment with God.
We experience the Big But of others all the time.	*Their* Big But 1) is easily recognizable, 2) is painful to us, 3) hinders the work of God, and 4) vilifies God's reputation.
We engage in our own Big But behavior.	*Our* Big But 1) is hard for us to recognize, 2) is painful to others, 3) hinders the work of God, and 4) vilifies God's reputation.
There are many examples of Big But-itis.	We examined 1) everyday examples, 2) New Testament Big Buts, and 3) Old Testament Big Buts.
Conclusion:	We experience the Big But of others and engage in Big But behavior ourselves. Big But-itis is a universal human problem that obstructs our view of God.
Encourage or discourage?	We can easily be discouraged with this universal problem, or we can be encouraged that God still uses us and refuses to give up on us even though we sometimes flaunt our Big Buts.

Discouragement can set in if we ruminate on the painful experiences created by the Big Buts of others. In fact, we can stew about it and get bogged down. Sometimes we like to waddle in a cesspool of pain rather than work our way out of a rut. Waddling in our sorry But acts as its own Big But, justifying and excusing our unwillingness to lift ourselves up.

Looking in the mirror is also uncomfortable, for it requires that we either turn away in discouragement, or that we actually do something about our But-ness. Reducing But size is no easy task. On one hand, we may view it as an impossible task, or at least unworthy of the effort, and on the other hand, the Lord urges us to be conformed to His image.

> Sometimes we like to waddle in a cesspool of pain rather than work our way out of a rut.

While the Big But Syndrome affects us all, it does not define us, nor does it have to conquer us. If nothing *could* be done about it, we might have reason to give up. If we could find no positive examples to lift our spirits, we might find reason to be discouraged. Our experience need not be subjugated to the Big But disease. There are many wonderful, God-honoring, and encouraging good Buts out there.

Let's call these good Buts, hmmm, let's see . . . how about Little Buts or Tiny Buts, so we can contrast them with the Big Buts already discussed. Big Buts are huge because they get in the way of living for God, obeying God, hearing God, and loving God. They are problematic because they eclipse our view of the Lord. Little Buts, on the other hand, are tiny because they don't hinder us in any way from seeing, obeying, loving, and living for God. In fact, they enhance our relationship with God. For Big Buts, God is small and their But is big. The opposite is true of Little Buts, for whom God is big and their But is tiny.

I call this the *"Eclipse of the Buts"* and it looks something like this:

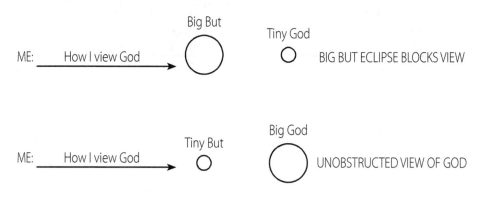

In the English language, "but" can be used to offer contrast. The book of Ephesians offers an example of this use as it pertains to submission:

Wives should submit to their husbands,
but husbands are to love their wives as Christ loved the church (Eph. 5:22–33).

Children should submit to their parents,
but fathers are not to provoke their children to anger (Eph. 6:1–4).

Slaves should submit to their masters,
but masters are not to threaten their slaves (Eph. 6:5–9).

The role of one is contrasted with the role of the other. One is to behave a certain way, and the other is to behave another way. Though we all use "but," the difference between a Big But and a Tiny But is whether the contrast is good or bad, big or little, and if it obstructs and hinders our view of God. While Ephesians reveals a contrast in submissive behaviors, the following chart contrasts the Big But of Gehazi with the Tiny But of the centurion.

BIG BUT CONTRAST

But	But Talk	Contrast	Result
Big But Gehazi 2 Kgs. 5	My master Elisha never takes money for the miracles he performs because he wants the Lord to get the glory, **but** Naaman is willing to pay, offered to pay, and there is no reason why I can't personally profit from Elisha's miracles. I will lie, get the money, and no one will be the wiser.	The contrast is between God's glory being enlarged, or Gehazi's greedy pocketbook being enlarged.	Gehazi is caught in his greedy lie and stricken with the very leprosy from which Naaman is healed. His view of God is obstructed.
Tiny But Centurion Mt. 8	My servant is in need of a healing, and Lord, I know You offered to come to my house, **but** You are so powerful and mighty all You have to do is say the word right now and he will be healed.	The contrast is between faith that requires coming and faith that requires only the words of Jesus for healing.	The servant is healed because of the great faith exhibited by the centurion. His view of God is enhanced.

Whether "but" is an actual word in a sentence, an attitude, or behavior, Big Buts use it as a means to condition, justify, or excuse their conduct and thinking, or reveal discontentment with God. Gehazi does just that. He covets money and views Elisha's miracles as a way to personally profit. So he schemes, lies, and actively engages in Big But behavior that skews his perspective and hinders his relationship with Yahweh. The result is disastrous. He acquires the very disease from which he is trying to profit.

In stark contrast, the centurion possesses an Itsy-Bitsy But. He is a powerful man who understands the nature of authority and the power of words. Instead of using his But to conceal God, he uses it to reveal God's power and glory. There is really no need for Jesus to come to his house and heal his servant. Jesus is so powerful, all He has to do is say the word. The Lord Himself is amazed as noted in Matthew 8:10, "Truly I say to you, I have not found such great faith with anyone in Israel." The centurion's Tiny But is not a hindrance, but a help. It reveals great faith and clears a path for the wondrous working of God.

Let's examine how Tiny Buts in the Bible clear a path for God to do great things.

New Testament Tiny Buts
Tiny But Joseph
Matthew 1:18–25

> Now the birth of Jesus Christ was as follows: when His mother Mary had been betrothed to Joseph, before they came together she was found to be with child by the Holy Spirit. And Joseph her husband, being a righteous man and not wanting to disgrace her, planned to send her away secretly. But when he had considered this, behold, an angel of the Lord appeared to him in a dream, saying, "Joseph, son of David, do not be afraid to take Mary as your wife; for the Child who has been conceived in her is of the Holy Spirit. She will bear a Son; and you shall call His name Jesus, for He will save His people from their sins." Now all this took place to fulfill what was spoken by the Lord through the prophet: "Behold, the virgin shall be with child and shall bear a Son, and they shall call his name Immanuel," which translated means, "God with us." And Joseph awoke from his sleep and did as the angel of the Lord commanded him, and took Mary as his wife, but kept her a virgin until she gave birth to a Son; and he called His name Jesus.

As a carpenter, Jesus works with his hands in a trade learned from his father. That's how it worked back then. If your father is a baker, then you are a baker. If your father is a butcher, then you are a butcher. Like father, like son. Woodworking is an honorable trade—one much needed and extensively utilized in those days. In an attempt to reconcile the miraculous ministry and power of Jesus with the carpenter they grew up with, the people of Nazareth wonder in Matthew 13:55–57,

> Is not this the carpenter's son? Is not His mother called Mary, and His brothers, James and Joseph and Simon and Judas? And His sisters, are they not all with us? Where then did this man get all these things? And they took offense at Him.

Marriages are often arranged by parents in the Middle East, even while children are very young. We don't know if this is true of Mary and Joseph, or whether their affection for one another grows on its own. Either way, they seem to love each other deeply. It is important for a man to find a wife, start a family, and contribute to the local community. Joseph is a skilled tradesman, engaged to be married, and will soon embark upon creating a family of his own.

Things are going along as planned until Mary unexpectedly becomes pregnant. Joseph's world is rocked to the core, and all his plans come crashing down. This is unexpected and unexplainable; yet, it is happening right before his very eyes. Mary's pregnancy occurs during the betrothal period, "when His mother Mary had been betrothed to Joseph, before they came together she was found to be with child by the Holy Spirit" (Mt. 1:18).

Betrothal is similar to our engagement period, except in those days a man and woman were promised to each other a year or more before the actual wedding ceremony and Mary would be considered the lawful wife of Joseph during this period. This is why Joseph is called her "husband" in Matthew 1:19 and why he "planned to send her away secretly" (divorce her).

Put yourself in Joseph's shoes; as a young carpenter you meet the girl of your dreams. She says "yes" when you ask for her hand in marriage. Proud as a peacock, you become engaged to this beautiful woman and the betrothal period can't end soon enough. You are ready to get on with your life, start a family, and contribute to the community. Betrothal is a waiting game, a time to honor the Lord, gather the dowry price, and look forward to the change your life is about to undertake.

Mary's youthful body begins to experience the changes pregnancy brings. She knows something is happening within her. In Luke 1:30–31, she is alerted to the Lord's surprise, "The angel said to her, 'Do not be afraid, Mary; for you have found favor with God. And behold, you will conceive in your womb and bear a son, and you shall name Him Jesus.'" Perplexed by such a statement, Mary responds in verse 34, "How can this be, since I am a virgin?" The answer comes in verse 35, "The angel answered and said to her, 'The Holy Spirit will come upon you, and the power of the Most High will overshadow you; and for that reason the holy Child shall be called the Son of God.'" Some ask how a young woman never having intimate relations with a man can become pregnant? The pregnancy occurs because the Holy Spirit comes upon her, and the power of the Most High overshadows her. In other words, God sanctions this event.

Joseph doesn't want to disgrace Mary in any way and decides to divorce her quietly. This way, she can preserve some dignity, and he can pick up the pieces and get on with his life. The Lord, however, has other plans. In a dream, what is revealed to Mary is also revealed to Joseph (Mt. 1:20–21),

> But when he had considered this, behold, an angel of the Lord appeared to him in a dream, saying, "Joseph, son of David, do not be afraid to take Mary as your wife; for the Child who has been conceived in her is of the Holy Spirit. She will bear a Son; and you shall call His name Jesus, for He will save His people from their sins."

There is benefit to hindsight, and in retrospect, many see this as the divine fulfillment of God's sovereign plan that Mary's conception fulfill prophecy (Is. 7:14; 9:6–7). Joseph believes in Yahweh, and along with all the Jews of his day, believes that the long-awaited Messiah will indeed come. Yet, the full impact of Mary's pregnancy escapes him. At this point, it is enough to obey the words of the Lord communicated to him in a dream. He takes Mary as his wife, she bears a son, and they name him Jesus, which means "God with us."

Why is Joseph considered a Tiny But? Why is he an example of small But size? Because, like us, there are often moments in our lives when we choose But size. We can enlarge our Buts to humungous proportions, and in so doing lose sight of God's work, or we can minimize our But dimensions, view God correctly, and watch Him work wonders in our life. Joseph chooses to keep his "But-print" tiny and his view of God large.

When Joseph discovers that his future bride is pregnant, his first thought is of her apparent unfaithfulness. You don't get pregnant by drinking from the community water fountain; you get pregnant when intimate relations occur between a man and a woman. He and Mary had remained pure with each other, so the only other explanation was her unfaithfulness.

According to Jewish law, unfaithfulness could lead to stoning or divorce. With a broken heart, Joseph opts to quietly divorce her. His love remains for Mary even though she *seems* unfaithful; he doesn't seek revenge or her public disgrace. This is Joseph's plan until the Lord intervenes and reveals that the child within Mary is a miracle by the Holy Spirit. Although his mind is perplexed over the "who, what, when, where, and how" of it all, his heart is relieved that Mary has indeed remained pure.

At this point, Joseph has a decision to make. His But can explode like a driver's side airbag, or it can remain small and inattentive. He could say, "Do you really think I am that stupid, Mary, to believe a story like that? You said your pregnancy is a miracle from God, *but* everyone knows you can't get pregnant without intimate relations. I had a dream that God spoke to me, *but* it was just a dream, probably caused by the stress of realizing the love of my life has been unfaithful." This is Big But-speak.

Joseph could have easily traveled the Big But path, but he didn't. Instead, he is grateful to God for the explanation, willing to endure the scorn and speculation of others, withholds intimate relations with Mary until after the child is born, and actively obeys without fully understanding all the implications of what God is doing. The result of Joseph's Tiny But is the fulfillment of messianic hopes and the joy of raising God's annointed. It doesn't get much better than that.

These kinds of situations happen to us all the time—certainly not on the scale of birthing the Messiah, but numerous choices throughout the hour, the day, and year. A time of choice arose in Jonah's life, for instance, and instead of reacting like Tiny But Joseph, Big But Jonah runs from the Lord. He had a choice, and he chose poorly. We too experience a lifetime of But-popping choices.

During my high school years, I struggled with the call of God upon my life. I enjoyed preaching, but I also loved police work. I enrolled in a law enforcement class at a community college during high school and absolutely loved it. I also accepted opportunities to preach during this time and absolutely loved that too. How could I make a decision? How was the Lord leading me?

I served as a reserve police officer in a large metropolis during my first year of college. Knowing that I would have to pass an eye exam to become a full-time police officer, I participated in orthokeratology to help correct my poor eyesight. The process of corneal reshaping continued until I could see well enough to pass the law enforcement eye exam.

I applied for a position in a small town but was rejected because the federal government was paying a portion of the new officer's salary, and I didn't meet the criteria for assistance. While I had more credentials and experience than the individual who obtained the position, I lost out.

With the small town rejection behind me, I applied to one of the largest cities in the nation and was rejected along with 97% of the other applicants. During a good portion of the grueling drive home, I wept before the Lord. I was over qualified for one position and under qualified for the other. After a period of reflection, I reached a point when I said, "Ok Lord, I get the hint. I will pursue full-time ministry and preach your ways," and that is exactly what I did.

It is a Joseph moment for me. The path I desperately desire to travel is blocked, not by accident but by divine design. My reaction to the roadblock becomes a choice for me. Will I allow my But to expand to epic proportions and say, "God, You know how much I want to be a police officer. I tolerated orthokeratology, gained experience and training, and I really wanted it Lord. Thanks a lot for disappointing me. Why is following You always about giving up the things I want?" That is Big But-speak.

Instead, I worked hard to remain pliable, open, sensitive, and trusting. Is this the Lord's intervention? Is He trying to tell me something? Is He whispering in my ear? Is this a time to pause, reflect, and listen? Of course it is. It is a Joseph moment, a moment of choice, and I chose to listen to God and align my will with His.

Joseph moments are often emotional and traumatic experiences for us, and during the height of it all, we sometimes feel like all hell is breaking loose. In retrospect, however, we comprehend the significance of the decision before us, and realize our decision is the correct one. In my case, I don't think I would have survived a law enforcement career. The day I was rejected from big city police work, two of the city's officers were shot. Though saturated with constant danger and stress, it is good work for sure. I still love police work, have immense respect for those who risk their lives to protect us every day, but in the end, I can say that it was not the road God had planned for me. In looking back, I would have it no other way.

What is your Joseph moment? Can you describe a time when something similar happened to you, when you chose to keep your But tiny and your view of God big? If so, look back and smile. Use the good choices you made in the past to encourage you in the present. It may be that you are going through one of those moments now. You don't know exactly what God is up to, but you know He has asked you to follow Him and trust Him with your life, your situation, and your path. Joseph surely doesn't grasp a momentous birth, but he obeys anyway. You may not grasp the intricacies and details of His leading, but a moment of choice is upon you. Choose carefully. Keep your Big But in check; don't let it pop and become a hindrance. Instead, keep your But tiny and your view of God large. In your Joseph moment, trust Him, yield to Him, and follow His leading. In the days to come you will look back with a smile on your face and say to yourself, "Boy, He sure knew what He was doing, even when I didn't."

Tiny But Centurion
Matthew 8:5–13

And when Jesus entered Capernaum, a centurion came to Him, imploring Him, and saying, "Lord, my servant is lying paralyzed at home, fearfully tormented." Jesus said to him, "I will come and heal him." But the centurion said, "Lord, I am not worthy for You to come under my roof, but just say the word, and my servant will be healed. For I also am a man under authority, with soldiers under me; and I say to this one, 'Go!' and he goes, and to another, 'Come!' and he comes, and to my slave, 'Do this!' and he does it." Now when Jesus heard this, He marveled and said to those who were following, "Truly I say to you, I have not found such great faith with anyone in Israel. I say to you that many will come from east and west, and recline at the table with Abraham, Isaac and Jacob in the kingdom of heaven; but the sons of the kingdom will be cast out into the outer darkness; in that place there will be weeping and gnashing of teeth." And Jesus said to the centurion, "Go; it shall be done for you as you have believed." And the servant was healed that very moment.

As a gifted teacher, Jesus displays tremendous ability to connect with an audience. In the opening verse of this chapter, we find Him teaching on a mountain with a great multitude of followers listening to His every word (Mt. 8:1). Upon finishing His public discourse, He travels to Capernaum and meets a centurion seeking a healing miracle.

Jesus was born in Bethlehem, raised in Nazareth, and adopts Capernaum as His own city once His home town of Nazareth disowns Him and His public ministry begins (Mt. 4:13–16; Lk. 4:16–31). Capernaum, located in Galilee, is situated on the western shore of the Sea of Galilee and is an important city on the route from Damascus to Tyre. Many miracles occur here. In fact, Jesus spends a great deal of time in Capernaum and engages in such extensive ministry that severe judgment will befall the residents for not believing in the midst of so many evidences (Mt. 11:23).

While in Capernaum, a centurion approaches Jesus requesting healing for his paralyzed servant who is suffering in great pain back home. Jesus' ministry is primarily to the Jews, and approaching Him for healing is a Roman officer in charge of one hundred men.

Although Jesus offers to travel home with him to perform the healing, the officer doesn't feel worthy of such a visit, nor does he see the need for it. It isn't that the house is a mess and his wife doesn't have time to clean before Jesus arrives; his request of Jesus reveals humility and recognition. The centurion recognizes who Jesus is and the authority He holds, and it prompts acute awareness of his own weaknesses and flaws.

> When our Big But gets out of the way, we are able to ascertain the magnificence of our Lord and our own diminutive status.

It reminds me of the prophet's vision in Isaiah 6. Upon seeing the Lord sitting on a throne and hearing the words, "Holy, Holy, Holy, is the LORD of hosts, the whole earth is full of His glory" (Is. 6:3), Isaiah cries out in 6:5, "Woe is me, for I am ruined! Because I am a man of unclean lips, and I live among a people of unclean lips; for my eyes have seen the King, the LORD of hosts." Unlike the prophet, the centurion doesn't see a vision, but he has a similar humbling response upon seeing the Son of God. When our Big But gets out of the way, we are able to ascertain the magnificence of our Lord and our own diminutive status.

The centurion does what so many of us do: we think through things and reason from our own operating sphere. Farmers think in terms of farming, and the centurion reasons from his military perspective. My father was a repairman, and I can't count the number of spiritual conversations where he processed the topic through the lens of repair work. Jesus understands this, and He often teaches with parables and stories so the audience can bring His words down into their world and easily apply new understanding to their own functional realm.

The centurion reasons that if one hundred men obey his commands, and he is merely a man with *limited* authority, then sickness must obey a man with *unlimited* authority and power. There is no reason for Jesus to visit his home when He has the power to merely say the words and sickness flees. This is an extraordinary act of faith at which Jesus marvels. His home town of Nazareth doesn't want anything to do with Him or His miracles. Capernaum will witness multiple evidences of His Lordship and still not believe. Yet, here is a Gentile, a Roman military officer exhibiting more faith than Jesus has seen in all of Israel.

Put in easily recognizable But-speak, the centurion's Tiny But-talk might sound like this:

Centurion:
My servant is at home paralyzed and in great pain. I will go see the great healer since He is now in Capernaum. Jesus, thank You for Your willingness to visit my home and heal my servant, *but* You are a man of ultimate authority and power. I command one hundred men and they do as I say, *but* You have power over all things. I believe in You so much that all You have to do is say the word and my servant will be healed.

This is Tiny But talk. By keeping his But small, his analysis of Jesus' ability to heal is unencumbered. His crystal-clear view of God is so big, he reasons that all Jesus has to do is *command* a healing. We all utilize some sort of "But" perspective, and the centurion is no exception; yet, he uses his But to reveal God, not conceal him.

This kind of faith is inspirational. Years ago, I received a small paperback book portraying the life of George Mueller who operated an orphanage in England. I marvel at his faith. He simply trusts God for everything. Who does that these days? Well, we all should, but we struggle in that department. He operated his orphanage on faith, believing God was able to provide for his needy children. Financial support arrives when needed. Groceries appear at just the right time. On occasions when there is no food to feed hungry tummies, George has the kids sit at the table, believing that provisions will come from the Lord. God does indeed provide! At just the right time, food is left on the outside porch and the children are fed. They sit at the table expecting food, and God feeds them. What great faith!

George Mueller's story bothers me, just as the centurion's story does. I am not so much concerned that others don't seem to live their life this way, as disappointing as that is; I am bothered because I struggle in my own life to walk this path. What if I lived with 100% commitment, 100% belief in God's ability and provision, 100% faith in His promises? What if I trust Him the way George Mueller does? What if I exhibit the faith of a centurion, how would that alter my life?

Isn't this what God desires? Doesn't He yearn for us to trust Him in everything? I can just hear Him saying, "Go ahead, trust me 100% with everything, and I will prove Myself absolutely true and faithful to you. Give it a try. Trust me."

Kudos to the Tiny But centurion. In a moment when the Big But of fear and unbelief could have easily seized control, he wisely keeps his focus on Jesus' ability and authority. Like Jesus, I marvel at this man's faith and seek to demonstrate it in my own life.

Tiny But Bleeding Woman
Matthew 9:20–22

> And a woman who had been suffering from a hemorrhage for twelve years, came up behind Him and touched the fringe of His cloak; for she was saying to herself, "If I only touch His garment, I will get well." But Jesus turning and seeing her said, "Daughter, take courage; your faith has made you well." At once the woman was made well.

The healing of a bleeding woman provides another fantastic Tiny But example. There is more to this story than initially meets the eye. Our modern day perspective merely sees a woman approaching Jesus, touching His garment, and moving on with a healing. In our society, all of this seems quite ordinary. Today, women move about freely without restraint or societal expectations of her proximity to a man. Today, women speak to men in public, and touching a piece of clothing is nothing unusual. Today, the modern medical community, through surgery or medicine, has a greater chance of correcting hemorrhaging problems than doctors of old. Today, women are no longer under ceremonial law as they were in Jesus' day.

When the Bible is read through twenty-first century lenses, we are apt to miss the richness and depth of meaning woven into the historical narratives. In harvesting the most from biblical study, it is imperative that we walk in the shoes of the original audience and understand the cultural milieu of the day. Once we understand as they would have understood, only then can we bring principles of application into our world.

An expanded version of this story, providing additional and significant information, is found in Mark 5:25–34. The bleeding woman has a medical condition and is unable to correct her problem. Fully aware of her physical need, she spends a fortune on doctor's bills seeking relief. At the end of the day, she is out of money, out of hope, out of doctors, and her condition actually worsens.

The lady is in dire straits with no hope left but Jesus. Unfortunately, many see Jesus as the emergency life raft rather than the very ship itself, and they often don't cry out to Him for help until all else fails. Instead of becoming our last resort, we do well to seek Him first. Here is the situation the woman finds herself in:

- *She has hemorrhaged for the last twelve years*
- *She endures much at the hands of doctors*
- *She spends all of her money seeking relief*
- *She grows worse, not better*

Though we don't know the exact nature of her bleeding problem, the very fact that she is bleeding is significant in light of Old Testament laws, especially Leviticus 15:19–30, which details the treatment of bleeding women. Considered ceremonially unclean, this designation has drastic implications for her life and relationship with others. Doctors can provide no cure, and without a healing she will forever be shunned, isolated, and unable to live a normal life. Here is how the laws in Leviticus affect her:

> **Whoever** she touches is unclean
> **Whatever** she touches is unclean

It is the *whatever* and *whoever* that is so devastating. If she sits in a chair, the chair is unclean. If she eats with a spoon, the spoon is unclean. Everything she uses becomes unclean. Not only are the "things" she touches unclean, but also the people she touches (the "whoevers"). She can't give her daughter a morning hug, be intimate with her husband, or enjoy a cup of coffee with a neighbor. She is banished to a life of solitude, loneliness, and social isolation. She certainly isn't going to be visiting the local restaurant for some challah bread, or attend one of the many Jewish festivals for fear of bumping into another person. She can't go out to eat with her husband or attend her child's school play. A life like this leads to continual pain, embarrassment, low self-esteem, and a sense of hopelessness.

Compounding her bleeding problem is the fact that she is a woman living in a patriarchal society. In her day, women had few rights and were often looked upon as second-class citizens. In fact, male Jews often thanked God in their prayers that they were not born a Gentile, a slave, or a woman. Females of that day lived in a different time and culture than our own, and one that, unfortunately, afforded them few rights and common courtesies.

Yet, with all of her cultural hindrances and ceremonial law restrictions, she reaches down deep and musters the courage to 1) seek Jesus out after hearing about Him, 2) make her way through a large crowd knowing she will in fact bump into others, 3) come behind Jesus so she is no distraction to His ministry, or seen as drawing attention to herself, and 4) reach out and touch the hem of His garment to gain healing without actually touching Him.

So the story of a woman moving through a crowd and touching a man's garment takes on greater significance as we understand her situation and the culture in which she lived. She risks being stoned, put in prison, or fined. What choice does she have? Her current pitiful existence isn't anything to write home about. In her mind, Jesus is the healer and she believes that if she can just touch the hem of His garment, the Great Physician will heal her. She hopes for a return to normalcy, a chance to enjoy the company of others, and to finally be declared clean.

As she touches His garment, Jesus senses His healing power leaving Him. Her blood problem is immediately healed and she knows it. When the Master seeks out who touched Him, she falls before Him, tells her story, and Jesus responds, "Daughter, take courage; your faith has made you well" (Mt. 9:22).

After twelve years of seeking medical relief, spending her life savings, living in social isolation, and having nothing to show for it except a worsening condition, her Big But could have easily burst wide open. In fact, we might even be tempted to justify it given her circumstances. Sarcasm could have ruled the day, but instead, we find a different attitude, a Tiny But attitude that allows her to experience the power of God in her life.

Let's contrast her *possible* Big But-speak with her *actual* Tiny But-speak:

Possible Big But Talk:
Woman:
I have had this stupid bleeding problem for twelve years now, ***but*** why do these things have to happen to me? I have spent my life savings on doctor bills trying to find a cure, ***but*** instead my condition only worsens. I have endured all the potions, tricks, and formulas these doctors prescribe, ***but*** look at me, I am poorer, more exhausted, more isolated, and more hopeless than ever before. I wish God would hear my prayers, ***but*** in fact, I am not even sure there is a God, or at least He is not listening to my cry for help.

Actual Tiny But Talk:

Woman:

I have endured this bleeding problem for twelve years, spent all my money trying to find a cure, and instead of getting better I am getting worse, *but* I heard of a man named Jesus who heals people. Maybe He can heal me. I have done everything I know to do in seeking relief, *but* if I can get to Jesus as He passes by I might have a chance of being healed. I know I am considered unclean and that I might actually be punished for doing this, *but* if I can just touch the hem of His garment, I know He will heal me. I know I have been down in the dumps at times, *but* maybe this is God's way of ministering to me and fulfilling my highest hope.

What a difference an attitude can make. If she goes the way of Big But-itis, she misses Jesus and forfeits her healing. Sarcasm and bitterness will obscure her vision of what could be. She chose, however, to keep her "But-print" very tiny. Sarcasm and bitterness are not allowed through the doorway of her life. Instead, she hopes in Jesus, seeks after Him, risks everything to get to Him, and firmly believes that He can meet her need. Because her But is tiny, her view of God is large. She receives her healing and walks away a changed woman. Her faith is bolstered, her body is healed, her mind is at peace, and her life is on the path to normal.

This story pangs my heart and reminds me of my first ten years of full-time ministry. In many ways, I was unprepared for the difficulties, problems, and setbacks faced by so many in my congregation. Folks I knew and loved experienced cancer, heart problems, brain surgery, divorce, marital issues, legal problems, emotional difficulties, spiritual concerns, job loss, death in the family; you name it I have seen it. We all look pretty shiny and new on Sunday morning as we paste a smile to our face and assure others that we are okay. In reality, we are deeply afraid they will find us out and discover our hurts, pains, flaws, and unpleasantries. We dare not take off our "pretender" mask, for to do so would risk embarrassment and the exposing of what we don't want others to see. We forget that virtually everyone in the church is doing the same thing.

It is quite a shock to discover the deep issues people face as I gently scratch the surface of their lives. It is as if I am enduring their pain with them and the weight of their problems fall upon my shoulders. It is something caregivers experience, hospice nurses learn to navigate, counselors are mindful of, and pastors must transfer to the strong shoulders of the Lord. I often thought to myself, "How can people endure so much pain and disappointment in life?"

The bleeding woman is a prime example of how Tiny But behaviors and attitudes *enhance* faith. Big But behaviors and attitudes *obscure* faith. When life seems overwhelming, the road you're on seems to lead nowhere, and you have given it your all, remember the story of the Tiny But bleeding woman. She meets Jesus, and He meets her need. She never gives up, even though she is exhausted. She keeps her attitude and behaviors positive. She maintains hope even when the situation seems hopeless. She pursues faith and Jesus commends her for it.

Tiny But Jesus
Matthew 26:36–39

> Then Jesus came with them to a place called Gethsemane, and said to His disciples, "Sit here while I go over there and pray." And He took with Him Peter and the two sons of Zebedee, and began to be grieved and distressed. Then He said to them, "My soul is deeply grieved, to the point of death; remain here and keep watch with Me." And He went a little beyond them, and fell on His face and prayed, saying, "My Father, if it is possible, let this cup pass from Me; yet not as I will, but as You will."

We have no problem viewing Jesus as divine. Our struggle emerges when we picture Him as a human being just like us. We may feel that highlighting His humanity in some way takes away from His status. Traditional Christianity believes Jesus to be both God and man; the Eternal Son who leaves His heavenly abode, cloaks Himself in human skin, and lives among us on this planet (Phil. 2:5–8). There isn't a theologian around who wholly comprehends this and can fully explain it. How someone can be both God and man at the same time baffles us. Yet, truth doesn't stand or fall on our understanding or approval.

For traditional Christians, that the Father would send the Eternal Son to live among us and be our Savior is absolutely breathtaking. It is the help we so desperately need and long for. Without His arrival on the scene, we would still be in bondage to our sin. But it is the human side of things that concerns us here; the fact that Jesus was fully human means that He was tempted as we are. "For we do not have a high priest who cannot sympathize with our weaknesses, but One who has been tempted in all things as we are, yet without sin" (Heb. 4:15).

Jesus didn't live in a holy bubble preventing Him from experiencing temptation. In fact, he experienced temptation more forcefully than any of us. We succumb quickly and easily, but Jesus withstood the full force of temptation and yet did not yield to its seductive power.

There were ample opportunities for Jesus to embrace the Big But Syndrome if He so desired. After being publicly baptized, He experiences forty days and nights of temptation in the wilderness with no Big But explosion. He could have easily retaliated against the religious elite of His day who tirelessly sought to trap Him and ruin His reputation, but He didn't. After speaking in His home town of

Nazareth, enraged townsfolk led Him to a cliff intending to throw Him off, yet Jesus had no Big But outburst toward them. After three years of mentoring His disciples and investing in their lives, they remained weak, afraid, selfish, and ignorant, yet no But-ness can be uncovered. Jesus could have easily become angry, disillusioned, or frustrated, but He didn't. He could have rebelled against God's divine plan during His trial and crucifixion, held a pity party, or used politically correct language and possibly lived, but He didn't. With His arms outstretched and His enemies mocking him, Jesus responds in Luke 23:34, "Father, forgive them; for they do not know what they are doing." This isn't the language of Big But-itis.

> When we look to others, place them on a pedestal, and hope to see sterling Christian examples, we always experience disappointment and frustration.

Knowing that Jesus was human and could be tempted raises His "But-ability" status. In other words, there are numerous opportunities, situations, circumstances, and temptations in His life where He could have exhibited Big But behaviors. While it was indeed possible for Big But eruptions to occur, Jesus keeps His But tiny so He can hear the voice of the Father and obey His will.

Jesus becomes an example to us, not only of who God is and what He is like, but an example of how we should live our lives. When we look to others, place them on a pedestal, and hope to see sterling Christian examples, we always experience disappointment and frustration. We fail, but Jesus doesn't. We sin, but Jesus doesn't. We don't always obey the Father, but Jesus does. He is the One we look to as embodying the nature and character of God, and how we should live to please the Father. Finally, when Phillip asks Jesus to show him the Father, Jesus replies, "He who has seen Me has seen the Father" (Jn. 14:9).

Even in His suffering, Christ is "leaving you an example for you to follow in His steps" (1 Pet. 2:21). Speaking of humility and service, Paul exhorts us in Philippians 2:5 to "Have this attitude in yourselves which was also in Christ Jesus." Jesus Himself indicates that He is an example in John 13:15, "For I gave you an example that you also should do as I did to you." Even in His death, we note that "the Son of Man did not come to be served, but to serve, and to give His life a ransom for many" (Mk. 10:45).

It's pretty clear that Jesus is someone we *can* and *should* look up to. Search all we may, we can't find one example of Big But-itis in Jesus' life, for there are none according to 2 Corinthians 5:21: "He made Him who knew no sin to be sin on our behalf, so that we might become the righteousness of God in Him." Peter describes Jesus as "a lamb unblemished and spotless" (1 Pet. 1:19). Imagine that—a human being without a Big But! That's what we long to see—someone who actually follows God, honors their word, employs truth and honesty, and is a shining example of what it means to follow the Father.

And now we find Jesus in the Garden of Gethsemane praying, "My Father, if it is possible, let this cup pass from Me" (Mt. 26:39). How do we reconcile His Tiny But with this prayer? In other words, isn't He asking the Father for permission *not* to endure the cross? Is this the beginning of Big But-itis in the life of Jesus, or is there more to the story?

This moment in Jesus' life isn't just any moment; it is time for *the* big moment in history, a moment that will forever alter human destiny. Traditional Christians believe this moment is the reason He leaves His heavenly abode. His entire life and ministry form one divine road to Jerusalem where He voluntarily offers up His life as a sacrifice to save us. Keenly aware of the gravity of this moment, Jesus tries to prepare His disciples for what is coming, "From that time Jesus began to show His disciples that He must go to Jerusalem, and suffer many things from the elders and chief priests and scribes, and be killed, and be raised up on the third day" (Mt. 16:21).

> This isn't an ordinary prayer in the life of an ordinary man during the course of an ordinary day.

As much as Jesus tries to prepare them, they are unwilling to fully support the mission. Peter actually pulls Jesus aside, rebukes Him, and declares, "God forbid it, Lord! This shall never happen to You" (Mt. 16:22). With the weight of the world upon His shoulders, and in the very moment He yearns for their support, His disciples decide to sleep. As Jesus prays in the Garden of Gethsemane, He is on His own.

This isn't an ordinary prayer in the life of an ordinary man during the course of an ordinary day. It is the moment in God's divine timeline when Jesus is about to face betrayal, false arrest, physical abuse, a sham trial, and crucifixion. It is the beginning of the end of His earthly existence.

Jesus knows what awaits Him, and He is willing to endure it for the sake of the kingdom. Yet, there is one particular aspect of His sacrificial death that is foreign to us: the crucifixion. Over the years, the American justice system has tolerated hangings, electrocutions, and lethal injections for those on death row, and not without great debate. But a crucifixion? We just don't do that in our modern age. A quick look at a Roman crucifixion helps us understand the weight upon our Lord's shoulders.

Throughout His ministry, Jesus endures the disrespect of many, but now He will be treated as a common criminal, unjustly accused and convicted in a mock trial. Once convicted and sentenced to die, His hands are tied above His head and clothing is stripped to expose His skin to the blows of a Roman legionnaire's whip until He is bruised, bloody, and nearly unconscious. Adding insult to injury, branches with thorns are woven into a wreath and placed upon His head, causing further discomfort and humiliation. That doesn't sound like a day in the park, does it?

After enduring such a whipping, Jesus is expected to carry His own cross to the killing zone, despite having little energy left in His gas tank. Once there, He lies on the crossbeam, arms outstretched, while nails are driven through His wrists to hold His upper body in place. His feet are then nailed to the wooden beam, and as He is hoisted up, the real agony begins. Fatigue, muscle spasms, and breathing difficulty take over. He must push Himself up by His feet just to breathe. His heart labors to pump blood, and His lungs cannot fully inhale or exhale. To ensure the prisoner is dead, the executioner drives a spear into His side. This wasn't the convenient "go to sleep and not wake up" exit we all hope for. In those days, it was one of the worst ways to die.

> ...there was no passion, no belief—only boring Wednesday ritual that was as dry as Thanksgiving leftovers.

Fully aware of what He is about to undergo, Jesus turns in prayer to His Heavenly Father. For the life of me, I don't know how Jesus endures all of this without a Big But explosion. If it were me, I would be screaming for justice, asking for my lawyer, cursing my accusers, and yelling at God for not saving me. In fact, I imagine my But would have been so large they would have had trouble even nailing me to a cross.

So great was His awareness of the situation, the gravity of His death, and the pain He would endure, He tells His disciples, "My soul is deeply grieved, to the point of death" (Mt. 26:38). It is no easy road. The path of discipleship is sometimes costly, demanding sacrifice, hardship, and even death as the great faith chapter of Hebrews 11 makes clear. In addition to excruciating physical pain, Jesus will soon bear the weight of the world upon His shoulders. Realizing this, He falls on His face and prays to the Father. Tempted to believe that Jesus' road to the crucifixion was effortless, we do well to remember the excruciating pain and suffering He endures in His resolve to obey the Father on our behalf.

I remember a Wednesday night prayer meeting at one church I pastored. A prayer list was distributed, and one by one we took turns praying for each item listed. Like a "to-do" list, we checked off each item, ensuring that we covered it all. We didn't fall on our face. We didn't sweat drops of blood. We didn't get on our knees. We didn't cry. We simply checked items off our list so we could say we did it, but there was no passion, no belief—only boring Wednesday ritual that was as dry as Thanksgiving leftovers. There is nothing wrong with prayer lists, or gathering on Wednesday to pray, but when our gathering becomes predictable legalism, devoid of passion or communion with the Father, it is nothing but meaningless routine. Jesus regularly prays to the Heavenly Father, but He does so as a way of life instead of a once-a-week event, and when He does pray, He is fully attentive, gives it His all, and on this occasion, falls flat on His face under the weight of so great a burden.

Luke's account indicates that Jesus actually sweats drops of blood under the intense burden. Many believe this is a condition called hematidrosis where, under great stress, the small capillaries under the skin burst and mix with sweat. Others feel that Luke is merely indicating that His sweat *was like* drops of blood. However the phrase is interpreted, we get the picture that a substantial load is placed upon His shoulders: the weight of the world.

Falling on His face, Jesus prays, "My Father, if it is possible, let this cup pass from Me; yet not as I will, but as You will" (Mt. 26:39). We must be careful to understand His prayer. He is not praying to get out of dying. In fact, quite the opposite is true. He wants to ensure that He is in absolute alignment with His Father's will—perfect oneness with the divine plan of God so He can actually fulfill and obey the Father.

What is always first and foremost for Jesus is knowing and doing the will of the Father who sent Him. In John 5:30 He says, "I do not seek My own will, but the will of Him who sent Me." Likewise, in John 6:38, Jesus declares, "For I have come down from heaven, not to do My own will, but the will of Him who sent Me."

For Jesus, enduring the Cross of Calvary is about accomplishing God's will. Had there been another way He may have been open to it, but there wasn't. For traditional Christians the world needed a Savior who was fully man as a representative for the human race. The world also needed a Savior who was fully God, so the atoning sacrifice could apply to all through faith. We are eternally grateful for the night of prayer in the garden. Jesus seeks confirmation, alignment, and absolute oneness with the will of the Father. Once He affirms His path down a difficult road, He walks it with courage and conviction, and as always, even in the most difficult segment of His life, His But is kept in check.

If there ever was a time for Jesus' But to explode, this would be it. He could have poured His heart out to the Father in anger, angst, frustration, and fear. He could have requested to stay longer with His disciples, for they still had so much to learn. He could have utilized His garden time accusing God of being unfair, uncaring, or simply too weak to create a different path. But He didn't. What is foremost in His mind is knowing and doing the will of God. The only thing Jesus is guilty of is being a great example of keeping His But tiny and His view of the Father large.

Putting Jesus' Tiny But actions into easy to recognize Tiny But-speak might look like this:

Jesus:
Holy Father, the momentous historical event You planned before the foundation of the world is now upon Me and I feel its weight upon My shoulders, **but** I want nothing more than to do Your will. My disciples have all fallen asleep and there is no one to count on, **but** I am glad that in this hour You are here with Me. I want to make sure this is the path You want Me to take. I don't want to make a wrong move, **but** I only want to confirm and fulfill Your will.

Even though Jesus was the hottest thing since sliced bread, well-liked by the populace and followed by crowds wherever He went, from a human perspective I can't help but think about the loneliness He must have experienced. No, I am not suggesting He is depressed or somehow warped in His personality. I only note that one can be alone even though surrounded by a multitude of people. I have experienced this very phenomenon to varying degrees throughout my own calling. People take up your time and emotional energy with never-ending requests. Always surrounded by others in great need, I gave and gave and at the end of the day, it was just me and the Lord.

Jesus is fulfilling the Father's mission, which few understand and support. Every move He makes is scrutinized by opponents whose sole desire is to destroy Him. His closest friends, the disciples, don't really grasp the situation, and in His deepest hour of need, it is just Him and the Father.

The cost of discipleship is not always an easy path. God calls each of us down different roads, some more difficult than others. As we seek to know and follow the Father's will for our lives, we may find it quite lonely at times. When we so desperately yearn for the support and encouragement of friends, it may not come. Instead, they may be sleeping in the garden. We can minister for the Lord among great multitudes and at the end of the day return home lonely and spent. God can call us to a ministry that others don't understand or endorse. Like Jesus, we can come to a point in our life and ministry when, under such burden, all else slips away and there we are, flat on our face before the Father. Nobody is around and it is just you and God. And that is enough! If He is your only friend in the entire world, it is enough. If He is your only source of strength and encouragement, it is enough.

It takes strong character to keep on keeping on in difficult situations. Challenging circumstances can easily become fertile environments for the growing of large Buts that interfere with successfully knowing and fulfilling God's will. Big Buts easily expose themselves during turbulent times when the heat is on. In the garden, when the heat is on, Jesus doesn't pick up His toys and go home. His commitment to the Father's will is unshakeable. When all is said and done in this life, it always comes down to you and the Father. Jesus knows this and when all else has gone by the wayside, the Father is right there with Him. And it is enough.

A divided heart is one reason our But pops out all too often. We want to live in both worlds. We desire to be holy, and yet enjoy sin at the same time. We want all the good things God has for us, but we want to enjoy the pleasures of the world, too. We want to intimately and passionately commune with the Father, yet we don't take time to cultivate the relationship. We want the rewards without the responsibilities. We want maturity and wisdom without the experiences that develop both within us. We have one foot in the boat and the other on the dock. As the boat pulls away, sooner or later we fall into the water.

> We want maturity and wisdom without the experiences that develop both within us.

When I was a youngster in elementary school, there came a time when our musical abilities were tested to help us choose the instrument we wanted to play. I longed to be a drummer. The tester asked that I keep one rhythm with my left hand slapping my knee and another rhythm with my right hand slapping the other knee. It doesn't sound like much, but having both hands doing different things is much harder than it appears, especially if you have no rhythm. The tester informed my father that another instrument would better suit my talents (or lack of them). I didn't care much for his advice and convinced my father to let me try the drums.

Dad brought home a snare drum, drum sticks, and basic instructional book. There I was, learning how to read drum notation in my bedroom, and counting . . . one, two, three, boom . . . one, boom, three, boom. I was bored out of my gord. This wasn't at all the drum playing I envisioned. Sitting in my room doing the one, two, three, boom routine wasn't to my liking. I wanted to have a full drum set, be in a band, play on stage, and sweat like a rock star. You see, I wanted the end result without the process. I wanted the reward without the risk and responsibility. It was nothing less than a grand illusion, a sustained effort in self-deception.

Not everyone has a drum story to tell, but I bet you can identify some area in your life where your commitment to the end result is undermined by your lack of interest in the journey it takes to get there. In the garden, Jesus is 100% committed to nothing else but the will of the Father. His heart isn't divided, distracted, or disengaged; it is focused on His mission. When it is only you and the Father there is little to get in the way, but when the Big But weeds of life fill the garden, it is difficult to find the cucumbers.

For many, God is nothing more than a cosmic slot machine dispensing candy and toys every time we put in a coin. He is something to be used, to lean upon only when we sense a need for Him. He is merely an addition to our lives, not life itself. Anything less than 100% commitment to the Lord is opening the doorway for Big But-itis. When our hearts are ablaze with love for Him, and our sole desire is to know Him and serve Him, we can do just about anything. Difficult roads, winding pathways, steep hills, off-roading, you name it—we can do it. When you are in love with the Father, you want nothing more than to align your will with His desires. That's what Jesus did in the garden. Is your heart divided? Does God have your attention? Are you 100% sold out? An undivided heart experiencing a "garden moment" becomes a precious occasion for communing with the Father. When it is just you and Him, it is enough.

Tiny But Stephen
Acts 7:54–60

Now when they heard this, they were cut to the quick, and they began gnashing their teeth at him. But being full of the Holy Spirit, he gazed intently into heaven and saw the glory of God, and Jesus standing at the right hand of God; and he said, "Behold, I see the heavens opened up and the Son of Man standing at the right hand of God." But they cried out with a loud voice, and covered their ears and rushed at him with one impulse. When they had driven him out of the city, they began stoning him; and the witnesses laid aside their robes at the feet of a young man named Saul. They went on stoning Stephen as he called on the Lord and said, "Lord Jesus, receive my spirit!" Then falling on his knees, he cried out with a loud voice, "Lord, do not hold this sin against them!" Having said this, he fell asleep.

Our last New Testament Tiny But example is Stephen, martyred in Acts 7 for his faith. Every time I read Acts 6–7 I am humbled, not only because of Stephen's deep commitment to Christ, but also because of the quality of his character.

Acts 6 identifies a problem in the early church: the neglect of Hellenistic Jewish widows in the distribution of food. Native Jewish widows, it seems, are given preference over other widows. While all were expecting to eat, only Jewish widows actually receive food. The widows receiving little to no food complain about the inequity.

Understanding their role to be teaching Scripture, the Twelve refrain from getting bogged down in such administrative and logistical issues. Their wise decision leads to the choosing of seven gifted men able for such work, whose qualifications are humbling. Here is a description of Stephen:

- *A man of good reputation 6:1*
- *A man full of the Spirit 6:1*
- *A man full of wisdom 6:1*
- *A man full of faith 6:5*
- *A man full of the Holy Spirit 6:5*
- *A man full of grace 6:8*
- *A man full of power 6:8*
- *A man who performs great wonders and signs 6:8*
- *A man who forgives his murderers 7:60*

Whenever God moves in great ways, there always seems to be resistance. Acts 6:7 says, "The word of God kept on spreading; and the number of the disciples continued to increase greatly in Jerusalem, and a great many of the priests were becoming obedient to the faith." Stephen engages in productive ministry by performing signs and wonders, proclaiming the gospel message, and bringing people to faith. He is so inspirational and convincing that even the priests are becoming followers of The Way, and that is what gets him in trouble—ministry with results.

His success brings out the enemy: men from a local synagogue. They arrive to argue with Stephen, strut their skills, and display their puffed-up knowledge. Instead, they run into a brick wall because "they were unable to cope with the wisdom and the Spirit with which he was speaking" (Acts 6:10). The battle begins. Like the giant Goliath against diminutive David, these men come prancing down the street to confront Stephen, believing they will surely bring him down with their superior skills and knowledge. Much to their chagrin, they are confounded, stifled, and unable to cope with the wisdom of his words and the Spirit behind them. It is futile to fight against God. Satan tries it in heaven, loses, and is kicked out, and these self-deceived men are fighting against a bold man backed by the Spirit of God. They will fail despite their best efforts.

Upon realizing that Stephen is too much for them, the men from the local synagogue raise false accusations for the sole purpose of stirring the crowd. It is the same tactic used against Jesus; accuse Him of blasphemy and paint Him as a rebel infidel. Their tactics work and before you know it, they are throwing stones at Stephen. Acts 7 encompasses Stephen's defense against the charges brought before him. In his lengthy sermon, he minces no words, telling it like it is. I suppose his words in Acts 7:51 don't go over too well: "You men who are stiff-necked and uncircumcised in heart and ears are always resisting the Holy Spirit; you are doing just as your fathers did." When Stephen finishes his fiery message, they move to stone him.

They lay their robes at the feet of Saul, freeing their arms for good aiming and powerful throws, and murder Stephen. Before he dies, Stephen sees heaven opening to receive him and in one last gesture of what a Tiny But looks like, he cries, "Lord, do not hold this sin against them!" (Acts 7:60)

Tiny But Stephen's Tiny But-speak might look something like this:

Stephen:

I have been told that I am a man of wisdom, faith, and full of the Spirit, *but* I know that it comes from You Lord. I know it is dangerous to go out and minister the way I do, *but* I just can't help proclaiming the good news. People see me performing signs and wonders, *but* it is really You working in me. Father, I have preached Your message to these false accusers and now they are stoning me, *but* Lord, please do not hold this against them.

Like Elijah challenging the prophets of Baal on Mt. Carmel, success in ministry brings out the enemy. In reality, Satan doesn't care if you read Scripture all day long, go to Bible studies, attend church, pray with friends, watch religious television, or share the good news, as long as you are unsuccessful and make no trouble for him. It's when you begin achieving results, making impact, and invading his territory that he gets upset and begins to fight back. Elijah successfully defeats the prophets of Baal, and Satan induces nasty Queen Jezebel to pursue Elijah's life. Stephen engages in powerful signs-and-wonders ministry, with many delivered from the kingdom of darkness to the kingdom of light. Outraged, Satan induces men from a local synagogue to silence him.

I watch my beloved Minnesota Vikings during fall football season. I enjoy the game. I follow the draft every year to see who we acquire. I discuss the season, players, and coaching staff with others who share my love for the Vikings. I watch the game with like-minded individuals, and we usually scream, holler, laugh, moan, groan, smile, exchange high fives, and roll our eyes, all in the same game.

But I am not a player. My involvement amounts to being a couch potato. I am not on the field. I am not breathing hard, running up and down the gridiron, sweating, tackling, and blocking. I am removed from the game. I am not an active participant. I am nothing but an excited spectator. No matter how I position myself on the couch, how much I yell and scream, or how many chicken wings I devour, I have absolutely no impact on the game.

It's the same way in the kingdom. Satan doesn't bother you too much as long as you are not an active player in the game. You can be as religious as you want; he doesn't care. You can talk about Jesus until you are blue in the face; he couldn't care less. It's when you get off the couch, put on the helmet and pads, and get on the field that he takes notice.

Big Buts hinder the team when they try to participate in the game. They struggle to run up and down the field, have little endurance for all four quarters, and even battle putting on the uniform. Even if they get on the field, to do so with a Big But jeopardizes the success of the team. Big Buts become liabilities rather than assets. It might be better for Big But Christians to remain on the couch where they do little damage instead of running on the field, flinging their Big Buts around, and bringing down the team.

It is spiritual success that brings out the enemy. Oh, he will let you grow a large church, initiate a television ministry, or have the appearance of success, but that isn't the kind of success that concerns him. You can be an unknown Christian from a rural town in western Oklahoma that nobody pays attention to, but you may be one giant threat to Satan because you get on your knees and engage the enemy. You are on the field, engaged in the game, participating, battling, winning, and finding success as you bind the enemy, hinder his plans, and take back wrongfully held territory. Stephen's Tiny But allows him to play the game and be successful. Though they stone him and take his life, they still do not win. Stephen's Tiny But gets the best of them, and in one final selfless act that testifies of God's grace, he forgives them and asks God to do the same.

Are you a player in the kingdom or a couch potato Christian? Are you merely struggling to survive in your own life, or are you taking back territory from the enemy? Does Satan leave you alone, or do you experience spiritual battles? Are you in condition to get on the field, or does your Big But make it hard for you to get off the couch? Stephen is a great example because his Tiny But-print allows him to get off the couch and onto the field, move in the power of the Spirit, and impact the lives of many people. Spiritual success brings out the enemy who employs But enlargement strategies so we become a hindrance and liability to our teammates. Stephen doesn't succumb to Big But-itis, even though he easily could have. Instead of a Big But bang as he is being martyred, Stephen's Tiny But gives testimony to the Lord, even in his death.

Old Testament Tiny Buts
Tiny But Joseph
Genesis 50:15–21

> When Joseph's brothers saw that their father was dead, they said, "What if Joseph bears a grudge against us and pays us back in full for all the wrong which we did to him!" So they sent a message to Joseph, saying, "Your father charged before he died, saying, 'Thus you shall say to Joseph, "Please forgive, I beg you, the transgression of your brothers and their sin, for they did you wrong."' And now, please forgive the transgression of the servants of the God of your father." And Joseph wept when they spoke to him. Then his brothers also came and fell down before him and said, "Behold, we are your servants." But Joseph said to them, "Do not be afraid, for am I in God's place? As for you, you meant evil against me, but God meant it for good in order to bring about this present result, to preserve many people alive. So therefore, do not be afraid; I will provide for you and your little ones." So he comforted them and spoke kindly to them.

There is hope in Joseph's story that despite the terrible injustices we bear, God is able to redeem them for His glory and our good. Wrongfully treated, Joseph has plenty of reason to be bitter, angry, and unforgiving. As his years in Egypt pass, Big But-itis could have set in like rigor mortis. Instead, Joseph's But becomes smaller, and his understanding and appreciation of God's grand design becomes crystal clear.

Joseph's story is a strange one indeed, with many twists and turns. With little effort, it could be turned into a best-selling novel. We have Jacob, father of a large family and an important figure in the history of Israel. He displays favoritism among his sons, loving Joseph more than all the others. The brothers know it. They feel it. It is undeniable. Jacob feels a special kinship with Joseph, since he is born during Jacob's older years. In fact, he honors Joseph by giving him a coat of many colors. No one else in the family receives such a special gift.

We have Joseph's brothers, who endure their father's favoritism toward Joseph. It is plain to them that Joseph is the favored son, and it makes them angry. They despise him—and in their eyes, he is nothing special. In reality, his most-favored status makes their lives miserable. His very presence is a constant reminder of how they never seem to measure up to Dad's expectations. Joseph represents all they despise about themselves, their father, and their brother.

We have Joseph himself, the favored son, who experiences the love of his father and the hatred of his brothers. The angry siblings solve their brotherly problem by selling Joseph into slavery and informing Dad that a wild beast killed him. After all, they reason, shepherding can be a dangerous job. Once in Egypt, Joseph's roller-coaster life involves highs and lows, from false accusations and imprison-ment to interpreting dreams and rising to second-in-command to Pharaoh. The game of life deals Joseph a bad hand, yet that losing hand becomes the providence of God. This is the stuff of Hollywood movies and best-selling novels.

Who in their right mind sells a sibling? What kind of family dynamic is this? Is Jacob's favoritism so offensive that his brothers believe this is the opportune moment for getting out of a prejudicial situation? Are the brothers just a little bit whacky, and this is nothing more than a severe case of sibling rivalry? We will never know for sure. Many siblings may feel like selling their brother or sister to the highest bidder, but in our society, they would be caught and punished. It is a cal-lous and selfish act for sure.

Bad things sometimes happen to good people. My father was one of those individuals. He didn't smoke, didn't drink, didn't chew, and wasn't overweight. He was a kind and gentle individual who loved his family and worked hard for the same company for forty years. Yet, from a physical perspective, he was dealt a bad hand. At the age of forty-three he underwent five-way bypass surgery. They sewed his chest up crooked, and one day he pulled a piece of wire from his leg, a forgot-ten souvenir from the surgeon. He endured nineteen angiograms, multiple hospital stays, numerous heart attacks, countless tests, aspiration into his lungs, placement on a respirator, multiple stents in his arteries that scarred over and closed, and finally, a second bypass surgery. Blood flow to his heart was so severely restricted that doctors informed him there was nothing more they could do. On top of that, he developed Parkinson's disease and lung problems associated with a chemical work environment. This ghastly hand couldn't have been dealt to a nicer guy. Life isn't fair, and bad things do happen to good people; just ask Joseph, or my father.

My father represents Mr. Average, the normal person who tries to do what is right and gets hit with Murphy's Law—anything that can go wrong, will go wrong. He didn't rise to second-in-command like Joseph, nor did he interpret dreams. In fact, since the age of forty-three, his life was one of chronic pain and uncertainty. Each night he went to bed wondering if he would wake up to see another day. Life can deal ordinary people a disastrous hand in many ways. The issue isn't being elevated to second-in-command or finding a pot of gold at the end of a rainbow; the point is that in whatever circumstance we find ourselves, whether being sold into slavery or facing severe medical issues, we do well to keep our Buts tiny and our vision of God big, just like Joseph.

I enjoy reading stories of individuals who endure great indignities or suffer severe loss. How do they respond and move forward after such a calamity? Joseph is one of those individuals I will enjoy speaking with in heaven about such issues.

We all know someone who has endured unspeakable things that would drag anyone under the water and hold them down. For some, their Big But goes ballistic with anger, resentment, and anti-God rhetoric, while others humble themselves, minimize But-ness, and gain a clearer view of God. Which one are you? Joseph is the latter and a good example of Tiny But talk during difficult times.

By no means do I intend to trivialize hardship and difficult circumstances. Nor do I imply that those enduring such hardship are involved in sin or that a vengeful God is punishing them from His large marble tribunal in the sky. We live in a broken world that affects us all in one way or another. God didn't promise us a rose garden when He called us to follow Him, but He *did* promise to be with us in our journey through this life.

While being appreciative of godly counselors who understand Scripture and the human condition, I often wonder if we are an over-medicated and over-therapeutic society. On the one extreme, zealous Christian counselors quote a few Scriptural passages, tell folks all they are doing wrong, belittle their faith commitment, shove a Bible down their throat, and expect them to get with the program. On the other extreme, self-reliant counselors without regard for Scripture, and whose approach to therapy is devoid of any wisdom from above, propose a multi-pill regimen, categorize clients according to the latest Diagnostic and Statistical Manual of Mental Disorders, and collect the insurance payment.

Neither extreme may have a category for Big But-itis. I am not the counselor type, and I have no desire to engage in such a difficult task, yet I can't help wondering what role But-ness plays in our mental health. In simple layman terms, those who experience great calamity seem to recover best when But size is reduced, especially through forgiveness. Terry Waite experienced this very phenomenon during his ordeal as a hostage in Lebanon from 1987–1991. His mission was to negotiate the release of other hostages, only to become one himself. Corrie ten Boom endured a similar experience as she helped Jews escape the Nazi Holocaust during WWII. Arrested in 1944 and sent to Ravensbruck concentration camp, she saw and endured great hardship. Yet, she forgave those who injured her in so many ways. I appreciate those who help navigate the bumps and potholes along life's journey, I just hope they don't forget how Big But-itis hinders us from knowing and experiencing our Lord.

The Joseph story presents numerous life lessons for further personal study. For instance, Joseph seems oblivious to his most-favored status and its effect upon his brothers. A bit on the cocky side, he proudly displays his robe of many colors mindful of how it distinguishes him from his siblings. He blabs about his dream of others bowing down to him. It isn't wrong for Joseph to share his dream, or wear his dazzling coat, but it may reveal a lack of wisdom and maturity on his part. When you are the most favored one, life seems pretty good. At this point, he may not have had the ability or willingness to empathize and put himself in his brothers' shoes. Later in his life, he is concerned for those less fortunate and oversees the distribution of food during a time of famine. Joseph has changed, matured, and grown up. His experiences soften him and enable him to empathize with others.

> In many ways, it is those closest to us who have the ability to inflict the greatest harm.

A wonderful friend of mine experienced the most-favored status in a slightly reversed manner. Growing up, she was the despised child, intentionally spurned by her parents in hurtful ways. Christmas is always a painful time as she remembers childhood years. She was the only one on Christmas day who didn't receive a gift from Mom and Dad. All the other siblings received gifts, and there she was, expectant, hopeful, and receiving absolutely nothing. This is merely one example of how her siblings secured most-favored status while she was despised and neglected. Everyone else obtained multi-colored robes but her. To this day, her siblings do not understand her perspective and feelings. After all, they always received Christmas gifts, and their most-favored status prevents them from empathizing and walking in her shoes.

Can you imagine being sold into slavery by your own family, just like Joseph? In many ways, it is those closest to us who have the ability to inflict the greatest harm. It is easier to accept being maimed by outsiders who know little about us than to be intentionally harmed by members of our own family. In my own life, this has been a difficult concept to accept. Within the church, I expected more from my spiritual family, and yet my greatest pains came from within the congregation itself. It is a member of Jesus' own inner circle of twelve who betrays Him. It is His own disciples who scatter during His arrest. It is Peter who denies ever knowing Him. It is the very people He came to help who cry, "Crucify Him. Crucify Him." The pain inflicted by those we love, trust, serve, and consider part of our family can lead to Big But-itis if we are not careful.

Joseph does something extremely helpful in reducing Big But-itis; he focuses on the big picture rather than every twist and turn of his life. He has the ability to view life from thirty thousand feet and sees the dimensions and boundaries of the forest below. It is possible to become fixated on one particular tree that prevents us from seeing the entire forest. Joseph, however, sees the bigger picture of what God is doing and has done in his life. "As for you, you meant evil against me, but God meant it for good in order to bring about this present result, to preserve many people alive" (Gen. 50:20). That's forest mentality. That's big picture viewing. That is the jug saying to the Potter, "Oh, I see why You made me and how my role fits in."

Had Joseph focused on his pain and misfortune, he would never have been able to see the larger plan of God for his life. The Lord was up to something much grander than Joseph could have ever imagined. Being sold into slavery is frightening. Being falsely accused of a crime you didn't commit is life-changing. Being unjustly confined in prison is humiliating. Being forgotten by a friend who promises to mention your situation to the king is excruciating. Knowing that your father believes you are dead when you are actually alive is heartbreaking.

As difficult as those circumstances are, they are overcome with a perspective of God's grand design. One way we overcome the But-ness of fixating on trees is to rise above them and view the forest. The Potter had a reason for creating you. Realizing He is the Grand Designer of our lives enables us to trust in His ability to guide and direct us in ways that honor Him and promote our good.

My son played basketball in his growing-up years. I was the father who practiced with him, taught him, played with him, and strategized with him. While he was the one on the court, we were in it together, each playing our own role. The time I enjoyed most was after the games when we downed pizza and pop while watching game video I had just recorded. I strategically sat on the bleachers where I could watch the plays unfold. My son, who was on the floor and in the thick of the battle, didn't have the perspective that I did. He was tree watching, while I saw the forest. As we watched the recorded game from a different perspective, he learned how plays developed, how to read picks, and how his game could improve. He gained a greater understanding and appreciation for basketball. In a similar way, God sees the game of life from a different vantage point. He sees things unfold, knows what's coming down the pike, and positions us exactly where we need to be in order to win the game.

But-ness entices us to question God, doubt His plan for our life, and focus on the trees in our life rather than the Grand Designer's plan as He leads us through the forest from a more informed perspective. Rising above the Big But trees and gaining a forest view entails a simple belief that God is in control. Either He is, or He isn't. We can't have it both ways. When good things come our way we thank the Lord for His blessing in our life, but when difficult situations arise, we believe God tucks His tail and runs away from us. Is He in control, or isn't He? It is a simple question. When life is viewed as the Master Designer strategically moving us to and fro, we realize He has not abandoned us. Life happens, but for Christians, life happens with a purpose. Paul notes in Romans 8:28, "And we know that God causes all things to work together for good to those who love God, to those who are called according to His purpose."

Some folks bounce around life like clothes in a dryer, free falling in extreme heat with no purpose and no hope of stopping the tumbling. Worrying about the future and regretting the past consumes their strength. Exhausted and weary, Big But-itis sets in, draining even more energy.

By recognizing God as the Master Weaver of our life, who sees the forest and leads us through the trees, we gain a more balanced perspective that looks like this:

- *Appreciate the past*
- *Live in the present*
- *Look expectantly to the future*

Big Buts often live the past in the present. They can't get over the bad hand dealt to them or their ungodly response in days gone by. They bring the past into the present, and in so doing, rob themselves of joy. They can't begin to ponder the future because they spend their present time reliving the past. They are stuck in an unhealthy and unproductive rut. Stuck-ness often equates to But-ness.

> Regret, anger, and hurt chain us to yesterday and prevent us from fully living in the present.

The past is exactly that—the past. It is water under the bridge, never to be relived again. It's like trying to put toothpaste back into the tube. The past is gone, for good or bad; it is no longer. Regret, anger, and hurt chain us to yesterday and prevent us from fully living in the present.

The past is certainly a part of our lives. While we can't undo what has already been done, how we choose to view events gone by either frees us for life in the present or binds us to the prison of the past. As I look back over my life, there have been ups and downs, good times and bad, mountain-top experiences and steep falls off the cliff. At times I have been a bonehead and other times truly used of God. What I don't do is relive the past in my present life. The memories, both good and bad, are still present, but I have learned to value and appreciate them. My past is used by God to shape and mold me. Some lessons I have learned and others I am still learning. The older I get, the more value and appreciation I place on yesterday. In looking back, I see the hand of God in so many ways that it encourages me and helps to control Big But-itis in the present.

While valuing and appreciating the past actually helps us successfully live in today's moment, navigating the present is not without its own challenges. A day in the past was at one time a present moment, and the present today will someday be in the past. Our actions, behaviors, and thoughts today are informed by the value, appreciation, and lessons learned from days gone by. Joseph looks back at his life and sees the hand of God written all over it. His ability to live in the present is encouraged by his appreciation of the past. He is grateful to even be alive after his brothers sell him into slavery. He refuses sexual overtures from his master's wife, and that encourages him to remain faithful to God. He appreciates the fact that a fellow inmate finally remembers him to Pharaoh. Rising to second-in-command in all of Egypt put him in a powerful position to help others, even those who sought his downfall.

Joseph knew he was mistreated and experienced great hardship, but he chose to view those events in light of God's grand design for his life. Had it not been for the past, he would have been unable to save his family in the days of severe famine. He humbly recognizes God's hand, and it encourages him in the present.

If we value and appreciate yesterday and live fully in the present, we are better able to anticipate God's leading in the future. We affirm the past by recognizing His grand design, live in the present knowing He guides our steps, and look forward to the Master Potter's future assignment. Whatever and wherever it is, we know He is in control and leads us toward His glory and our good.

By appreciating the past, living in the present, and looking expectantly to the future, Joseph is able to forgive his brothers for their ill-treatment, minister to them, see his father again, and provide sustenance to his family. Once cocky and without empathy for his brothers, Joseph now weeps with love at the sight of them. God has accomplished a great work in his life and uses him to bless others.

When we are dealt a bad hand and endure the ill-treatment of others, focusing on the Grand Designer and His greater purpose for our life helps reduce Big But-itis. Live in the present by appreciating and valuing the past, listen carefully to His still, small voice today, and look forward to His next steps for you.

Tiny Buts Shadrach, Meshach, and Abednego
Daniel 3:13–18

Then Nebuchadnezzar in rage and anger gave orders to bring Shadrach, Meshach and Abed-nego; then these men were brought before the king. Nebuchadnezzar responded and said to them, "Is it true, Shadrach, Meshach and Abed-nego, that you do not serve my gods or worship the golden image that I have set up? Now if you are ready, at the moment you hear the sound of the horn, flute, lyre, trigon, psaltery and bagpipe and all kinds of music, to fall down and worship the image that I have made, very well. But if you do not worship, you will immediately be cast into the midst of a furnace of blazing fire; and what god is there who can deliver you out of my hands?" Shadrach, Meshach and Abed-nego replied to the king, "O Nebuchadnezzar, we do not need to give you an answer concerning this matter. If it be so, our God whom we serve is able to deliver us from the furnace of blazing fire; and He will deliver us out of your hand, O king. But even if He does not, let it be known to you, O king, that we are not going to serve your gods or worship the golden image that you have set up."

The fiery furnace narrative is one of the all-time greatest Tiny But stories ever found in the Old Testament. I am tempted to use words like "bestest" and "amazinable" to reveal my intense delight, but since they aren't real words, I can't. You will just have to believe me when I say how much I admire Shadrach, Meshach and Abed-nego for their courage, commitment, and Itsy-Bitsy But.

There seems to be an alluring, yet adverse interest with golden images in the Old Testament. While Moses is on the mountain top receiving the Ten Commandments, Aaron is busy collecting gold jewelry from the wilderness wanderers to fashion a golden calf to worship. It is a low point in the history of Israel, and of all people, Aaron? He knew better than that!

Nebuchadnezzar, on the other hand, is a deeply troubled soul who believes in himself rather than Yahweh. Consolidated power is his drink of choice. As king of the Babylonian Empire, he is known for conquering Judah, sacking Jerusalem, destroying the Temple, and driving the Jews into exile. In his spare time, he builds the infamous hanging gardens of Babylon. Now, he constructs a large object standing nine feet wide by ninety feet high, and at its dedication ceremony, decrees that everyone must bow down and worship the image. The price for disobedience is a personal tour of a fiery hot furnace, a most unpleasant demise.

When Shadrach, Meshach, and Abed-nego rebuff the order, blabber mouths run to the king and report their refusal to obey. Infuriated that someone is challenging his authority, the three men are summoned to account for their behavior. One more chance is afforded for a change of mind; obey the king's decree, or be thrown into the incendiary blaze. Nebuchadnezzar closes the little pep talk with mocking words, "What god is there who can deliver you out of my hands?" (Dan. 3:15). What insolence! He is nothing more than a floppy puppet in the hand of the Lord, acting as if he controls the entire world.

Listen to the phenomenal Tiny But-speak of Shadrach, Meshach, and Abed-nego in Daniel 3:16–18:

O Nebuchadnezzar, we do not need to give you an answer concerning this matter. If it be *so,* our God whom we serve is able to deliver us from the furnace of blazing fire; and He will deliver us out of your hand, O king. ***But*** even if He does not, let it be known to you, O king, that we are not going to serve your gods or worship the golden image that you have set up.

To address the king in this manner takes some guts. In their deepest being, they know God is able to save them, if He chooses, and if not, they accept the inevitable outcome of becoming crispy critters for the kingdom. With a fire blazing behind them and a furious king in front of them, they stick to their guns.

This is an opportune time for Big But-itis to work its magic. If its initial inflammation doesn't scare them to bow down the first time they hear the music, standing face-to-face with the king ought to kick the disease into high gear. When the choice is between worshipping God or worshipping an image, even at the king's command and under the threat of death, the right thing to do isn't difficult to ascertain. This isn't one of those decisions requiring an internal wrestling match to discover the will of God. His will has already been revealed in Exodus 20:3–4.

> You shall have no other gods before Me. You shall not make for yourself an idol, or any likeness of what is in heaven above or on the earth beneath or in the water under the earth. You shall not worship them or serve them; for I, the Lord your God, am a jealous God.

For Shadrach, Meshach, and Abed-nego, the issue wasn't *what* they should do, but whether they *will* obey what God has already revealed, even in such strenuous circumstances. In this situation, knowing what is right is easy; obeying when your life is at stake is more difficult.

Had Big But-itis carried the day, Shadrach, Meshach, and Abed-nego would have found a way to bow down, worship the image, save face, and devise a legitimate sounding rationale to alleviate any guilt. Between the three of them, they could have conspired to help each other feel virtuous while succumbing to the Big But Syndrome. Their discussion might have sounded something like this:

Meshach:
Hey Shad, I've been thinking about bowing down before the king's image. We have a pretty good ministry going on here and it would be a shame to lose it. God needs us here to be witnesses for Him, don't you think?

Shadrach:
That's a good idea Meshach. I wonder if we could bow down just this once, get it over with, and then get on with our ministry. It seems to me that God would certainly understand our unique situation. What do you think Abed-nego?

Abed-nego:

Well, Scripture is quite clear that we are not to worship other gods or bow down before idols of any kind, but I am not sure God had this particular circumstance in mind when those words were penned so long ago. These are different times. We probably could do it once, given the circumstances, and ask forgiveness if need be, and then get on with helping others live obedient and faithful lives unto the Lord.

The three of them could have conjured up a reasonable-sounding excuse to save their own skin, but they didn't. To a man, not one of them backed down from what was right and what they knew to be the clear teaching of Scripture. Big But-itis tried to sneak in through the backdoor, only to realize it was shut tight and locked. This is a day when Tiny Buts prevail to the glory of God.

Their obedient refusal to worship the image angers the king. Shadrach, Meshach, and Abed-nego are kind in their approach but firm in their defiance of the king's command. Nebuchadnezzar is used to being feared, not confronted, and was "filled with wrath, and his facial expression was altered toward Shadrach, Meshach and Abed-nego. He answered by giving orders to heat the furnace seven times more than it was usually heated" (Dan. 3:19). Just as he promised, he binds the three men and tosses them into the intense fire.

As the king looks on with prurient interest, he notices four unbound men walking around in the fire when he expected instant incineration. God intervenes and sends His messenger to protect these three godly individuals. When they come out of the furnace, everyone notices that "the fire had no effect on the bodies of these men nor was the hair of their head singed, nor were their trousers damaged, nor had the smell of fire even come upon them" (Dan. 3:27). It's hard to get out of a restaurant these days without some twinge of smoke smell. It was as if Shadrach, Meshach, and Abed-nego hadn't even been near a fire. King Nebuchadnezzar recognizes the miraculous deliverance and decrees that no one should speak evil of the Lord.

Had I been in their shoes and faced similar circumstances, would I bow or would I obey? Would I justify saving my own skin, or would I simply do the right thing, no matter what the cost? I have a sneaky suspicion that I would bow to save my own skin, dishonor God with some lousy excuse, and miss out on His prosperous blessing for my life.

Shadrach, Meshach, and Abed-nego represent the kind of devoted followers we admire and desire to emulate. Conditions were ripe for a Big But tsunami to slam into their lives, yet, Tiny Buts triumph. Big Buts don't have to erupt; they *can* and *should* be held in check. Several key attitudes help Shadrach, Meshach, and Abed-nego maintain Tiny Buts in a Big But situation.

They are intimately familiar with Scripture.

Knowledge of Scripture is essential for overcoming Big But tsunamis. Since the founding of America, our generation may be the most biblically illiterate of all. With churches in every neighborhood, Christian bookstores in virtually every town, famous preachers pummeling the airwaves, and easy access to printed and digital Bibles, we are without excuse. The issue isn't a lack of information, for the ubiquitous word of Scripture abounds everywhere, and in nearly every form; the issue is one of priority.

If you continually overdraw your bank account, you soon realize the sting of extra bank fees. So what do you do? You learn to balance a checkbook and keep track of your balance. If you continually drive your car until it runs out of gas, you realize how costly this is in time and convenience. So what do you do? You learn to keep appropriate levels of gasoline in the tank. If you continually fall in your faith for lack of knowledge, you realize how costly this is in terms of spiritual growth and success. So what do you do? Increase your understanding by ensuring that Bible study is a high priority in your daily routine.

This is not a difficult concept to grasp. In any other area of life, we invest time and energy to avoid costly mistakes. We ensure appropriate funds are in the bank and keep gas in the tank, but when it comes to dedicating ourselves to Bible study, we remain quite content to plop our butts down in a Sunday morning pew once a week while being spoon fed from the pulpit.

Advanced degrees in theology or biblical studies are unnecessary for understanding Scripture. All you really need is an interest and commitment of time. Without interest or commitment, Scripture remains a mystery. Increased knowledge doesn't come by chance or osmosis; it comes by reading, meditating, and studying. Shadrach, Meshach, and Abed-nego clearly understand the directive of God in the matter of worshipping idols. The issue is settled. God's desire is clear. They know what Scripture teaches because they are familiar with it. If you want success over But-ness, become familiar with the words of Scripture as a daily preventative.

They recognize that God is the Potter and they are the clay.

This allows them to rest in the sovereignty of the Maker and His wisdom for their life. Standing before the king and testifying of the Lord isn't a mere coincidence; rather, it is a divine appointment. Shadrach, Meshach, and Abed-nego face a challenging situation. Their response literally becomes a life or death decision. Being secure in the Potter's ability and the purpose of His design allows them to say, "God can save us if He desires, but whatever happens, we will not bow down to any image." If you want success over But-ness, life must be lived on the Master's terms. We are players in the production, not the producers of the play.

Shadrach, Meshach, and Abed-nego are 100% committed to doing what is right despite their circumstances.

Do Christians have a price tag on their loyalty? In other words, at what point does our commitment to Christ fly out the window? Will we chuck it all for $1,000, or $5,000? Will we throw it all away for fame, fortune, or power? Will our commitment go down the drain for one-night of sensual pleasure? Will we readily cast aside our commitment knowing that by bowing to the king's image, we can avoid certain death?

Price tags, I imagine, change from person to person and from circumstance to circumstance. Whatever the price may be, the very fact that there is a point where we would sacrifice our commitment to God is truly bothersome. For Shadrach, Meshach, and Abed-nego, there is no "price tag" theology. Offer what you will, their answer is always the same. Fame, fortune, sensual pleasure, power and control—you name it, the answer is always, "Not for sale!"

With a foundational knowledge of Scripture, an acknowledgment of God's purpose for our life, and a sold-out commitment to follow no matter the circumstance, Big But-itis is starved of the essential nutrients necessary for its growth and expansion.

Tiny But Joshua

Joshua 24:14–15

> Now, therefore, fear the LORD and serve Him in sincerity and truth; and put away the gods which your fathers served beyond the River and in Egypt, and serve the LORD. If it is disagreeable in your sight to serve the LORD, choose for yourselves today whom you will serve: whether the gods which your fathers served which were beyond the River, or the gods of the Amorites in whose land you are living; but as for me and my house, we will serve the LORD.

Our final Old Testament Tiny But is Joshua, who displays unwavering commitment to Yahweh. Joshua is there in the beginning and witnesses the exodus from Egypt. He is there in the end, conquering and possessing the Promised Land. Extensive experience fills his life and he is a "been there, done that" kind of guy. Born in Egypt, he and his friend Caleb realize that Egypt is a place of hardship and restraint for the Hebrews. He knows of Moses and Aaron, and personally experiences the Lord's miraculous deliverance from the bonds of slavery.

Traveling in the desert with Moses, he watches God miraculously provide food, water, and clothing that doesn't wear out. He hears the former slaves curse their current conditions, complain against their leaders, and look backward, pining for the chains of Egypt with one eye, and with the other, straining to see what God's next steps will bring. He witnesses the pillar of cloud by day and the pillar of fire by night. He observes the Shekinah glory surrounding the Tent of Meeting and the glow upon Moses' face after being in the presence of God.

As one of the spies sent to survey the Promised Land, he and Caleb communicate a positive report and encourage the assembly to move forward with God's divine plan. The people nearly stone him for this. As a commander in Israel's army, Joshua leads the charge against Jericho, a formidable fortress in Canaan that must be overtaken. The city isn't conquered by Israel's great military prowess, strategic planning, or Joshua's leadership strength; it is captured unconventionally, by blowing trumpets, marching around the city wall, and shouting. How is that for a plan of attack? For most of us, that isn't a plan, but a death wish. Yet Joshua obeys, and if God wants him to march around a city blowing trumpets, then that is what he is going to do. The strong fortress walls tumble down and Israel conquers Jericho with little resistance. It is yet another one of God's astonishing miracles Joshua witnesses.

As the personal minister and servant of Moses, the great leader builds into the life of Joshua, mentoring and marking him for a time when he would take over the reins. Joshua isn't impatient, doesn't badmouth his mentor, and refuses to manipulate events or circumstances to advance his career. Instead, he is content with pleasing the Lord in whatever role he is called to perform. Called as a commander, he is a noble one. Called as a spy, he is first-class. Called to serve Moses, he ministers with love and loyalty. It is Joshua who accompanies him partway up the mountain as Moses receives the Ten Commandments.

Joshua has seen it all, both good and bad, the mountain tops and the valleys. Through thick and thin, he remains faithful. His commitment to Yahweh is resolute. Not once do we find him vacillating in his allegiance and devotion to the Lord.

Recognizing Joshua's genuine character, his deep trust in the Lord, and his heart to serve, Moses calls him before the assembly and publicly declares to the people, "I am a hundred and twenty years old today; I am no longer able to come and go, and the LORD has said to me, 'You shall not cross this Jordan'" (Dt. 31:2). It is time for Moses to step aside and make room for Israel's next leader. God chooses Joshua to replace him. "Behold, the time for you to die is near; call Joshua, and present yourselves at the tent of meeting, that I may commission him" (Dt. 31:14). The Lord commissions Moses' successor, saying, "Be strong and courageous, for you shall bring the sons of Israel into the land which I swore to them, and I will be with you" (Dt. 31:23).

Moses' role was to free the people from Egyptian bondage; Joshua's role is to conquer and possess the Promised Land. Joshua has the experience, the big picture, the right heart attitude, and a resolute belief in God's calling and abilities. The Israelites are at a crossroad; will they remain in the wilderness, or move forward to claim what has been promised?

It is a watershed moment in Israel's history. While Joshua has served with distinction and faithfulness in times past, he has never before been the leader of an entire nation. This is a big moment in his life with long-lasting repercussions for the future of Israel. How will Joshua react to his new calling and responsibilities? Will we see the battle of the Buts emerge?

Joshua accepts the Lord's commissioning and conquers six nations and thirty-one kings in possessing the Promised Land. He embraces the calling of God upon his life without a battle of the Buts. Joshua's history of allegiance, devotion, obedience, faithfulness, and servant mindset pays huge dividends in this very moment. Often we want great responsibility without the proving ground that readies us for such a role. This principle is summed up in the parable of the unrighteous steward when Jesus says, "He who is faithful in a very little thing is faithful also in much; and he who is unrighteous in a very little thing is unrighteous also in much" (Lk. 16:10). What keeps Joshua's But from erupting in fear, doubt, and arrogance at a time when great things are expected from him, is years and years of faithful obedience to God. When the time arrives for an increased role in the kingdom, his response is second-nature. His training pays off. There is no battle of the Buts.

> Often we want great responsibility without the proving ground that readies us for such a role.

Joshua realizes the tremendous responsibility placed upon his shoulders. He will not be successful without the Lord's help and anointing. At this critical juncture, when the time to go forth and conquer arrives, he takes a stand, and challenges the people to commit themselves to the Lord, saying, "choose for yourselves today whom you will serve" (Josh. 24:15). The last time he challenged the assembly to follow God, they attempted to stone him. Yet, he doesn't back down and lets them know what decision he has made, "as for me and my house, we will serve the LORD" (Josh. 24:15).

Divided loyalties contribute to spiritual failure, as Jesus mentions in Mark 3:25: "If a house is divided against itself, that house will not be able to stand." Where do your loyalties reside? What captures your heart? Joshua's words for a nation at the crossroad are apropos for us today. God doesn't want a piece of our heart; He wants all of our heart. He doesn't want to be a compartment in our life; He wants to be our very life.

In my younger years, I fell head over heels for a young girl of missionary parents. She captured my heart and I traveled many miles out of state to visit her. I wrote letters, treated her right, and did all that was within my power to win her over. But she had divided loyalties. She liked me, and at times had feelings for me, but I knew I didn't have her heart.

I had a piece of it, but not all of it. No matter how hard I tried, her fractured heart brought me pain. A heart must be given, rather than compelled. Obedience out of obligation or guilt isn't a heart motivated by love, but one forced through coercion or compulsion. When a heart is forced, the receiving party feels used, unappreciated, unloved, and senses broken devotion. But when a heart is freely given and fully committed, the receiving party experiences unspeakable joy, love, and acceptance.

> A heart must be given, rather than compelled. Obedience out of obligation or guilt isn't a heart motivated by love, but one forced through coercion or compulsion.

God wants our heart. Joshua gives his whole heart to the Lord without one ounce of divided loyalty. Though he had multiple opportunities to embrace half-hearted allegiance and perform out of obligation and guilt, he didn't. His But remained tiny because his heart was absolutely in love with God, fully engaged, and fully committed—no holding back. If we desire to move forward and conquer the Promised Land God has for our lives, our hearts must likewise be fully committed to Him.

Bible Tiny But Summary

In this chapter, we discovered that not all Buts are bad. We notice Big Buts more so than Tiny Buts because the former are so painful and tend to stick with us a bit longer. Like dragons whose fiery breath leaves nothing but charred timber and a scorched earth, Big But-itis produces unwanted and negative effects in our lives. But-ness becomes as dragon breath to us, yet God is able to use these adverse experiences and turn them into learning lessons for our good and His glory. This doesn't mean that He advocates, supports, or condones Big But-itis or painful experiences; for He would much rather we exhibit Tiny Buts and enjoy Him forever. Yet, fully aware that we live in a broken world where sooner or later we get hit with pain, He doesn't allow us to be overcome but creates a path for moving us on to the other side, stronger and better.

We all use the "but" word in sentences and have some sort of But perspective from which we operate on a daily basis. While the painful effects of Big But-itis seem to grab the headlines, we must not forget the many Tiny Buts out there that inspire, encourage, and motivate us. The difference between a Tiny But and a Big But is that one obstructs our view of God, while the other enhances it. The question isn't whether we are using the "but" word, or possess a But perspective, for the answer to that question is an unqualified "yes." We all use "but" and we all view God and circumstances through some sort of But lens. The questions to ask are, "Do I possess a Big But or a Tiny But? Does my But perspective obstruct my view of God and hinder my relationship with Him, or does it enhance my view of God and advance my relationship with Him?"

Big Buts filter circumstances through the perspective of how actions and thoughts can be conditioned, justified, or excused because of discontentment with God. Given the same situation, a Tiny But filters circumstances through the perspective of how actions and thoughts can unconditionally, without justification or excuse, be aligned with the Father's will in order to experience contentment with God. These are two very different ways of living, looking at the world, and viewing God. Big Buts obstruct; Tiny Buts enhance. How we choose to react is up to us. We can allow Big But-itis to set in, or we can look for God's handiwork in all situations. The choice we make leads to the outcome we experience.

We examined numerous Old and New Testament Tiny But examples that bring inspiration, hope, and strength to our lives. Jesus lived life without one Big But explosion and becomes a trustworthy example for us. Shadrach, Meshach, and Abed-nego are unwilling to bend in their commitment to Yahweh, no matter what the cost. Despite being sold into slavery and cast into prison, Joseph finds within his Tiny But heart to forgive those who wronged him and becomes a blessing to his enemies. The bleeding woman who is socially isolated, religiously unclean, and living a pitiful existence risks all to meet the Great Physician. Thrilling! Inspirational! These are the stories that bring tears of joy to our dry eyes and cause us to say, "Yes, that's the way it should be. I want to live my life like that."

THE TINY BUT PERSPECTIVE

Tiny But Definition:	A Tiny But is a perspective or behavior that unconditionally, and without justification or excuse, aligns itself with the Father's will and experiences contentment with God.
We experience the Tiny But of others some of the time.	**Their** Tiny But 1) is easy to identify, though not as prevalent, 2) is inspirational to us, 3) advances the work of God, and 4) enhances God's reputation.
We engage in our own Tiny But behavior.	**Our** Tiny But 1) is easy to identify, though not as prevalent, 2) is inspirational to others, 3) advances the work of God, and 4) enhances God's reputation.
There are many examples of Tiny Buts.	We examined 1) New Testament Tiny Buts, and 2) Old Testament Tiny Buts.
Conclusion:	Not everyone experiences or engages in Tiny But behavior, but when they do, they inspire others and their view of God is unobstructed.
Encourage or discourage?	Tiny But perspectives can have a powerful impact, yet their scarcity could discourage us. When we intentionally employ Tiny But behaviors and thinking, we experience God, help others experience him, and we are encouraged.

Now that we know the difference between a Big But and a Tiny But, I created a Top Ten Big But list and a Top Ten Tiny But list. Your list may look different than mine, but it helps us understand the differences on a practical level.

EXCUSES VERSUS DECLARATIONS

Top Ten Big But Excuses	Top Ten Tiny But Declarations
1. But, I don't want to.	1. But, I will go wherever You lead me.
2. But, it's not my fault.	2. I stumbled, but please forgive me.
3. But, I can't.	3. I can't, but You can.
4. But, I am afraid.	4. But, You protect and provide for me.
5. But, only on the condition that…	5. But I will, without condition.
6. But, I want my way.	6. Not my will, but Yours.
7. But, I am an exception.	7. But, I yield to You in all things.
8. But, I don't trust you.	8. I believe, but help my unbelief.
9. But, I might as well give up.	9. But, I can do all things through Christ.
10. But, it's not fair.	10. But, I yield to Your sovereignty.

THE BIG BUT SOLUTION

T his book contends that all Christians wrestle with Big But-itis. I even divulged a secret of my own: I have Big But flare-ups myself. Examples from the Old and New Testament help us identify a few of the many potential Big But issues out there. Since Big Buts can erupt at any time over any issue, resolution becomes more difficult because of the sheer volume of possible Big But problems. Discovering and applying a specific solution for each particular item is overwhelming.

For the sake of argument, if there are one thousand objects of But-ness, then we need to develop one thousand unique solutions for one thousand specific Big But problems. As culture changes and progresses over time, new issues of But-ness emerge, and fresh solutions must be developed to address each newfangled Big But issue. This is time consuming, burdensome, and maybe impossible. Carrying around a Big But Solution Manual for every infinite object of But-ness is impractical (not to mention extremely heavy). This puts us back into the realm of legalism, trying to invent a rule for every situation that currently exists or could possibly exist in the future. Surely, there has to be a better way.

Clustering similar Big But issues around eight magnets brings the infinite number of objects down to a manageable amount. Instead of thousands of specific solutions unique to each problem, we now have to memorize only eight different solutions—one for each cluster. But what if a new cluster is added or if others create different clusters? What about all the specific details, offshoots, and exceptions to be considered for each cluster? Take fear, for instance—is there a specific solution for fear of the dark, a different one for fear of risk, one for fear of losing a job, or fear of being asked to pray in public? By clustering similar issues of But-ness, we can more easily identify at-risk areas in our lives, but it does little to reduce the actual number of solutions required. While there is enough similarity for placement into one category over another, there are still many nuanced differences that beg for distinction. While there may be commonality, there is no unanimity, or identical issues.

Clustering allows us to identify and understand But-ness in our life. We recognize that we are not alone; most believers struggle with similar Big But problems. Trying to learn thousands and thousands of solutions for the infinite issues of But-ness is impractical. I can't even remember why I opened the refrigerator door most of the time. I am not convinced that I could even remember eight cluster solutions. And realizing there are differences within the clusters makes me question whether eight solutions could adequately accommodate all of the nuanced differences. Is it possible to find a single process, a single antidote, a single solution that can be utilized for all matters of But-ness, no matter what the issue? If there were such a thing, I could remember something like that. Here comes the big top megaphone announcement. Drum roll, please. Walla! Ladies and gentlemen, please give it up for the Big But Cleansing Cycle introduced in this chapter!

The Big But Cleansing Cycle is one cycle, one solution, one process for all objects of But-ness. It doesn't matter whether you put one thousand items through the cycle or eight clusters; this single cycle works for all of them. Whatever enters the cycle is filtered of its contaminants and since the process is ongoing, our thoughts, values, and behaviors are continually being cleansed. No more discovering, memorizing, and applying thousands of specific solutions. No more wrestling with eight cluster solutions. Now, we have one cleansing solution for all objects of But-ness that helps us move from a Small God, Big But perspective to a Big God, Tiny But viewpoint.

Big But Spotters

I am a problem solver. I help organizations, individuals, and groups with competing interests work together in finding mutually agreeable solutions. Throw into the mix limited resources, varying educational levels, diverse personality types, assorted past experiences, hidden agendas, and you have the necessary ingredients for a human Molotov cocktail. Togetherness can trigger this incendiary device and send people packing.

Resolving issues and exploring solutions to problems requires participation from everyone involved. That's right, participation. Occasionally, someone only wants to point out problems rather than contribute toward a solution. They are Big But spotters, skilled in observing and registering all the wrong things others are doing. While it is certainly important to identify issues in need of resolution, finger-pointing must give way to participatory engagement for agreement to occur. Yet, there are those who only want to finger-point, and they become obstacles to forward movement.

After reading about Big But-itis and its destructive influences to this point, you may think I am merely finger-pointing, the very thing I am against. The problem isn't the identification of issues, but finger-pointing *only*, and in an effort to obfuscate solutions. In this chapter, I actually propose a solution to the Big But problem. If all we do is assign blame, we accomplish nothing. Spotting Big Buts is useless unless we know how to overcome them and help others conquer the debilitating disease. By necessity, discovering and applying an antidote that frees us from the malady is essential. It is time to focus on the Big But Solution.

Three Easy Steps . . . Right!

My eyes typically roll in disgust whenever Christians promote three easy steps to—you name it—overcoming alcoholism, discovering God's will, being a better spouse, raising righteous teenagers, etc. It is like saying the solution for someone in poverty is to get rich. This is lollipop Christianity, and I loathe it. The three easy step method smacks of slick marketing campaigns that induce others to buy a product, like an 1800s elixir for what ails you. It is nothing more than a boastful claim with little results.

Let's take something simple, for instance, like putting on our shoes in three easy steps: 1) lift foot, 2) insert foot into shoe, and 3) tie shoelaces. Pretty simple, isn't it? So I give it a try, only to discover that I am unable to lift my foot because of a severely strained muscle. Can I bypass step one? Can I put my shoe on without lifting my foot? Do I search for new shoes that allow me to put them on without lifting my foot, a sandal perhaps? Should I lie sideways to put them on as an alternative method? I can't even begin step one.

> I am all for simplifying things and making them easy to grasp, but not at the expense of misleading people or dumbing down substantive issues.

Now I try to insert my foot into the shoe (step two), only to find that it will not go in. What if my foot is swollen? What if the shoe size is incorrect? Does it matter what type of shoe it is? Are the instructions different for sandals, cowboy boots, snow boots, or penny loafers? Does it matter which foot goes into which shoe, or is the key merely to insert a foot?

The third step is to tie the shoelaces. What if the shoe is a slip-on and has no shoelaces? What if the shoelaces are too short, or broken, or absent? What if the shoe is a boot with buckles and zippers? What if the current style is to leave laces untied? What if I don't know how to tie shoelaces?

As you can see, three easy steps become more complex than we imagined. It might make for a catchy marketing campaign, but in reality, it lacks substantive depth to really be helpful. I am all for simplifying things and making them easy to grasp, but not at the expense of misleading people or dumbing down substantive issues. Just where the balance between simplicity and substance lies is likely subjective and arguable depending on one's priorities and goals, yet we must be careful with the easy step process as it often frustrates people. They engage in the easy steps with gusto, but rarely find success because they are shallow instructions, never digging below the surface to core issues.

In overcoming Big But-itis, I could throw out an easy three-step process, but that would be misleading and make superficial what is really core issue material. What I will put forth, however, is a Big But Cleansing Cycle that acts to filter out contaminants in our thinking and behavior. No matter what comes in the front end, fear, unbelief, greed, pride, etc., it all goes through a filtering process that helps move us from But-ness to But-less, from a Big But, Tiny God outlook to a Big God, Tiny But viewpoint. It is not simply three steps and we are done; it is a way of being, a way of thinking, and a way of filtering that which is negative and harmful. It is nothing inventive, there is no wow factor, and it isn't rocket science, but it is a solid way to reduce Big But flare-ups. Before revealing the Big But Cleansing Cycle, let me discuss what it is designed to do.

Filtering Contaminants

The Big But Cleansing Cycle is designed to filter out the bad and keep the good. It is not a one-time pill we swallow, but a way of thinking. It is not some magic potion I mixed up in the darkness of my basement that cures all our illnesses. It is more like a furnace filter that screens circulated air so we don't breathe nasty pollutants into our lungs. This is the antidote for an inflammation of Big But-itis. When bitten by the Big But bug, we need some way to reduce the inflammation and become whole again. The Big But Cleansing Cycle helps us do that.

While on vacation in beautiful Wind River Canyon, Wyoming, my father warned us to be careful of rattlesnakes. We listened hard for the rattling of their tails. The bite from its deadly venom could result in death, since we were miles from the nearest town and lacked an antidote. When bitten by the Big But bug, the Big But Cleansing Cycle acts as an antidote; yet, instead of a one-time shot in the arm for a solitary event, this antidote is more like a constant intravenous drip.

A beautiful river also winds its way through Wind River Canyon. It isn't the dirty, brown river I grew up with in Iowa, but a crystal clear river. Rocks punch through its surface and the river bed can be seen with the naked eye. It is absolutely stunning. I can't wait to go there again and experience the beauty of God's creation.

What often escapes the casual observer is the vital role river rocks play in the health of the stream. As water tumbles over and through the rocks, a cleansing action occurs that removes impurities from the river. The rocks, in essence, help purify the water.

A final filtering illustration might be helpful. I have a love affair with fish aquariums. While growing up, my freshwater aquarium contained guppies, neon tetras, swordtails, and algae suckers, while I always yearned for a school of silver dollar fish. Coming home from school one afternoon, I discovered one of my swordtails, known for jumping out of the water, lying on the floor outside the aquarium. Frolicking one day, he must have accidentally jumped out of the tank and landed on the carpet thinking to himself, "Oops!" I picked him up, put him back in the tank, and in short time, he was swimming to live another day. I guess the timing of my arrival was fortuitous for my fish friend.

As a contained ecosystem, aquariums quickly turn to green muck if not cleaned on a regular basis. Aquarium water is purified through a filter system. A pump circulates water through several layers of charcoal, rocks, and foams that absorb or trap pollutants, while sustaining life in the fish tank. Without this filtering devise, fish die.

The Big But Cleansing Cycle isn't intended to be a one-time fix for an ongoing problem. Instead, it acts as a continuous filtering system designed to sustain abundant life, create clarity of thought, and remove contaminants so we can experience God more abundantly.

The Big But Cleansing Cycle

The various stages of the Big But Cleansing Cycle could be stated this way:

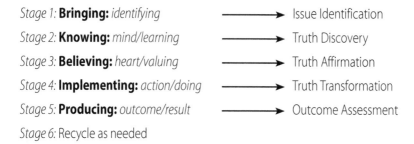

Stage 1: **Bringing:** *identifying* ⟶ Issue Identification

Stage 2: **Knowing:** *mind/learning* ⟶ Truth Discovery

Stage 3: **Believing:** *heart/valuing* ⟶ Truth Affirmation

Stage 4: **Implementing:** *action/doing* ⟶ Truth Transformation

Stage 5: **Producing:** *outcome/result* ⟶ Outcome Assessment

Stage 6: Recycle as needed

Before discussing the various stages of the filtering process, it is helpful to see the cycle in chart form and in an illustrated diagram.

BIG BUT CLEANSING CYCLE CHART

STAGE	TITLE	TASK	QUESTIONS
1	Issue Identification	Identifying and exposing the issue.	What is the issue(s) causing Big But-itis?
2	Truth Discovery	Learning what God has to say about the issue.	What is true and what is false about this issue?
3	Truth Affirmation	Choosing to value God's truth over lies.	Will I choose to believe lies or God's truth?
4	Truth Transformation	Implementing behaviors, skills, and attitudes that advance truth in our lives.	How should I live in light of the truth discovered? What behavior, skills, and attitudes will help advance truth in my life?
5	Outcome Assessment	Evaluating the result of transformational changes.	Has Big But-itis been reduced? Is there still work to be done?
6	Recycle As Needed		

Stage 1 Filter: *Issue Identification*

Rest assured, we can bring any issue or problem to God. He is not intimidated or repulsed by the fact that we have so many. He desires that we bring our needs before Him; nothing is too big or too small. Matthew 11:28–30 reveals the loving heart of Christ toward the heavy burdens we carry:

> Come to Me, all who are weary and heavy-laden, and I will give you rest. Take My yoke upon you and learn from Me, for I am gentle and humble in heart, and you will find rest for your souls. For My yoke is easy and My burden is light.

In like manner, I Peter 5:7 urges us to cast "all your anxiety on Him, because He cares for you." Don't ever be ashamed or afraid to bring issues before the Lord, no matter how personal, embarrassing, or repulsive they may be. He invites us to do so, because He cares so much about us.

For the most part, we pretty much know what our issues are. No matter how hard we rationalize, hide, or justify them, deep down inside we recognize the But-ness within. If we lack patience, we know it. If we are fearful, we know it. If we lack faith, we know it. If we are rude, self-serving, or half-hearted in our commitment to God, we know it. It is time to quit fooling ourselves and playing childish cat-and-mouse games with God. He already knows what we know, so why try to hide

It is time to quit fooling ourselves and playing childish cat-and-mouse games with God.

it from Him? Just admit the issues straight on and bring them directly to Him. He knows how to handle them better than we do, and He has the power and authority to actually help us.

BIG BUT CLEANSING CYCLE

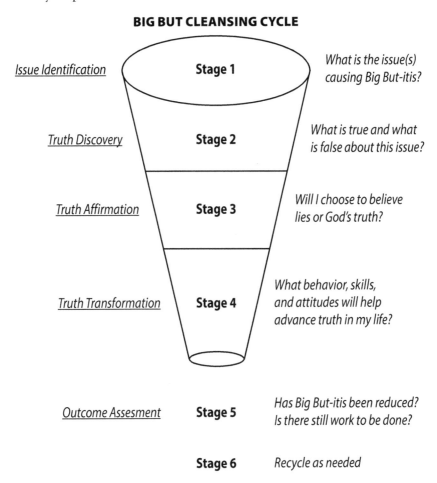

Issue Identification	**Stage 1**	*What is the issue(s) causing Big But-itis?*
Truth Discovery	**Stage 2**	*What is true and what is false about this issue?*
Truth Affirmation	**Stage 3**	*Will I choose to believe lies or God's truth?*
Truth Transformation	**Stage 4**	*What behavior, skills, and attitudes will help advance truth in my life?*
Outcome Assesment	**Stage 5**	*Has Big But-itis been reduced? Is there still work to be done?*
	Stage 6	*Recycle as needed*

There may be times, however, when we know that *something* is wrong, but we just can't quite pinpoint what it is. In times like these, re-examining the Big But Cluster List may help determine if our experience falls into one of the categories. Don't be afraid to simply ask God to reveal troublesome issues of But-ness.

God speaks to us in many ways, but most often: 1) through His Spirit who indwells us, 2) through Scripture, and 3) through other people, events, things, or circumstances. If you ask God's Spirit to uncover problematic issues within you, He will. Be prepared to listen. You may not like what is revealed, but it is the first step on the journey to wholeness. Nothing gets resolved if the Big But issue isn't identified and acknowledged.

Stage 2 Filter: *Truth Discovery*

Once we have surfaced the Big But issue, we need to discover what God says about it. After all, that which really matters on any subject is what our Creator has to say. Since He knows all, sees all, holds all power, and created all, it stands to reason that He might actually have something important to say on the matter.

In this stage of the Big But Cleansing Cycle, we ask ourselves what is true and what is false about the issue. Truth is the groundwork for building a meaningful and abundant life. Truth is solid, immovable, and the foundational bedrock from which all else stands.

> Without a resurrection, we are merely hopeless, deceived individuals pitied by the world for believing a lie.

Take the resurrection of Christ, for example. It is one of those pillar doctrines that without it, everything else crumbles like a house of cards. If Christ did not rise from the dead and conquer death, then we must agree with the Apostle Paul who said in I Corinthians 15:19, "If we have hoped in Christ in this life only, we are of all men most to be pitied." Without a resurrection, we are merely hopeless, deceived individuals pitied by the world for believing a lie.

A foundation of sand may be pleasing when the sun is shining, the wind is calm, the rain is withheld, and we don't have to think about death, but foundations of sand are unable to withstand the realities of life. Sand foundations may look pretty on the outside and are relatively easy to build, but they are a complete waste of time since they are absolutely worthless.

However, expose the lie to truth, and we have a whole different ballgame. After revealing what life would be like without a resurrection, Paul now states the truth in I Corinthians 15:20: "But now Christ has been raised from the dead, the first fruits of those who are asleep."

Truth 1:
Christ is indeed resurrected.

Truth 2:
Christ is the first fruits of those who are asleep. This means that death is not the end. We ourselves will experience a resurrection just like Jesus, the "first fruit."

If I am wavering in fear that I might be stuck in the ground, rotting away forever into nothingness upon my death, or if I am concerned about a friend who dies from cancer at the tender age of twelve, the foundational truth of I Corinthians 15:20 becomes a solid base to stand upon when issues of doubt come my way. When the sun doesn't shine, the winds howl with maniacal ambition, and the pounding rains fall, the foundational truth of our resurrection remains. We are able to smile even when mortality knocks on our door knowing in the depths of our being that death is conquered. That is truth, and nothing can tear it down.

Light is one of the metaphors Jesus uses to describe Himself, "I am the Light of the world; he who follows Me will not walk in the darkness, but will have the Light of life" (Jn. 8:12). There are many positive qualities of light to be considered in Jesus' statement, but one thing light does is expose what is in the dark. Jesus indicates that He is also truth (Jn. 14:6). Light exposes darkness and truth exposes what is false. In fact, Jesus says in Luke 12:2–3, "There is nothing covered up that will not be revealed, and hidden that will not be known. Accordingly, whatever you have said in the dark will be heard in the light, and what you have whispered in the inner rooms will be proclaimed upon the housetops."

> When the sun doesn't shine, the winds howl with maniacal ambition, and the pounding rains fall, the foundational truth of our resurrection remains.

Not only does light expose darkness and truth expose falsehood, but the Bible also indicates that when we come into contact with the truth, it sets us free, "and you will know the truth, and the truth will make you free" (Jn. 8:32). We experienced this personally upon placing our trust in Christ, "for you were formerly darkness, but now you are Light in the Lord; walk as children of Light" (Eph. 5:8). Colossians 1:13–14 says it this way: "For He rescued us from the domain of darkness, and transferred us to the kingdom of His beloved Son, in whom we have redemption, the forgiveness of sins."

Having been transplanted from darkness to light, we are now emboldened to live in that truth and light. "The night is almost gone, and the day is near. Therefore let us lay aside the deeds of darkness and put on the armor of light" (Rom. 13:12). The Gospel of John adds, "For everyone who does evil hates the Light, and does not come to the Light for fear that his deeds will be exposed. But he who practices the truth comes to the Light, so that his deeds may be manifested as having been wrought in God" (Jn. 3:20–21).

Light exposes darkness, and truth exposes lies. When we pursue truth, we find freedom. As Christians, our very lives have experienced transformation from the kingdom of darkness to the kingdom of light and because of that, we are encouraged to live in light and truth. This is exactly what this stage of the Big But Cleansing Cycle is all about; bringing truth and light to bear on the issue at hand. Why? Because to continue holding on to Big But issues is to stand on foundations of sand and remain in darkness, chained to the fetters of lies. What we desire is freedom, and freedom comes from acknowledging Big But issues and exposing them to the truth. As truth and light are brought to bear upon the darkness, we are well on our way to experiencing the freedom we so desperately desire.

Let's say that I struggle mightily with self-identity. Every time I begin to feel good about myself in Christ, the enemy swoops in and snatches away any sense of stability I manage to gain. He causes me to question my sonship and entangles truth with lies so it becomes difficult to discern the difference. His half-truth strategy confuses me and I become powerless and timid.

I do the right thing by correctly identifying the Big But issue causing me so much anguish, and I do the right thing by bringing it to God instead of trying to handle it on my own. I got that right. Now, I ask God to reveal the truth about this lie and expose the darkness with light. I begin to search the Scriptures and find the following verses concerning who I am in Christ:

Eph. 1:1, 1 Cor. 1:2 Phil. 1:1; Col. 1:2	I am a saint.
2 Cor. 5:17	I am a new creation in Christ.
1 Pet. 1:9-10	I am a member of the people of God, a chosen race, royal priesthood, holy nation.
1 Jn. 3:1-2	I am a child of God.
Jn. 15:15	I am a friend of Christ.
Jn. 15:16	I am chosen of Christ to bear His fruit.
Eph. 1:3	I am blessed with every spiritual blessing.
Rom. 8:17	I am a joint-heir with Christ sharing in His inheritance.
1 Cor. 3:16; 6:19	I am a temple of God where the Holy Spirit dwells.
Eph. 2:10	I am the workmanship of God.
Eph. 4:24	I am righteous and holy.
Rom. 5:1	I am justified.
Rom. 8:1	I am free from condemnation.
Phil. 3:20	I am a citizen of heaven.
Eph. 2:6	I am seated in the heavenlies with Christ.
Col. 1:13	I am delivered from Satan's kingdom to God's kingdom.
1 Thess. 5:5	I am a child of light, not of darkness.
1 Pet. 2:11	I am an alien and stranger in this world since I belong to God.
1 Pet. 5:8	I am the enemy of Satan.

This is quite an impressive truth list. I can build upon a foundation like this. If I delve further, I discover that my identity in Christ results in additional truth helpful to my situation. Because of my new identity in Christ, the following statements are true:

Rom. 5:1	I have been justified and have peace with God.
Rom. 5:5	The love of God has been poured out within my heart.
Rom. 6:1-6	I am free from the bondage of sin.
Rom. 8:1	I will not experience the condemnation of God.
Rom. 8:28	All things work for my good.
Rom. 8:29-30	I will be glorified one day.
1 Cor. 2:12	I have been given the Holy Spirit so I might freely know the things of God.
1 Cor. 2:16	I have the mind of Christ.
1 Cor. 3:9	I am God's fellow worker.
1 Cor. 3:23	I belong to Christ.
1 Cor. 6:20	I was bought with a price.
1 Cor. 12:7	I have been given a spiritual gift(s).
2 Cor. 1:21-22; 5:5	
Eph. 1:13-14	The Holy Spirit indwells me and is given to me as a pledge of what is to come.
2 Cor. 5:18-20	I am God's ambassador and have been given the ministry of reconciliation.
2 Cor. 5:21	I am the righteousness of God.
Gal. 2:20	I have been crucified with Christ and the life I live is Christ living in me.
Gal. 4:1-7	I am adopted by God as His child and am an heir of God.
Eph. 1:3	God has blessed me with every spiritual blessing.
Eph. 1:4-8	God chose me before the foundation of the world to be His adopted child, and has poured out His grace upon me.
Eph. 2:5	I am made alive together with Christ.
Eph. 2:6	I have been raised up with Christ and seated with Him in the heavenlies.

Eph. 2:18; 3:12 *Heb. 4:16*	I can approach God with confidence and boldness.
Eph. 6:10-18	I have been given the armor of God.
Col. 1:14	I have redemption and the forgiveness of sins.
Col. 2:7	I am firmly rooted in Christ and am being built up in Him.
2 Tim. 1:7	I am given the Spirit of power, love, and discipline.
Heb. 2:11	I am assured that Christ is not ashamed to call me His brother.
1 Pet. 1:3-5	I have a living hope of obtaining my inheritance which God is protecting for me.
2 Pet. 1:3-4	I am granted, by God, everything I need to live a life of godliness.

Wow, this is a boatload of truth to digest, but it certainly ensures that my identity is secure and strong in Christ. Not all issues will be so prolific in Scripture; yet, even one verse is enough to stand upon with unwavering faith. Where no Scriptures address a particular Big But issue, we still have the Spirit of God who speaks to our hearts: "But when He, the Spirit of truth, comes, He will guide you into all the truth; for He will not speak on His own initiative, but whatever He hears, He will speak; and He will disclose to you what is to come" (Jn. 16:13).

Many today seem to think that God is silent in this age because the written Scripture is among us. This mindset forces us to choose between a God willing to communicate directly with us or a silent God who communicates only through Scripture. How silly is this? It is true that the written Scriptures are "living and active and sharper than any two-edged sword, and piercing as far as the division of soul and spirit, of both joints and marrow, and able to judge the thoughts and intentions of the heart" (Heb. 4:12). God does indeed disclose Himself to us through Scripture, but He also speaks to us through the Holy Spirit who indwells us. In fact, the Spirit within us "helps our weakness; for we do not know how to pray as we should, but the Spirit Himself intercedes for us with groanings too deep for words" (Rom. 8:26).

We are to walk in step with the Spirit (Gal. 5:16), produce the fruit of the Spirit (Gal. 5:22–23), and follow Him into all truth (Jn. 16:13) as He teaches us (Jn. 14:26). It is the Spirit who bears witness to our spirit (Rom. 8:16), and those who follow His leading are the children of God (Rom. 8:14). He is the Helper, the Comforter, the Teacher who mediates the presence of Christ within us.

The belief that God is silent in this age, except for the holy writings, nullifies the doctrine of the priesthood of all believers. If believers have immediate and experiential access to the throne of God, there must be communication directly occurring between God and us.

We often deify Scripture, thinking that it is somehow God Himself, but it isn't. It is one form of His communication to us. Without a doubt, Scripture is important to our Christian walk, but it is not exclusive of God's ability and desire to directly communicate with us. Like a friend, God is able to reveal things to us, instruct us, and speak to us on a daily basis. The Spirit of God within helps us in this endeavor. If God only speaks through Scripture, however, then the doctrine of the priesthood of believers makes no sense. If you run into a Big But issue that is difficult to identify, or there is scant Scripture on the topic, you can always go directly to God, for you are a priest in His kingdom with direct access to the Father. God uses people, circumstances, Scripture, His Spirit, His still, small voice, and a host of other phenomena to speak to our heart. He is not silent. He is alive and well and communicates with us today in diverse ways. He will help us discover truth.

> The rubber meets the road when we *choose* to believe, when we *choose* to make truth a priority and reality in our lives.

Stage 3 Filter: *Truth Affirmation*

After acknowledging a Big But issue and discovering what God has to say about the matter, we are now ready for the next stage in the cycle: believing and valuing God's truth. In this phase we ask, what will I believe in light of God's truth about the issue? It is not enough to merely *know* the truth intellectually, for that is merely the gathering of information. It is what we *do* with that truth that really matters. The rubber meets the road when we *choose* to believe, when we *choose* to make truth a priority and reality in our lives. This is an all important step as it connects the truth in our mind with the impetus of our heart.

If, after discovering the truth, we choose not to walk according to it, we disable the driveshaft connecting our "knowing" with our "believing" and wonder why our life is awry and God seems so distant. King David realizes this as he pens these words: "Your word I have treasured in my heart, that I may not sin against You" (Ps. 119:11). We tend to emphasize the cognitive without understanding its impact upon the practical. In other words, David treasures the truth of God's Word with the purpose of influencing the way he lives his life. Since Scripture is alive and active, it has the ability to travel from the head to the heart and from the heart to our behavior.

Contrary to popular sentiment, it *is* important what we believe. We live in a pluralistic society allowing assorted religious beliefs to co-exist. Contemporary culture values tolerance of belief. If the co-existence of various beliefs is all that is meant by "tolerance of belief," then all we are saying is that people have a right to believe what they want. This is not a problem, and something we all readily agree with. Instead, what is meant by "tolerance of belief" is that every religious belief system is equally true, and this is nonsensical gibberish, devoid of all logic.

> Instead, what is meant by "tolerance of belief" is that every religious belief system is equally true, and this is nonsensical gibberish, devoid of all logic.

If my favorite color is yellow and yours is blue, then we can rightly say that my favorite color is true for me, and your favorite color is true for you. But these are personal preferences, not universal, absolute truths. It may be true for me that I own a Fender Stratocaster electric guitar, and it may be true for you that you own a Gibson Les Paul. What is true for me is different than what is true for you.

However, these aren't the kind of truths we are considering, for they are not absolute and universal.

When talking about truth that acts as a solid foundation for belief and behavior, and is applicable to everyone, contradictory statements cannot both be true when utilized in the same sense at the same time. This is referred to as the law of noncontradiction. If a truth is absolute, then it applies to everyone, and if it is true, then truth statements cannot be self-contradictory. For instance, you are either pregnant or you are not. You cannot be both pregnant and not pregnant at the same time. Contemporary culture would have us believe that both can be true. This isn't tolerance of belief; it is foolishness. One belief system cannot proclaim that Jesus is resurrected from the dead, and another maintain that He is dead, and both be true. One belief system cannot advance that we obtain heaven only by the atoning work of Christ's death, and another claim that we attain our true end only through reincarnation. They are contradictory beliefs and cannot both be true at the same time. Yet, to acknowledge the contradictory nature of such "tolerance of belief" is to incur the wrath of contemporary culture and risk the label of intolerant bigot.

What we believe does indeed matter. It impacts what we value, and our values impact how we live our lives. In a world of competing beliefs with a default view toward accepting all of them as equally valid, choosing to believe and value God's truth becomes paramount to walking in a manner that pleases Him while allowing us to experience His abundant life.

Our thinking is so entwined into our behavior that Proverbs 23:7 says, "For as he thinks within himself, so he is." We are encouraged to protect our heart in Proverbs 4:23: "Watch over your heart with all diligence, for from it flow the springs of life" and I Peter 1:13 states, "Therefore, prepare your minds for action, keep sober in spirit, fix your hope completely on the grace to be brought to you at the revelation of Jesus Christ." In fact, 2 Peter 3:17 instructs us to be on the alert. "You therefore, beloved, knowing this beforehand, be on your guard so that you are not carried away by the error of unprincipled men and fall from your own steadfastness."

Clearly, what we believe influences how we live, and because of that, we are instructed to guard our hearts and minds. Actions and behaviors begin as thoughts. The mind becomes the control room for triggering behavior. If we lived out every thought that crossed our mind, we would be on one wild ride, never exercising restraint and never processing or evaluating our thoughts to determine which ones are true and worthy of action. Our mind, what we believe and think, becomes a strategic battlefield for spiritual warfare with the enemy.

> Our mind, what we believe and think, becomes a strategic battlefield for spiritual warfare with the enemy.

Satan provides David with the idea to number Israel against God's desires. David acts upon those thoughts and displeases God. Judas Iscariot values thirty pieces of silver more than he values Jesus. His thinking leads to a colossal downfall and eventually to his death. Ananias and Sapphira believe they can deceive God about profits realized from the transfer of property. They value money over honesty before God and forfeit their lives. After spying a bathing woman on a rooftop, David can quickly move away. Instead, he allows his mind to wonder toward sin. His impure thoughts lead to lies, murder, and the death of an illegitimate child.

Knowing how important our thinking and belief is to our actions, Paul encourages us in Romans 12:2, "And do not be conformed to this world, but be transformed by the renewing of your mind, so that you may prove what the will of God is, that which is good and acceptable and perfect."

This stage of the Big But Cleansing Cycle asks for a decision. It is a turning point in our thinking. Will we intentionally choose to believe and value truth, or will we continue following a lie? It is time for "taking every thought captive to the obedience of Christ" (2 Cor. 10:5). It is a time to think and believe the things of God.

> Finally, brethren, whatever is true, whatever is honorable, whatever is right, whatever is pure, whatever is lovely, whatever is of good repute, if there is any excellence and if anything worthy of praise, dwell on these things. The things you have learned and received and heard and seen in me, practice these things, and the God of peace will be with you (Phil. 4:8–9).

So what will you believe? What will you value? What will you choose? Each phase of the Big But Cleansing Cycle is essential. What good is it to identify the Big But issue in our life, discover God's truth about the matter, and then choose not to believe that truth? We must absolutely resolve in our heart and mind to

> We must absolutely resolve in our heart and mind to believe what is true, no matter how difficult it may be and no matter how intense our swim against the opposing current.

believe what is true, no matter how difficult it may be and no matter how intense our swim against the opposing current. Since behaviors begin as thoughts, this step is absolutely critical to our long-term success.

In my previous example of a Big But identity problem, I surface the issue and bring it before the Lord. I ask Him for guidance in showing me the truth about myself. As I scour Scripture and ask God to speak to my heart about the matter, there is a great deal of truth for me to digest. It is all in front of me. I read it. I understand it, and my heart is touched by the Holy Spirit. When the lie surfaces and I believe that I am at odds with God, that somehow He is always against me and disappointed in me, I discover the truth that I am actually a child of God (1 Jn. 3:1–2), a friend of Christ (Jn. 15:15), a citizen of heaven (Phil. 3:20), and a joint-heir with Christ (Rom. 8:17).

The question now is will I believe it, deep down, and with all that I am? The choice is before me. Will I choose to waddle in the lie, or will I embrace the truth that I am a beloved child of God? Will I turn my attention to truth with full commitment, desire, and resolve, or will I allow feelings to hijack truth and transport me away in a torrent of emotional ups and downs? This is where the rubber meets the road. Success in the Christian life always requires faith on my part. What I believe is indeed important, for it means the difference between abundant living and constant struggle.

Stage 4 Filter: *Truth Transformation*

So far, the Big But Cleansing Cycle has taken us down the path of issue identification and truth discovery, leaving us with a choice whether or not to believe that truth. Now, the pursuit turns toward intentionally

> What I believe is indeed important, for it means the difference between abundant living and constant struggle.

implementing behaviors, skills, and attitudes that draw forth positive expression in our lives. Since we now know the truth and choose to believe it, we ask practical questions like, "How should I live to reflect the truth discovered? What behaviors, skills, and attitudes will help advance truth in my life rather than detract from it? What behaviors and attitudes am I currently exhibiting that keep me in a Big But rut?" In other words, our behaviors and attitudes come under intense scrutiny.

The previous stages have been cognitive actions—mental functions of identifying, discovering, and believing. We now go from thinking to movement, and from believing to practical application. We have surveyed the mountain and it is now time to pack up our gear and begin the rigorous climb. It is time for intentionality, hard work, and sweat, for changing behaviors and attitudes is no easy assignment. While we long to experience breathtaking views from the mountain top, we dare not forget that learning, growing, and changing is the climb itself. There is no mountain-top exhilaration without a toilsome mountain climb. Though taxing and exhaustive, it is the journey we are most concerned with—the process of becoming like our

> There is no mountain-top exhilaration without a toilsome mountain climb.

Lord in thought, word, and deed. When the mind, heart, and behavior converge, there is bound to be turbulence as the tributaries meet the river. In this stage we buckle our seat belts and focus on our part in the change process.

Knowledge Alone

Some folks are content to merely identify Big But issues. They have no true intention of changing their behavior, for that would entail work, but it sure is good to put a label on the problems. Others are content with the mere accumulation of knowledge. They have no real intention of changing their behavior, for that would be difficult, but it sure is good to know what God says about the issue. There are also those who not only know the truth, but firmly believe the truth. They have no genuine intention of changing their behavior, for that would be demanding, but it sure is good to believe the right things when so many believe the wrong things.

These perspectives misunderstand the very purpose of identifying, knowing, and believing; they are not ends unto themselves. Keeping these things cloistered in some inner chamber of the mind is worthless until they find practical expression with how we actually live. Without this connection, knowledge is nothing more than powerless and irrelevant pieces of information stored on our already-fragmented human hard drive.

Knowledge alone cannot produce the transformation truth requires. What good is extensive Bible expertise without a practical outworking of that knowledge into our life? What good is it to memorize copious passages of Scripture only to live like hell? After all, even the demons know the truth and choose not to follow (Jas. 2:19).

The Pharisees are great "knowers," congratulating themselves for their bountiful knowledge of Scripture and God's laws. But it does little to change their heart and revolutionize their behavior. Their converts act just like them, as Jesus notes in Matthew 23:15, "Woe to you, scribes and Pharisees, hypocrites, because you travel around on sea and land to make one proselyte; and when he becomes one, you make him twice as much a son of hell as yourselves."

Prior to following Christ, Paul was a "knower" with vast intellectual capacity, excelling beyond his peers. He reflects in Philippians 3:4–6,

> I myself might have confidence even in the flesh. If anyone else has a mind to put confidence in the flesh, I far more: circumcised the eighth day, of the nation of Israel, of the tribe of Benjamin, a Hebrew of Hebrews; as to the Law, a Pharisee; as to zeal, a persecutor of the church; as to the righteousness which is in the Law, found blameless.

Yet, with all of his training and education, he is unprepared for the requisite intersection of mind, heart, and behavior. One day, the convergence joins together for Paul who writes in Philippians 3:7–8,

> But whatever things were gain to me, those things I have counted as loss for the sake of Christ. More than that, I count all things to be loss in view of the surpassing value of knowing Christ Jesus my Lord, for whom I have suffered the loss of all things, and count them but rubbish so that I may gain Christ.

Though his thirst for understanding is insatiable, the knowledge he obtains as a distinguished Pharisee is incomplete. He knows a great deal but doesn't comprehend the many details pertaining to Christ or the heart of God. Incomplete knowledge can lead to inappropriate behavior, such as persecuting followers of The Way. But when Paul encounters the risen Christ on his trip to Damascus, he comes face-to-face with truth and his conduct begins to change. Healthy, God-honoring behaviors are rooted in truth that transforms us.

Intentional Transformation

The intentionality of this stage cannot be overstated. All too often we give up too quickly, when in reality, we are partners with God in this transformational dance.

There are at least five good reasons why we should commit ourselves to the process of truth transformation instead of giving up at the first twinge of pain.

1. The assurance of pursuing the right path.
2. We are inspired by Scripture.
3. The Spirit of God empowers us.
4. The example of Christ inspires us.
5. We can risk change without loss.

The assurance of pursuing the right path.

Climbing the mountain may take time, and we may face unexpected obstacles along the way. Yet, despite our many stumbles, at least we know we are climbing the right mountain. Great disappointment would overcome us if we discovered half-way to the peak that we had our mountains mixed up. Our investment of time, energy, finances, and hard work is not wasted, for our caboose is hitched to the right train heading in the right direction. We are motivated to persevere, because we are pursuing truth.

We are inspired by Scripture.

Scripture encourages us to guard our minds, take up and put on the armor of God, persevere, and move forth in ministry, knowing that Christ is with us. Here are a few sample Scriptures challenging us to engage in the transformation process:

Ephesians 6:10–13
Finally, be strong in the Lord and in the strength of His might. Put on the full armor of God, so that you will be able to stand firm against the schemes of the devil. For our struggle is not against flesh and blood, but against the rulers, against the powers, against the world forces of this darkness, against the spiritual forces of wickedness in the heavenly places. Therefore, take up the full armor of God, so that you will be able to resist in the evil day, and having done everything, to stand firm.

Proverbs 4:23
Watch over your heart with all diligence, for from it flow the springs of life.

James 4:7
Submit therefore to God. Resist the devil and he will flee from you.

2 Corinthians 10:5
We are destroying speculations and every lofty thing raised up against the knowledge of God, and we are taking every thought captive to the obedience of Christ.

Romans 12:1–2
Therefore I urge you, brethren, by the mercies of God, to present your bodies a living and holy sacrifice, acceptable to God, which is your spiritual service of worship. And do not be conformed to this world, but be transformed by the renewing of your mind, so that you may prove what the will of God is, that which is good and acceptable and perfect.

Galatians 6:9
Let us not lose heart in doing good, for in due time we will reap if we do not grow weary.

John 16:13
But when He, the Spirit of truth, comes, He will guide you into all the truth.

Acts 1:8
But you will receive power when the Holy Spirit has come upon you; and you shall be My witnesses both in Jerusalem, and in all Judea and Samaria, and even to the remotest part of the earth.

2 Peter 1:3
. . . seeing that His divine power has granted to us everything pertaining to life and godliness.

Matthew 28:18–20
All authority has been given to Me in heaven and on earth. Go therefore and make disciples of all the nations, baptizing them in the name of the Father and the Son and the Holy Spirit, teaching them to observe all that I commanded you; and lo, I am with you always, even to the end of the age.

The Spirit of God empowers us.
There is no need to search for the Holy Spirit; He resides within us. According to Ephesians 1: 13–14, when we believe the truth of the gospel, we are given the Holy Spirit:

> In Him, you also, after listening to the message of truth, the gospel of your salvation—having also believed, you were sealed in Him with the Holy Spirit of promise, who is given as a pledge of our inheritance, with a view to the redemption of God's own possession, to the praise of His glory.

He comes with power (Acts 1:8) to teach, guide, comfort, and intercede for us (Jn. 14:26, Rom. 8:14, 26). When we walk in step with the Spirit and allow His power to flow through us, we no longer fulfill the desires of the flesh. "But I say, walk by the Spirit, and you will not carry out the desire of the flesh" (Gal. 5:16), rather, we produce the fruit of the Spirit, "But the fruit of the Spirit is love, joy, peace, patience, kindness, goodness, faithfulness, gentleness, self-control; against such things there is no law" (Gal. 5:22–23).

The point is, "If we live by the Spirit, let us also walk by the Spirit" (Gal. 5:25). According to Peter, we have all the necessary tools for a successful climb, "seeing that His divine power has granted to us everything pertaining to life and godliness, through the true knowledge of Him who called us by His own glory and excellence" (2 Pet. 1:3).

The example of Christ inspires us.
It is one thing to be told how to do something and another to be shown. Most of what we encounter today is, "Do as I say, not as I do." Scripture not only inspires us to engage in austere mountain climbing, but the life of Jesus provides a sterling example of unconquerable resolve.

We find in Him an unmatched determination to do the Father's will at all times. He could have comfortably remained in the glorious heavens as the Eternal Son, but instead, lowers Himself to our level and enters into human flesh according to Philippians 2:5–8,

> Have this attitude in yourselves which was also in Christ Jesus, who, although He existed in the form of God, did not regard equality with God a thing to be grasped, but emptied Himself, taking the form of a bond-servant, and being made in the likeness of men. Being found in appearance as a man, He humbled Himself by becoming obedient to the point of death, even death on a cross.

This would be like us deciding to leave the comforts of home to become an earthworm. It is a colossal disparity, and to think that a holy God emptied Himself into human flesh is absolutely stunning. He didn't have to, but He did. He resolved to love us and save us, and He followed through on it, even when it meant lowering Himself to our "earthworm" level.

For Jesus, His forty days and nights of temptation was no leisurely walk through golden fields of daisies. Sometimes we make Him out to be Superman, but to do so actually decreases His value, if we mean that He is incapable of yielding to temptation in the first place. In fact, Satan tempts Jesus precisely because He has the capability to fail. For Jesus, it is a mountain to climb. Yet, He resolves to obey, trust the Father, and overcome the full force of temptation for forty days. Most of us would have capitulated the very first day.

During His earthly ministry, Jesus constantly runs into disbelief and anger from those who dislike His message. One day they hail Him as the promised Messiah, and the next they scream for His death. Finally, the religious elite orchestrate His downfall by bringing baseless accusations against Him. After a false arrest, a mock trial, and a severe beating, they nail Him to a cross like a common criminal. In their mind, they are finally ridding themselves of a troublemaker, but what they don't realize is that all along Jesus is merely obeying His Father. His death is part of God's ordained plan to save all humanity, even those who commit this heinous crime against the Savior.

Jesus knows the plan, accepts the plan, and resolves to work the Father's plan with diligence, even as He hangs on that despised crossbeam. According to 1 Peter 2:21–23, Christ is an example for us:

> For you have been called for this purpose, since Christ also suffered for you, leaving you an example for you to follow in His steps, who committed no sin, nor was any deceit found in His mouth; and while being reviled, He did not revile in return; while suffering, He uttered no threats, but kept entrusting Himself to Him who judges righteously.

It takes plenty of courage to unjustly endure such things without fighting back or muttering derisions under one's breath. In Jesus, we have a superb example of mountain climbing resolve.

We can risk change without loss.

This fifth reason why we should commit ourselves to the process of truth transformation is absolutely astounding. My heart skips a beat every time I ponder its marvelous implication. One reason why we don't risk change is because of the possibility of failure or loss. Status quo brings with it a feeling of stability, while the risk of change can bring uncertainty.

Investing in the stock market is risky no matter how much one knows about the securities business. People risk hard-earned money hoping the investment is a good gamble. With optimism, they anticipate a positive return. They invest money hoping to change their current financial situation to one of increased wealth. But sometimes it doesn't work out that way. The stock market is volatile, and if things don't go as planned, the anticipated return can actually become a significant loss. Sometimes when you risk, you lose.

But what if there was a way to invest without the risk of loss? What if you could invest your principal knowing that it has the potential to increase, but never decrease? If I handed you $100,000 dollars and told you to invest it in the stock market, make as much money as you can, and take risks knowing that you can never lose your initial $100,000, would you do it? Of course you would. Only fools would turn down an offer like that. The risk is minimal and the reward astronomical.

The risk we take in committing ourselves to truth transformation doesn't have anything to do with the stock market, but the principle remains the same. We understand risk when it comes to money, but we don't readily grasp the principle when it comes to our spiritual life. Simply put, we can work on changing ourselves to be more like Christ because there is no risk involved, only reward.

> Truth becomes personal when it becomes practical.

The purpose of truth is not merely to collect accurate and logical perspectives, but rather to influence the way we live our lives for Christ's kingdom. Truth has impact. For instance, the truth that Jesus is the Messiah is merely a piece of correct information until that truth finds expression in our lives, that is, until He actually becomes *our* Messiah. Truth becomes personal when it becomes practical.

We are children of God, saved, forgiven, and empowered by the indwelling Holy Spirit. Nothing can change that. No matter how badly we falter, what Christ has done for us is forever ours. We don't lose what He has given us every time we stumble, make a mistake, or screw up. Our secure status becomes our $100,000 principal that can never be diminished. We have nothing to lose. We can, and should, pursue becoming more like Christ because if we fail, we just pick ourselves up and keep going, growing, learning, and conforming to His image. We don't lose our $100,000. The reward is enormous and the risk is minimal. It would be folly not to pursue truth transformation and please our Lord with so little to risk and so much to gain.

There are several reasons why we can be successful engaging in the difficult task of molding our thoughts, words, and deeds after Christ. We can be successful in truth transformation because:

- *We are no longer under bondage to sin.*
- *The ultimate outcome is already determined.*
- *We are already accepted and forgiven by God.*

We are no longer under bondage to sin.

Bondage to sin in our former way of life always led to errant behavior. Alienated from a holy God, pleasing Him was impossible. Paul cautions us not to return to those days: "It was for freedom that Christ set us free; therefore keep standing firm and do not be subject again to a yoke of slavery" (Gal. 5:1). This concept is emphasized again in Romans 6:5–7,

> For if we have become united with Him in the likeness of His death, certainly we shall also be in the likeness of His resurrection, knowing this, that our old self was crucified with Him, in order that our body of sin might be done away with, so that we would no longer be slaves to sin; for he who has died is freed from sin.

Our freedom from the bondage of sin emanates from the work of Christ. "For you have been bought with a price: therefore glorify God in your body" (1 Cor. 6:20). The purchase price was Christ's sinless, substitutionary, atoning sacrifice on our behalf, "He made Him who knew no sin to be sin on our behalf, so that we might become the righteousness of God in Him" (2 Cor. 5:21). The result of this truth in our life is seen in John 8:36: "So if the Son makes you free, you will be free indeed" and Romans 8:1, "Therefore there is now no condemnation for those who are in Christ Jesus."

Freedom *from* sin means freedom *to* serve God. We have been transferred from one kingdom to another. "For He rescued us from the domain of darkness, and transferred us to the kingdom of His beloved Son, in whom we have redemption, the forgiveness of sins" (Col. 1:13–14). Trapped in bondage to sin is like running the 100-yard dash tethered to shackles on our feet and arms while carrying a 200-pound weight on our shoulders. There is no way to successfully outrun the competition to the finish line. The race is over before it even begins.

But what if we were set free from those obnoxious shackles and could freely move our hands and feet as fast as we desired? What if the 200-pound burden on our back was suddenly lifted from us? We are now free to run fast and cross the finish line. Sure, at times we stumble and fall for various reasons, but I John 1:9 encourages us, "If we confess our sins, He is faithful and righteous to forgive us our sins and to cleanse us from all unrighteousness."

So get up and run, let it rip, get going. You are no longer constrained in your ability or desire to serve the living God. Risk, risk, risk, for your $100,000 is safe and cannot be lost. The shackles holding you back are unlocked and lying on the ground beside you. What are you waiting for?

> Freedom from sin means freedom to serve God.

This stage of the Big But Cleansing Cycle entails hard work, sweat, and intentionality. What good is it to have the shackles sitting on the ground next to us if we are unwilling to run, work, and risk? Our freedom was bought with a great price so we could serve and please the Father; there is no time for sloth or self-pity. Having been set free, don't act like you are still in bondage. Risk, risk, risk, and get a move on up that mountain with full vigor. The reward is great and the risk is minimal.

The ultimate outcome is already determined.

Another reason why we can risk without loss is because the ultimate outcome is already determined. While battles and skirmishes continue to break out, some we win and some we lose, the outcome of the war is never in doubt. The death, burial, and resurrection of our Lord sealed the victory. Our enemy's fate is clearly specified in Revelation 20:10. " And the devil who deceived them was thrown into the lake of fire and brimstone, where the beast and the false prophet are also; and they will be tormented day and night forever and ever."

Not only do we have assurance of the war's outcome, our inheritance is also guaranteed, because it is protected by God Himself. It will be there for us when we need it (I Pet. 1:3–7),

> Blessed be the God and Father of our Lord Jesus Christ, who according to His great mercy has caused us to be born again to a living hope through the resurrection of Jesus Christ from the dead, to obtain an inheritance which is imperishable and undefiled and will not fade away, reserved in heaven for

you, who are protected by the power of God through faith for a salvation ready to be revealed in the last time. In this you greatly rejoice, even though now for a little while, if necessary, you have been distressed by various trials, so that the proof of your faith, being more precious than gold which is perishable, even though tested by fire, may be found to result in praise and glory and honor at the revelation of Jesus Christ.

With confidence, we can begin the mountain trek knowing that a slip-up won't cost us the war; whether we stumble or make great progress, our inheritance in Christ is secure. God Himself is protecting it for us. Heaven will be there when we need it.

We are already accepted and forgiven by God.
Much like the rich young ruler, many kingdom trekkers live life trying to earn God's favor. Basking in God's grace and fully embracing His favor is difficult for them. Engaging in truth transformation is just another opportunity to come up short, so why even try?

> We can quit running on the hamster wheel trying to get God to like us.

But the beauty of being in Christ is that we *already* measure up—not by anything we've done, but solely because of what Christ has done for us. Our new status is child of the king, joint-heir with Jesus, forgiven, cleansed, and empowered ambassador for Christ. We pursue truth transformation not to *earn* God's grace, but *because* of God's grace. We are the recipients of His undeserved mercy and love, and the appropriate response is to conform our life to His desires out of pure gratitude for what He has done, what we have received, and what He promises in the future. A grateful heart proclaims, "Lord, my heart overflows with thanksgiving and I want to be more like my Savior. Please change me."

We are adopted children of God and our position is secure. "But as many as received Him, to them He gave the right to become children of God, even to those who believe in His name" (Jn.1:12). As we initiate the process of Christ-like transformation, we are encouraged with the truth of Romans 8:31, "If God is for us, who is against us?" and Romans 8:37–39,

But in all these things we overwhelmingly conquer through Him who loved us. For I am convinced that neither death, nor life, nor angels, nor principalities, nor things present, nor things to come, nor powers, nor height, nor depth, nor any other created thing, will be able to separate us from the love of God, which is in Christ Jesus our Lord.

Appreciating these truths, Paul states with confidence in Romans 5:3–5,

> We also exult in our tribulations, knowing that tribulation brings about perseverance; and perseverance, proven character; and proven character, hope; and hope does not disappoint, because the love of God has been poured out within our hearts through the Holy Spirit who was given to us.

The truth of the matter is that we don't have to earn anything. We can quit running on the hamster wheel trying to get God to like us. In fact, we are already friends of God, "No longer do I call you slaves, for the slave does not know what his master is doing; but I have called you friends, for all things that I have heard from My Father I have made known to you" (Jn. 15:15). This means that we can change, grow, and embrace the risk of transformation without fear. We can, and should, be conformed to the image of Christ, not out of obligation, fear, or an eye toward earning God's approval, but because He loves us, accepts us, forgives us, no longer condemns us, and is rooting for us. We desire change because we love Him, desire to please Him, and are motivated by a grateful heart.

> With anything less than perfection, legalism is in our face and pointing a finger at our failure.

If we stumble along the route, then we stumble. God doesn't zap us with fire from heaven and suddenly we lose all of the benefits gained through Christ simply for a flub-up on our part. As a loving Father, He reaches down, helps us up, dusts us off, smiles and says, "Let's try that again." Many strive for perfection in this life, but the headlines in today's newspaper reads, "It ain't gonna happen!" Try as we might, sooner or later we slip and fall. With anything less than perfection, legalism is in our face and pointing a finger at our failure. God, on the other hand, is about the journey and His loving, forgiving smile encourages us to get up and get moving on up the mountain.

I heard a story that reflects this very issue. It goes something like this: participants at a conference were asked to summarize their life as if it were chapters in a book. One participant wrote the following:

Chapter One:
Was walking one day, turned down a dark street, and fell into a deep hole. It was dark and it took me a long time to crawl out, but I did.

Chapter Two:
Was walking one day, turned down a dark street, and fell into a deep hole. It was dark and it took me a long time to crawl out, but I did.

Chapter Three:
Was walking one day, turned down a dark street, and fell into a deep hole. It was dark and it took me a long time to crawl out, but I did.

Chapter Four:
Was walking one day, turned down a dark street, and saw a big hole. I tried to go around it, but I fell into the hole. It was dark and it took me a long time to crawl out, but I did.

Chapter Five:
Was walking one day, turned down a dark street, and saw a big hole. I walked around the hole.

Chapter Six:
Was walking one day, saw a dark street, turned the other way and walked down a different street.

That pretty much sums up the journey, doesn't it? Legalist would beat us to a pulp at chapter one and leave us feeling guilty, doomed, and unwilling to continue on. But remember, God is about the journey. He is with us through every chapter, even when we walk down the wrong street. The journey is about choosing the right streets to walk, but it takes a mountain climb for us to reach the peak. God is gracious and kind, and we continue the journey because of who He is and what He has done for us. It is called gratitude.

Beginning The Climb

At this point, people want specifics. During the climb, do I read my Bible in the morning or evening? Which version do I use? How long should I read? Should I start with the Old Testament or the New Testament? Should I get a study Bible? What if I don't like reading? What if I don't understand it? How should I meditate? What is meditation? How long should I meditate? What position should I be in to meditate? The questions are never-ending and are most often useless.

Since living for Christ is about learning, growing, and becoming more like our Lord, every voyage is different and no one path fits all of us. God gifts individual believers and leads them on the road He chooses. The Potter not only crafts the clay, He also leads the finished product into suitable experiences needed for its refinement.

When we hear things like "every voyage is different" and "no one path fits all of us," many want to read into such statements new age elements, or universalist teaching that all paths lead to God, or that we can each do our own thing apart from scriptural teaching or the Spirit's leading. That is not the point I am trying to make. Quit reading between the lines; there is nothing there but white space.

Let me say it one more time, as clearly as I am able, once we become a follower of God, His Spirit leads each of us to the paths, experiences, and situations in our spiritual walk that best results in the learning and growth needed to become more like Christ.

Though our paths to growth and learning may be different, the journey always leads to the same end of becoming conformed to the image of Christ. While I am unwilling to provide the specific details many seek (that is God's role as He leads each individual), a few observations may be useful; broad strokes for consideration.

Ask God What To Do

We seek a spreadsheet of rules, criteria, and stipulations to follow as we check off our list of things to do for the kingdom. But the journey isn't about checking things off; it is about communing with God, moving and dancing to His lead. What does He want you to do? If you don't know, ask Him. After all, aren't you a priest in His kingdom? Don't you have direct access to His throne? Don't you have the Holy Spirit indwelling and empowering you? Quit looking for a rule to follow and instead, listen to God and follow His leading. This is what Jesus did.

Don't misunderstand. I am not at all suggesting that we not consult Scripture, for that would be foolish. One of the ways God speaks to us is through Scripture, which the Holy Spirit makes active in our lives. My broad stroke advice is to find time to quiet your mind and heart and listen for the still, small voice of God. It may be through Scripture, prayer, meditation, or some other means, but the key to communing with our Creator is to jettison all the noise and become quiet enough to hear His voice. Jesus often found time away from the clamoring crowd to quiet His heart in preparation for hearing the Father's voice.

To begin keeping lists, seeking rules, and monitoring a spreadsheet is to go back to legalism and the hamster wheel. Instead, seek God Himself. Ask Him and He will answer. Seek Him and He will be found.

Seek Advice From Other Godly Climbers

Be careful with this one. Not every climber on the mountain has worthwhile advice to share. If we listened to every voice, insanity would soon envelope us. Instead, find those whose life is exemplary, who emulate Christ in an admirable way, and seek them out. Most individuals don't mind sharing their experiences, failures, and learning, as long as the seeker is genuine. Many godly mountain climbers have stories to share, much like the Psalmist, whose experiences comfort and encourage others. Maybe God's still, small voice will come to you through a seasoned journeyman.

Hold Yourself Accountable

Mentoring is a hot topic these days, and I am one of its biggest supporters. I love the concept and wish more of it was occurring within the local church. Finding someone with whom we can talk things over, share what's going on in our lives, and who seeks to comfort, clarify, and confront us at appropriate times is positive. I am all for it.

However, I also want to bring personal responsibility back into the picture. It happens, on occasion, that instead of engaging in the hard work of mountain climbing, we blame others for our failures. In our mind, we would have been successful if others had done so and so. This is nothing but legendary scapegoating and grandiose deception. I celebrate mentors and encourage you to find one, but the ultimate responsibility rests with you. Hold yourself accountable to be accountable to God. When all is said and done, God isn't going to look at your life in light of others; you stand or fall on your own two feet.

This is where true grit comes into play. I said mountain climbing is hard work, and I meant it. Sometimes we reach plateaus with luscious green grass, acrobatic waterfalls, and beautiful sunsets, and at other times we climb straight up on sheer ice, unable to see the way ahead, with howling winds causing our hands and feet to go numb.

My son played basketball as a young lad. I knew that throughout the season he could be challenged, frustrated, and possibly consider hanging up his shoes, so I sat him down and had a talk with him before he even tried out for the team. I told him he could try out for the team, but if he made it, he had to stick it out through the entire season. Once begun, quitting was not an option. I brought up the various issues that might arise such as disliking his coach, not getting enough playing time, loathing his position, detesting the travel, conflict with teammates, interference with homework, etc. Finally, I asked him if he wanted to continue in light of these possible obstacles. He committed himself to playing, never once thought about quitting, and learned some valuable lessons about perseverance.

Hold yourself accountable. In other words, be diligent, honor your commitment, persevere, and don't give up, even when you feel you want to.

Seek Professional Counseling If Needed

I never cease to be amazed at the obstacles trekkers face when mountain climbing. Our issues aren't always "dig deep, more grit, stick it out" problems. Instead, many of them are deep, serious, and traumatic. We don't say to the rape victim, "Come on, just get over it!" How do we respond to family issues of physical and sexual abuse? We must go deeper than a "git 'er done" mentality. Seeking professional help from well-qualified Christian counselors is valuable. There will be plenty of opportunities for digging deep and sticking it out during the counseling sessions.

> Successfully climbing the mountain involves faith and risk, but not stupidity.

Notice I encourage "professional counseling." This is purposeful. Many pastors, although willing, have no formal training or expertise in the subject matter. They may be able to share Scripture verses and possess general insight into generic subjects, but rarely do they possess the knowledge and training needed to treat more than theological questions or surface issues. Because they hold the office, many feel they must also possess all the answers. Some merely quote Scripture, often out of context, or shove legalistic Bible passages down throats. Thank goodness, not all are this way, but it is tragic, especially when someone needs professional help. On the other hand, Christians are often cheap. While they may need and desire professional counseling, they are typically unwilling to pay for it.

Professional Christian counselors are trained to spot underlying issues, help resolve those issues, and appropriately apply Scripture to the situation at hand. Professional Christian counselors are precious gifts from God who bring needed healing and perspective to life's issues. Their role is to help get you back on your feet again so you can continue your journey. Mountain climbing can be a difficult excursion and professional Christian counseling may help along the way.

Use Common Sense

Sometimes we get lost in stupid. I apologize for being so blunt, but some of the dazzling mind games we play borders on lunacy. We pray to win the lottery when God tells us to work hard and be good stewards of what has been entrusted to us. We lie to ourselves, believing we can regularly associate with a corrupt crowd and not be negatively influenced. In other words, our walk with God involves a great deal of common sense.

Obviously, there will be times when things don't make sense to us or God asks us to stretch our wings and soar—that is the stuff faith is made of. Just because it doesn't make sense to us doesn't mean it is nonsense. Successfully climbing the mountain involves faith and risk, but not stupidity. Don't jump off the cliff and in mid-air ask to sprout wings. Don't leap in front of a freight train and suddenly ask for the powers of Superman. God isn't into these kinds of tricks that make a mockery of our faith. Even Jesus declines the devil's tricks during His wilderness temptation.

Take Time To Journal

Climbing mountains is intense, involving highs and lows, rugged terrain and soft plateaus, times of exertion and moments of rest. The climb lasts a lifetime, and one of the best activities I can recommend is journaling. Writing down our thoughts, musings, struggles, prayers, and learning is a worthwhile endeavor. It captures, in tangible form, snapshots of our mountain climbing experiences. It strengthens us as we reflect on the presence and help of God throughout our journey. We gather courage, refill our faith tank, and lift our hearts in praise realizing how far we have climbed and how much we enjoy our emerging intimacy with the Lord.

Get Moving

Quit talking about climbing and start climbing. The journey begins with a step, even if it is a tiny one. Talking does nothing, moving gets us heading in the right direction. We often know what Scripture says, so why are we waiting? When is a good time to begin obeying the Lord?

As is the case with a vehicle, it is much easier to steer a car when it is moving. Rarely does God provide a detailed roadmap before the journey begins; He reveals just enough for us to take the next step. Instead of worrying about every nook and cranny of the climb, He leads us as we move forward in faith.

As we seek to implement behaviors, skills, and attitudes that enhance Christ-likeness, we discovered at least five strong reasons for committing ourselves to the process of truth transformation:

1. The assurance of pursuing the right path.
2. We are inspired by Scripture.
3. The Spirit of God empowers us.
4. The example of Christ inspires us.
5. We can risk change without loss.

Since this stage involves blood, sweat, and tears, many want a specific roadmap with infinitesimal details regarding every aspect of each step taken. But this is the last thing we need; some cookie-cutter approach to the Spirit's work in our lives. If God is alive and active, as we believe Him to be, then we can go directly to Him and ask that He lead and guide our lives. Rather than provide specific details for this stage, I offered a few broad suggestions for consideration:

1. Ask God what to do.
2. Seek advice from other godly climbers.
3. Hold yourself accountable.
4. Seek professional counseling if needed.
5. Use common sense.
6. Take time to journal.
7. Get moving.

Let's say I am committed to pursuing truth transformation in my own life and am willing to begin mountain climbing regarding the Big But issue causing me so many problems. I successfully complete stage one of the Big But Cleansing Cycle by identifying the Big But issue, an identity crisis in my life. No more hiding in the shadows, I have surfaced and named the issue. Stage one complete.

In stage two, I seek God's truth about the matter. I search Scripture and communicate with my Creator to learn what He has to say about the issue. My Big But identity crisis is built on lies and God's truth exposes the many falsehoods underlying my thinking. I discover a truth list concerning my identity in Christ that is quite impressive.

Eph. 1:1, 1 Cor. 1:2 *Phil. 1:1; Col. 1:2*	I am a saint.
2 Cor. 5:17	I am a new creation in Christ.
1 Pet. 1:9-10	I am a member of the people of God, a chosen race, royal priesthood, holy nation.
1 Jn. 3:1-2	I am a child of God.
Jn. 15:15	I am a friend of Christ.
Jn. 15:16	I am chosen of Christ to bear His fruit.
Eph. 1:3	I am blessed with every spiritual blessing.
Rom. 8:17	I am a joint-heir with Christ sharing in His inheritance.
1 Cor. 3:16; 6:19	I am a temple of God where the Holy Spirit dwells.
Eph. 2:10	I am the workmanship of God.
Eph. 4:24	I am righteous and holy.
Rom. 5:1	I am justified.
Rom. 8:1	I am free from condemnation.
Phil. 3:20	I am a citizen of heaven.
Eph. 2:6	I am seated in the heavenlies with Christ.
Col. 1:13	I am delivered from Satan's kingdom to God's kingdom.
1 Thess. 5:5	I am a child of light, not of darkness.
1 Pet. 2:11	I am an alien and stranger in this world since I belong to God.
I Pet. 5:8	I am the enemy of Satan.

Now that I have identified the Big But problem and discovered God's truth about the issue, stage three kicks in with a choice to be made. Will I believe and embrace God's truth or will I continue believing Big But lies? I choose to believe God's truth realizing that freedom from Big But-itis must have truth as its foundation, for it is truth that will set me free (Jn. 8:32).

Once I choose to set my course toward God's truth, stage four begins; the difficult work of implementing behaviors, skills, and attitudes that enhance truth, not detract from it. My life, behaviors, habits, thoughts, attitudes, etc., are scrutinized to rid myself of unhealthy ways of living and thinking. I seek to replace them with positive mannerisms.

> If I am an alcoholic, don't lock me in a liquor store overnight and ask me to resolve my problems.

For instance, if I realize that I always seem to stumble when I am out with a certain crowd on Friday nights, I must bravely alter my Friday night schedule and seek a new crowd to associate with that evening. Who could I hang out with and where could I go that would enhance the truth of my identity in Christ rather than detract from it? If I am an alcoholic, don't lock me in a liquor store overnight and ask me to resolve my problems. We must be smart and honest with ourselves in making necessary changes that help us progress up the mountain.

If I discover upon close examination that my identity issues are magnified when I am around my parents, I might visit a professional counselor to help me overcome this association. If I find that my self-talk is always negative and that I have a tendency to see the glass as half-empty, I may discipline myself and change my thinking habits to become more positive. I may decide to memorize key Bible passages as ammunition against negative thoughts that creep in.

The point is that my resolve to believe and act upon the truth of stage three motivates me to engage in the difficult task of truth transformation in stage four. The fruit of belief is action; a movement toward change. I am willing to change because I realize the risk is minimal and the reward is great. My heart, filled with gratitude toward my Lord, wants nothing more than to please Him, no matter how difficult the road. So, I move forward and partner with God in helping me become more like Christ. This kind of commitment leads to the fifth stage, assessing the outcome.

Stage 5 Filter: *Outcome assessment*

There comes a point when we look back and assess how far we have come, much like the quality assurance inspector on the assembly line who checks the widgets rolling down the conveyor belt. He ensures they are manufactured to exact specifications.

In our case, when a Big But issue enters the Big But Cleansing Cycle, by stage five, we expect to have less of a Big But problem. If the Big But contaminants are not fully filtered out, we just send the issue through the cycle again and again until they are removed.

In our sample Big But identity issue, by the time I get to stage five, I should be able to examine the outcome. In other words, has my identity crisis been reduced? Is it completely gone? Am I strong in my understanding, belief, and implementation of behaviors, skills, and attitudes that enhance the truth of my identity, or am I still wrestling with certain elements?

> The fruit of belief is action; a movement toward change. I am willing to change because I realize the risk is minimal and the reward is great.

Let's say that I have come a long way regarding my identity issue. I confirm in my mind, heart, and behavior that I am a redeemed child of God, valued and loved by my Heavenly Father. Accepting and embracing this truth has changed my self-identity in many ways. However, I still struggle with understanding and believing the fact that I have been transferred from the kingdom of darkness to the kingdom of light as described in Colossians 1:13. For some odd reason, I still feel as though I am in Satan's kingdom when in reality I am in God's kingdom. This negative and incorrect attitude interferes with my Christian walk.

Though I have come far, this unwanted trait is still hanging on to my life. So I cycle the issue again and allow the filters to further reduce the contaminated thinking. This time I visit a professional counselor who helps me understand my behaviors from a new perspective. I also visit with my pastor who shares additional Scriptures and personal experiences from his own life that are extremely helpful. When I examine the widget off the assembly line a second time, it looks good, meets specifications, and there is no need to send it through the cycle again. My thinking and behavior are good to go for the time being. One year later, however, I sense an inflammation of this same Big But issue arising in my life.

Back to the cycle it goes. In this last stage, we merely assess how far we've come and what areas need to be recycled for continued filtering. Some stains are stubborn to get out and must cycle through the various stages multiple times. The issue isn't whether it takes one time through the cycle or a thousand times, the issue is that we are continually filtering out contaminants like rocks filter a river and aquariums filter tank water. The filtering process continuously purifies.

Once we get this cycle down, it becomes a natural way of thinking and we are able to progress through the stages with agility and speed. The initial surfacing of a Big But issue may take time to come to light, but once it has been identified, recycling through this stage is simple. If I have already discovered God's truth about the matter, I may only need to refresh my memory in stage two, not necessarily dig it all up again. My commitment to believe and act upon that truth in the next stage may also be quickly reaffirmed.

What consumes the most time in recycling Big But issues is stage four—implementing behaviors, skills, and attitudes that enhance God's truth in our life rather than detract from it. Once we go through stages 1–3, the rubber meets the road in stage four. We experience greater success in our Christian walk when our behaviors align with our goal of becoming like Christ. This is an important stage in the Big But Cleansing Cycle.

Over time, the Big But Cleansing Cycle becomes second-nature. We now have a framework from which to operate: 1) identify the issue, 2) discover what God says about it, 3) choose to believe God's truth, 4) implement behaviors, skills, and attitudes that enhance God's truth, 5) assess the outcome, 6) recycle the issue if needed.

Keep in mind that the Big But Cleansing Cycle is merely a tool for truth transformation. It is not the only helpful apparatus, nor is it in any way a replacement for God or the Holy Spirit. It merely helps us implement God's truth into our life. This process readily and humbly acknowledges that it is not an end unto itself, but a practical way of moving us toward Christ-like behaviors that honor God and positively impact our lives. It relies heavily upon the truth of Scripture, access to and communion with a living and caring God, and the Holy Spirit who leads us in truth and empowers us toward successful Christian living.

The Big But Conclusion

Finally, the Big But book is complete. I took a humorous approach to a serious topic with the high hope that some of it might actually stay with you. Whether I failed or succeeded, I do not know, and I probably never will. But I have a sneaky suspicion that when you least expect it, something you hear or observe will remind you of the term "Big But" and a smile will come upon you. Let's hope it's not at a somber funeral service or a quiet church ceremony where you might erupt in laughter and embarrass yourself. This Big But book will remain latent in your mind until its memory is jogged, reminding you to keep your But tiny and your view of God large.

Big But-it is *a perspective or behavior that conditions, justifies, or excuses our conduct and thinking, or reveals discontentment with God.* It prevents us from seeing, serving, and pleasing our Lord. A Tiny But is a perspective or behavior that unconditionally, and without justification or excuse, aligns itself with the Father's will and experiences contentment with God. Tiny Buts are tiny because they don't hinder us in any way from seeing, obeying, loving, and living for God.

This is my prayer for you, that your But size would be drastically reduced so you can experience the abundant life God has for you.

 # ENDNOTES

1. Ravi Zacharias, *Jesus Among Other Gods*, Thomas Nelson, Nashville: TN, 2000, pg. 19-20.

2. Copyright © Terry S. Wise, *I Must*, March 28, 1982.

3. Corrie ten Boom, *Clippings From My Notebook*, Thomas Nelson, Nashville: TN, 1982, pg. 33.

4. Howard Taylor, *Hudson Taylor and the China Inland Mission*, London: The China Inland Mission, 1927, pg. 176.

5. Chuck Swindoll, *Moses: A Man of Selfless Dedication*, Word, Nashville: TN, 1999, pg. 17.

6. Warren Wiersbe, *The Bible Exposition Commentary: The Pentateuch*, Victor, Colorado Springs: CO, 2003, pg. 195.

7. Leslie T. Lyall, *A Passion for the Impossible: The Continuing Story of the Mission Hudson Taylor Began*, London: OMF Books, 1965, pg. 37.

8. A.J. Broomhall, *Hudson Taylor and China's Open Century, Book Two: Over the Treaty Wall*, London: Hodder and Stoughton and Overseas Missionary Fellowship, 1982, pg. 192.

9. Roger Steer. *Hudson Taylor: Lessons in Discipleship*, OMF International, 1995, pg. 34.

APPENDIX A

SAMPLE BIBLE BIG BUT LIST

Old Testament

Genesis 3
Adam: Sure I ate the forbidden fruit, **but** Eve made me do it.

Eve: Sure I ate the forbidden fruit, **but** the devil made me do it.

Genesis 4
Cain: Yes, I killed Abel, **but** my offering should have been accepted too.

Genesis 11
City of Babel: Of course we built a tower, **but** we wanted a name for ourselves.

Genesis 12
Abraham: Yes, I lied to Pharaoh about Sarah being my wife, **but** I had to protect myself.

Genesis 16
Sarah: I know God promised me a child, **but** Abraham should have relations with Hagar to ensure we have an heir, just in case.

Genesis 20
Abraham: Of course I lied to King Abimelech about Sarah being my wife, **but** I had to protect myself.

Genesis 21
Sarah: Sure I treated Hagar badly, **but** I now have my son and she is a threat to me.

Genesis 27
Jacob: Yes, I lied to my father Isaac, **but** I wanted to steal the blessing reserved for Esau.

Genesis 29

Laban: I know I told Jacob that he could marry Rachel after seven years of service, **but** I had to lie so that Leah could get married and I could get more work out of Jacob.

Genesis 37

Joseph's brothers: Yes, we sold Joseph into slavery, **but** we couldn't stand him, for he was Jacob's favorite.

Genesis 39

Potiphar's wife: It is true, my lie caused Joseph to wind up in prison, **but** I wanted to sleep with him, and he wouldn't let me.

Exodus 4

Moses: I know You will be with me in leading Your people from Egypt, **but** I would sure feel better if Aaron were with me too. The three of us would make a better team.

Exodus 5–12

Pharaoh: Your God demands that I let the Hebrews go, **but** I am the leader around here.

Exodus 15

Wandering Hebrews: We are free from the Egyptians, **but** we will die out here without water. Why did God lead us here only to let us die from lack of water?

Exodus 16

Wandering Hebrews: We would have been better off dying in Egypt, **but** here we are hungry and without meat.

Exodus 17

Wandering Hebrews: We gladly followed you, Moses, into this God-forsaken wilderness, **but** we don't even have water. We should have stayed in Egypt.

Exodus 32

Wandering Hebrews: Sure we made a golden calf as a god to lead us, **but** we were afraid something happened to Moses on Mt. Sinai, and we didn't want to be without a leader.

Numbers 11

Wandering Hebrews: We fondly remember the fish, cucumbers, and onions we used to eat in Egypt, **but** out here there is nothing to eat but manna. Even our appetite is gone.

Moses: I know you called me to lead these people out of Egypt, **but** why did You give me such a complaining, grumbling bunch of misfits. The burden is too great. If this is going to continue, You might as well just kill me right now.

Numbers 12

Miriam and Aaron: You think you are pretty high and mighty Moses, **but** we think you were wrong to marry a Cushite woman, and you aren't the only one God has ever called. We are getting tired of your leadership.

Numbers 13–14

The 10 Spies: Sure the land is prosperous, flowing with milk and honey, and sure it is able to sustain us, **but** did you see the size of their soldiers and the walls of their cities? Surely, we cannot overtake them. We are but grasshoppers in their sight and in ours.

Numbers 16

Korah: Sure I am leading the congregation against Moses and Aaron, **but** who do they think they are, assuming to be the leaders of the congregation?

Israel: Why of course we are grumbling, **but** we have a right to grumble because Moses and Aaron are responsible for causing the death of so many.

Numbers 20

Moses: I know You told me to strike the rock in Meribah once, **but** I was upset and angry so I struck it twice.

Numbers 21

Israel: You sure delivered us Lord, **but** for what . . . to die in a wilderness where there is no food, no water, and any food we do eat is miserable.

Numbers 22–24

Balaam: Okay Lord, I won't take money from Balak or curse Israel as You request, **but** I will inform them that introducing Baal worship will be a way to bring Israel down.

Numbers 25

Israel: We know we are to worship only the Lord God, **but** while we are camped here at Shittim we might as well play harlot with the daughters of Moab and worship Baal.

Joshua 7

Achan: I know the Lord banned us from taking certain spoils of war, **but** I couldn't pass up a beautiful mantle from Shinar, 200 shekels of silver, and a bar of gold 50 shekels in weight.

Joshua 9

Joshua: Yes, we made peace with the Gibeonites when we shouldn't have, **but** we didn't think to ask for the counsel of the Lord, so we were deceived.

Joshua 22

Sons of Israel: Sure we were ready to slaughter our brothers in the Lord and fight against them over the offensive altar, **but** we didn't think to get all the facts until it was almost too late.

Judges 11

Jephthah: Yes, I killed my own daughter who was innocent, **but** I made a vow to the Lord that must be kept, even though it cost me my own daughter.

Judges 16

Samson: Yes, I made a Nazarite vow and lost my strength and life by telling Delilah the secret to my strength, **but** it wasn't my fault; she twisted it out of me.

Judges 19

Levite: I did give my virgin daughter and concubine to wicked men who raped them, and yes, I cut my concubine into twelve pieces and sent them to the twelve tribes of Israel, **but** I thought it was best to sacrifice my own family than that of guests I took in from the city square.

1 Samuel 2

Eli's Sons: We know you brought meat to sacrifice to the Lord, **but** we don't want leftovers; we will take your offering by force if we have to.

1 Samuel 8

Israel: We know the Lord has been leading us, **but** we want a king to lead us like all the other nations.

1 Samuel 15

King Saul: Oh, I know the Lord commanded me to conquer Amalek and not spare their king, their people, or their possessions, **but** I did obey . . . mostly. What is wrong with that? I spared the king, and I spared the best of the sheep and oxen to sacrifice to the Lord.

1 Samuel 17
Goliath: I am big and strong and no one from Israel can beat me, **but** you send a boy with sticks and stones to fight me. Am I a dog? Your God cannot protect you.

2 Samuel 3
Joab: Yes, I murdered Joab, **but** he didn't deserve to live. He needed to be punished for his role in killing my brother Asahel in the battle at Gibeon.

2 Samuel 11
King David: Yes, I know Bathsheba is the wife of another, **but** I want her. Yes, I arranged the death of her husband, **but** how else was I to cover up the fact that I got her pregnant?

2 Samuel 13
Amnon: Yes, I realize it is wrong to sleep with my sister Tamar, **but** I wanted to, and I did.

Absalom: I know it is not my prerogative to determine life and death, **but** Amnon deserves to die for violating my sister Tamar.

2 Samuel 15
Absalom: I know David is my king, **but** I want to be king, so I will manipulate things to get the people on my side and overthrow David.

2 Samuel 24
King David: I knew that taking a census would not please the Lord, **but** I did it anyway because I felt more secure knowing how many people were in Israel.

1 Kings 11
King Solomon: Yes, the Lord instructed us not to marry foreign women from among the nations because they might turn our hearts away from Him, **but** I want lots of wives and concubines so I will disobey.

1 Kings 12
King Rehoboam: Of course I was counseled that it would be wise for me to listen to the people, **but** I had to show them who was boss, so I spoke harshly to them.

1 Kings 13
Disobedient prophet: It is true, the Lord commanded me not to eat bread, drink water, or return the way I came, **but** I listened to a lying prophet and did the very thing the Lord commanded me not to do.

1 Kings 19
Elijah: Yes, I just watched the Lord miraculously conquer 450 prophets of Baal, **but** vicious Queen Jezebel wants me dead, so I will just sit under this juniper tree and ask the Lord to take my life.

1 Kings 21
King Ahab: I know that the vineyard I covet is owned by Naboth who won't give it to me, **but** Jezebel has a plan to kill him so I can get what I want.

2 Kings 5
Naaman: Sure I want to be healed, **but** dip in the filthy Jordan River seven times? I would be better off dipping in the rivers of Damascus.

Gehazi: My master Elisha won't take money from Naaman so glory goes to God, **but** why should I pass up this financial opportunity? Nobody will know, and I will prosper.

2 Kings 19
Sennacherib: I am the great king of Assyria, powerful and not to be refused, **but** you can cry to your God all you want and I will still destroy you.

1 Chronicles 13
Uzza: I know the ark is holy and we are not to touch it, **but** I will just steady it a bit.

1 Chronicles 21
David: I know I am to trust God for winning battles, **but** I would feel much better if I took a census to know where I stand against my enemies.

2 Chronicles 16
Asa: I know God protects those who rely on Him, **but** I would feel more secure if I could sign a treaty with the king of Aram for protection.

2 Chronicles 23
Athaliah: I know Yahweh is the God of Judah, **but** I want to promote my god, Baal, and will do everything in my power to see that Baal is worshipped, not Yahweh.

2 Chronicles 24
Faithless priests: We know that Joash commanded us to collect the levy from the people since Athaliah drained the funds, **but** we will take our time in completing the task.

Joash: I know your father Jehoiada was kind to me, **but** I don't like your words, so I am going to kill you Zechariah.

2 Chronicles 25
Amaziah: I know that Yahweh is the one true God, **but** I will bring back idols from Edom and bow down and worship them.

2 Chronicles 26
Uzziah: I have been pretty successful in all of my endeavors, **but** I can do whatever I want, like burn incense on the altar of the Lord.

2 Chronicles 28
Ahaz: I am king of Judah and know I am to worship Yahweh, **but** I will make images for the Baals.

2 Chronicles 33
Manasseh: I know I am to worship Yahweh, **but** I will mislead Judah into idolatry.

Ezra 4
King Artaxerxes: I know the Jews want to rebuild the house of God in Jerusalem, **but** I will stop them.

Job 42
Jobs friends (Eliphaz, Bildad, Zophar): Job, you say you haven't sinned before God, **but** listen to us; we know why you are going through this, and you are wrong in your assessment of things.

Jeremiah 20
Jeremiah: Lord, You have deceived me. Why did I ever come forth from the womb? Pashur is persecuting me, **but** You are nowhere to be found.

Daniel 3
Nebuchadnezzar: Shadrach, Meshach and Abed-nego, you say your God is able to save you, **but** what god is there who can deliver you out of my hands?

Jonah 4
Jonah: I knew this would happen. I preach your judgment to Nineveh as requested, **but** instead You bring mercy.

New Testament
Matthew 2
King Herod: You wise men go and search for this new king and report back to me what you find so I too can worship Him, **but** what I am really going to do is make sure He never becomes king.

Matthew 7
Hypocrite: I see the obvious speck in my brother's eye, **but** I neglect the log in my own eye.

Matthew 8
Scribe: Teacher, I will follow You wherever You go, **but** first permit me to bury my father.

Matthew 9
Scribe: Jesus, You just told the paralytic that his sins were forgiven, **but** only God has the right to do that, and You aren't God. You are a blasphemer.

Matthew 11
Cities of Chorazin, Bethsaida, and Caperaum: We have witnessed the majority of Jesus' miracles, **but** we still will not believe.

Matthew 12
Pharisees: Jesus, You say You are lord of the Sabbath, **but** Your disciples do what is not lawful on the Sabbath; therefore; You cannot be anything but a lawbreaker.

Pharisees: We know Jesus casts out demons, **but** He does it by the authority of Beelzebul.

Pharisees/scribes: We will believe You, **but** only after You give us a sign.

Matthew 13
Nazareth: Jesus, we see Your miraculous power, **but** aren't You Joseph the carpenter's son? We would believe You, but we are offended at Your claims, since we know You grew up among us.

Matthew 14
Disciples: We know the people are hungry, **but** why are You looking to us for food, Jesus? This place is desolate, so send the people away. We only have five loaves and two fish, **but** that is not enough to feed so many.

Peter: I want to get out of this boat and walk to see Jesus, **but** wait, I am on water. This isn't right. I am afraid, and I am sinking.

Matthew 15
Pharisees/scribes: You claim to be from God, **but** Your disciples transgress the tradition of the elders.

Dicsiples: You want us to feed the multitude? **But** we only have seven loaves of bread and a few small fish. That certainly isn't enough.

Matthew 16
Pharisees and Sadducees: We will believe You, **but** first show us a sign from heaven.

Matthew 17
Disciples: We tried to cast out a demon, **but** we were unsuccessful because of our lack of faith.

Peter: Lord, I think forgiving my brother up to seven times is good enough, **but** You teach seventy times seven.

Matthew 19
Rich young ruler: Teacher, I have kept the law, so what good thing must I do to obtain eternal life? **But**, I don't want to sell my possessions and give to the poor.

Matthew 20
Vineyard workers: **But** it is unfair to pay the late workers the same amount as us.

Sons of Zebedee: We sure like following You Jesus, **but** we seek preference above the others. Please ensure that in Your kingdom, we get to sit next to You—one on Your right and one on Your left.

Matthew 21
Chief priests and elders: We are the ones in authority, **but** by what authority are You doing these things?

Matthew 22
Pharisees: Teacher, we know You are good and honorable, **but** is it lawful to give a poll-tax to Ceasar, or not?

Sadducees: We don't believe in a resurrection, **but** if there is one, whose wife will she be?

Matthew 26
Disciples: You just poured perfume upon the head of Jesus, **but** that is such a waste when it could have been sold and given to the poor.

Judas: I sure like Jesus, **but** if I betray Him, I can make 30 pieces of silver.

Peter: You think I am a disciple of Jesus, **but** I deny ever being with Him.

John 6
Phillip: **But** we can't feed this many people with only five loaves of bread and two fish.

John 8
Pharisees: We caught this woman in adultery and the law commands us to stone her, **but** what do You say?

John 9
Pharisees: We know you claimed to have been blind and that Jesus healed you, **but** Jesus couldn't have possibly healed you.

John 11
Mary: Lazarus is dead, **but** had You been here, Lord, this would not have happened.

Chief priests and Pharisees: Jesus is outperforming us, **but** we can't let Him take away our place and our nation. We must kill Him.

John 12
Judas: Mary, you have wasted a pound of very costly perfume on Jesus, **but** the perfume could have been sold for 300 denari and given to the poor.

John 13
Disciples: We know there is no rank and file servant to wash the feet of supper guests, **but** we aren't going to stoop so low to wash their feet.

John 18
Judas: I am giving You a kiss, Lord, **but** what I am really doing is betraying You.

John 20
Thomas: You say you have seen the resurrected Lord, **but** I won't believe until I can put my hands in the place of the nails and in His side.

Acts 5
Ananias and Sapphira: We can lie about the proceeds from property we sold, **but** no one will ever know the difference, not even God.

Acts 7
Men from the synagogue: We don't like your ministry, **but** in order to shut you up, we will lie saying we heard blasphemous words from you.

Acts 23
Jews: We cannot stand Paul and what he preaches, **but** we will make an oath not to eat or drink until we have killed him.

1 Corinthians 1
Corinthian church: Sure, we are the local church in Corinth, **but** I am of Paul. **But** I am of Apollos. **But** I am of Cephas. **But** I am of Christ.

1 Corinthians 6
Corinthian church: Sure, we believe that Christ rules in our hearts and Scripture is our authority, **but** if we don't get our way, we file lawsuits against each other and appeal to a higher authority.

James 2
Recipients of his letter: All are welcome in our church, **but** if you are wealthy, you are especially welcome and get to sit in a place of honor.

SAMPLE BIBLE TINY BUT LIST

Old Testament

Genesis 6
Noah: The rest of humankind is corrupt, **but** I will live a righteous life before the Lord.

Genesis 12
Abraham: Lord, You have called me to pack up and hit the road without knowing where You are leading me, **but** I will obey and begin the journey.

Genesis 22
Abraham: Dear God, You fulfilled Your promise of giving me a son, **but** I am willing to give him back to You if that is Your desire.

Genesis 24
Servant: My master Abraham has asked me to find a bride for his son Isaac, **but** I won't be able to find one without Your help and guidance. Please lead me to the right woman.

Genesis 50
Joseph: My brothers, you meant to harm me when you sold me into slavery, **but** God meant it for good and has used it to preserve life.

Exodus 33
Moses: I have been leading this complaining group of people for a long time, **but** I cannot lead them any farther unless Your presence goes with us.

Numbers 13
Caleb and Joshua: The land God promised us is filled with milk and honey and it also contains fortified cities for us to conquer, **but** with God leading us, we should go and possess the land.

Numbers 25
Phinehas: The people are being led astray into idolatry by these two leaders, **but** this goes against God's desires, and I will jealously show my loyalty to God.

Joshua 24
Joshua: Choose this day whom you will serve, **but** as for me and my household, we will serve the Lord.

Judges 3
Ehud: Israel has served Eglon the king of Moab for too long, **but** God has called me to deliver us from Moabite bondage.

Judges 4
Deborah: We are under bondage to Jabin, the king of Canaan, **but** God will deliver us from his hand in battle. Let us go forth, for the Lord is going out before us.

Judges 7
Gideon: Midian is oppressing us, **but** God has commanded us to conquer Midian with only 300 men. Let's do it!

Judges 16
Samson: God, I am sorry that I have failed You, **but** please strengthen me just this one last time to avenge the Philistines.

Ruth 3
Ruth: My husband has died and I have no way to survive, **but** God will show favor upon me as Boaz redeems me.

I Samuel 1
Hannah: Lord, my womb is closed and I am provoked by Peninnah, **but** if You will give me a son, I will give him back to You all the days of his life.

I Samuel 3
Samuel: I heard something; someone calling me; **but** here I am Lord, speak to me.

I Samuel 14
Jonathan: **But** since the Lord is not restrained to save by many or by few, let us go over to the Philistine garrison and overtake them.

I Samuel 17
David: This Philistine giant thinks he can mock the living God, **but** God will be with me as I fight him for the honor of the Lord.

I Kings 3
Solomon: Dear Lord, You have made me king in place of my father David, and I am young and inexperienced, **but** I ask that You give me wisdom so I can discern between good and evil.

I Kings 18
Elijah: Baal was unable to consume the false priests' sacrifice, **but** God will reveal Himself as the only true God by consuming a water-soaked sacrifice.

2 Kings 18
Hezekiah: I am now king of Judah, **but** I will cling to the Lord, follow Him, and keep His commandments.

2 Kings 23
Josiah: This land is filled with idolatry, **but** I covenant with You, Lord, to walk after You, keep Your commandments, testimonies, and statutes, and I will begin initiating reforms immediately.

Ezra 5
Darius: The house of God is in ruins, **but** I command that you rebuild the house of God.

Ezra 9
Ezra: Lord, I am embarrassed and ashamed to lift my face to You because Your people have greatly sinned against You throughout its history, **but** now I confess their sin to You and intercede for them and seek Your favor.

Nehemiah I
Nehemiah: Lord, today I bring up the rebuilding of Jerusalem with the king, **but** You can give him an attentive ear and compassion toward rebuilding Your holy city.

Esther 4
Esther: I am not allowed to see the king without being summoned, **but** I will trust God in the matter in order that I might save my Jewish people.

Job 42
Job: Lord, I have been going through a rough time without understanding, **but** now I repent in dust and ashes for my behavior and thinking and ask that You instruct me.

Ecclesiastes 12
Solomon: I have tried just about everything in life to find happiness, **but** the conclusion of it all is to fear God and keep His commandments.

Isaiah 6

Isaiah: I see the Lord sitting on His throne, lofty and exalted, **but** woe is me, for I am but a man of unclean lips.

Isaiah 37

Hezekiah: Sennacherib, king of Assyria is attacking us, **but** God, deliver us from his hand that all kingdoms of the earth may know that You alone are God.

Jeremiah 18

Jeremiah: I have been preaching Your words to the people, **but** now I see that we are but clay in the Potter's hands, and You are able to do as You desire.

Daniel 1

Daniel: I have been taken captive by Nebuchadnezzar, **but** I will remain faithful to God and will not eat of the king's choice food.

Daniel 3

Shadrach, Meshach, Abed-nego: You can order us to bow down and worship the image, **but** we will not do it. God is able to save us, but even if He doesn't, we will not bow down to your image.

Hosea 1

Hosea: I have taken Gomer the harlot as my wife, **but** You have commanded me to marry her as a symbolic message to Your people.

Haggai 1

Haggai: The people say it is not yet time to rebuild the house of the Lord, **but** You say it is time, and so I will begin rebuilding Your house.

New Testament

Matthew 1

Joseph: My betrothed is pregnant and I was going to send her away quietly, **but** God has asked me to take Mary as my wife, and I will obey Him.

Matthew 2

Wise men: King Herod told us to report back to him when we found the Christ-child, **but** God instructs us not to return to Herod, and we will obey the Lord.

Matthew 3

John the Baptist: I baptize you with water for repentance, **but** He who is coming after me is mightier than I and I am not fit to remove His sandals.

Matthew 8
Centurion: Lord, I know You are willing to come to my house, **but** You are so powerful all You have to do is speak the words and my servant will be healed.

Matthew 9
Bleeding woman: I have been hemorrhaging for 12 years, **but** if I could just touch the hem of Jesus' garment, I know I would be healed.

Matthew 11
John the Baptist: I am in prison for preaching truth and I don't understand what is happening, **but** I will take my doubt to Jesus and see what He says about the matter.

Matthew 14
Peter: Lord, I see You walking on the water in the midst of the storm, **but** if You bid me to come, I will walk out to You.

Matthew 16
Peter: Others say You are Elijah, John the Baptist, or Jeremiah, **but** You are the Christ, the son of the living God.

Matthew 23
Jesus: You perceive yourselves as spiritual giants, **but** woe to you scribes and Pharisees because you shut the kingdom of heaven from men.

Matthew 26
Jesus: Father, if it is possible, let this cup pass from Me, **but** I want nothing more than Your will to be done.

John 3
John the Baptist: He must increase, **but** I must decrease.

John 4
Samaritan woman: I will gather up the townspeople to come hear Jesus, **but** this couldn't be the Christ, could it?

John 9
Blind man: What I do know is that I once was blind, **but** now I see.

Acts 2
Pentecost crowd: Peter, we have listened to your sermon and are touched to the core of our being, **but** what shall we do?

Acts 3
Peter: Silver and gold I do not have, **but** what I do have I give to you, in the name of Jesus, rise and walk.

Acts 4
Peter and John: You have instructed us not to preach about Christ, **but** we cannot stop speaking about what we have seen and heard.

Acts 7
Stephen: You have rejected my words and are stoning me for my belief in Christ, **but** Lord, please do not hold this against them.

Acts 9
Paul: I was going about persecuting followers of The Way, **but** You intervened on my way to Damascus, and now I am a follower myself.

Acts 15
Jerusalem council: We are wrestling with the requirements for salvation, **but** now we proclaim that it is by the grace of God alone.

Acts 16
Jailor: God has rescued you from prison, **but** what must I do to be saved?

Acts 21
Paul: I know you are weeping for me, but I am ready not only to be bound, **but** even to die at Jerusalem in the name of the Lord Jesus.

Romans 1
Paul: I am eager to preach the gospel to you, **but** I am not ashamed of the gospel, for it is the power of God for salvation to everyone who believes.

1 Corinthians 15
Paul: If Jesus has not been resurrected from the dead then we are of all men most pitied, **but** Christ has been raised from the dead.

Philippians 3
Paul: I will count everything in this life a loss **but** the knowledge of knowing Jesus Christ.

BIG BUT CLUSTER LIST

- Fear and Worry
- Doubt and Unbelief
- Control
- Misconception of God and the Bible
- Less Than Total Commitment
- Myopic Vision of God's Plan
- Misconception of Ourselves
- Pain, Disappointment, and Anger

APPENDIX

BIG BUT CLEANSING CYCLE

Stage 1: **Bringing:** *identifying* ⟶ Issue Identification

Stage 2: **Knowing:** *mind/learning* ⟶ Truth Discovery

Stage 3: **Believing:** *heart/valuing* ⟶ Truth Affirmation

Stage 4: **Implementing:** *action/doing* ⟶ Truth Transformation

Stage 5: **Producing:** *outcome/result* ⟶ Outcome Assessment

Stage 6: Recycle as needed

APPENDIX

BIG BUT CLEANSING CYCLE CHART

STAGE	TITLE	TASK	QUESTIONS
1	Issue Identification	Identifying and exposing the issue.	What is the issue(s) causing Big But-itis?
2	Truth Discovery	Learning what God has to say about the issue.	What is true and what is false about this issue?
3	Truth Affirmation	Choosing to value God's truth over lies.	Will I choose to believe lies or God's truth?
4	Truth Transformation	Implementing behaviors, skills, and attitudes that advance truth in our lives.	How should I live in light of the truth discovered? What behavior, skills, and attitudes will help advance truth in my life?
5	Outcome Assessment	Evaluating the result of transformational changes.	Has Big But-itis been reduced? Is there still work to be done?
6	Recycle As Needed		

APPENDIX

BIG BUT CLEANSING CYCLE DIAGRAM

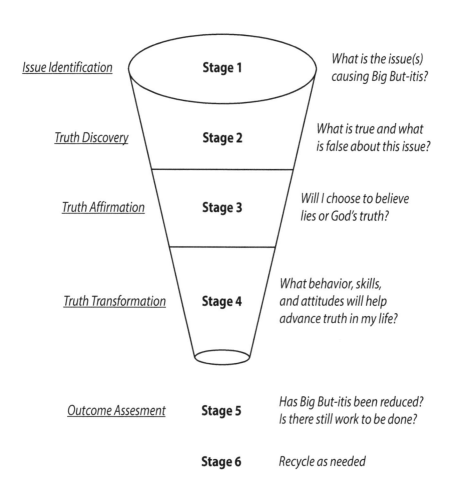

Issue Identification — **Stage 1** — *What is the issue(s) causing Big But-itis?*

Truth Discovery — **Stage 2** — *What is true and what is false about this issue?*

Truth Affirmation — **Stage 3** — *Will I choose to believe lies or God's truth?*

Truth Transformation — **Stage 4** — *What behavior, skills, and attitudes will help advance truth in my life?*

Outcome Assesment — **Stage 5** — *Has Big But-itis been reduced? Is there still work to be done?*

Stage 6 — *Recycle as needed*

233

CPSIA information can be obtained
at www.ICGtesting.com
Printed in the USA
LVHW082328261022
731688LV00014B/871

9 780986 061318